DAREDEVIL

THE MAN WITHOUT FEAR!

MARVEL KNIGHTS

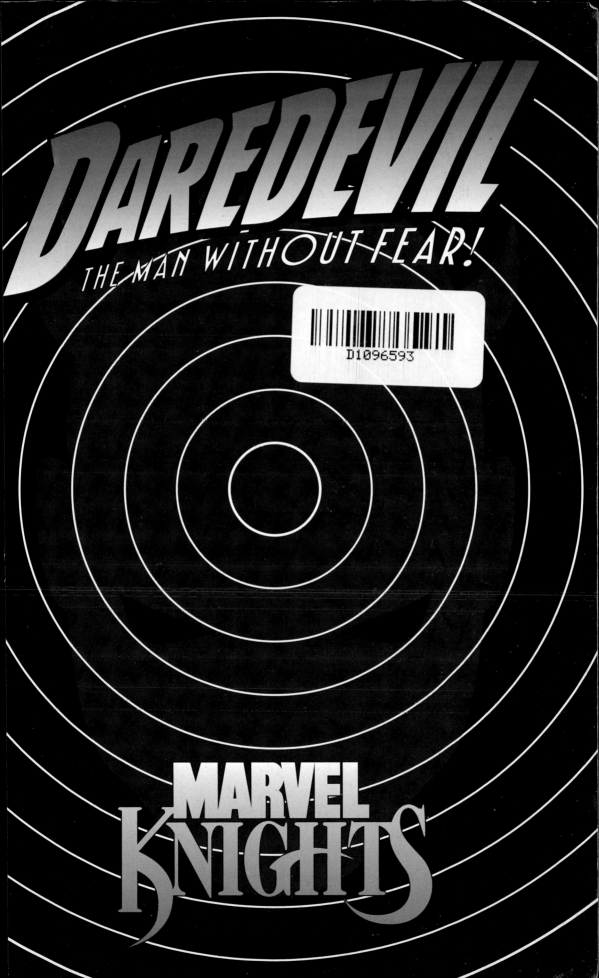

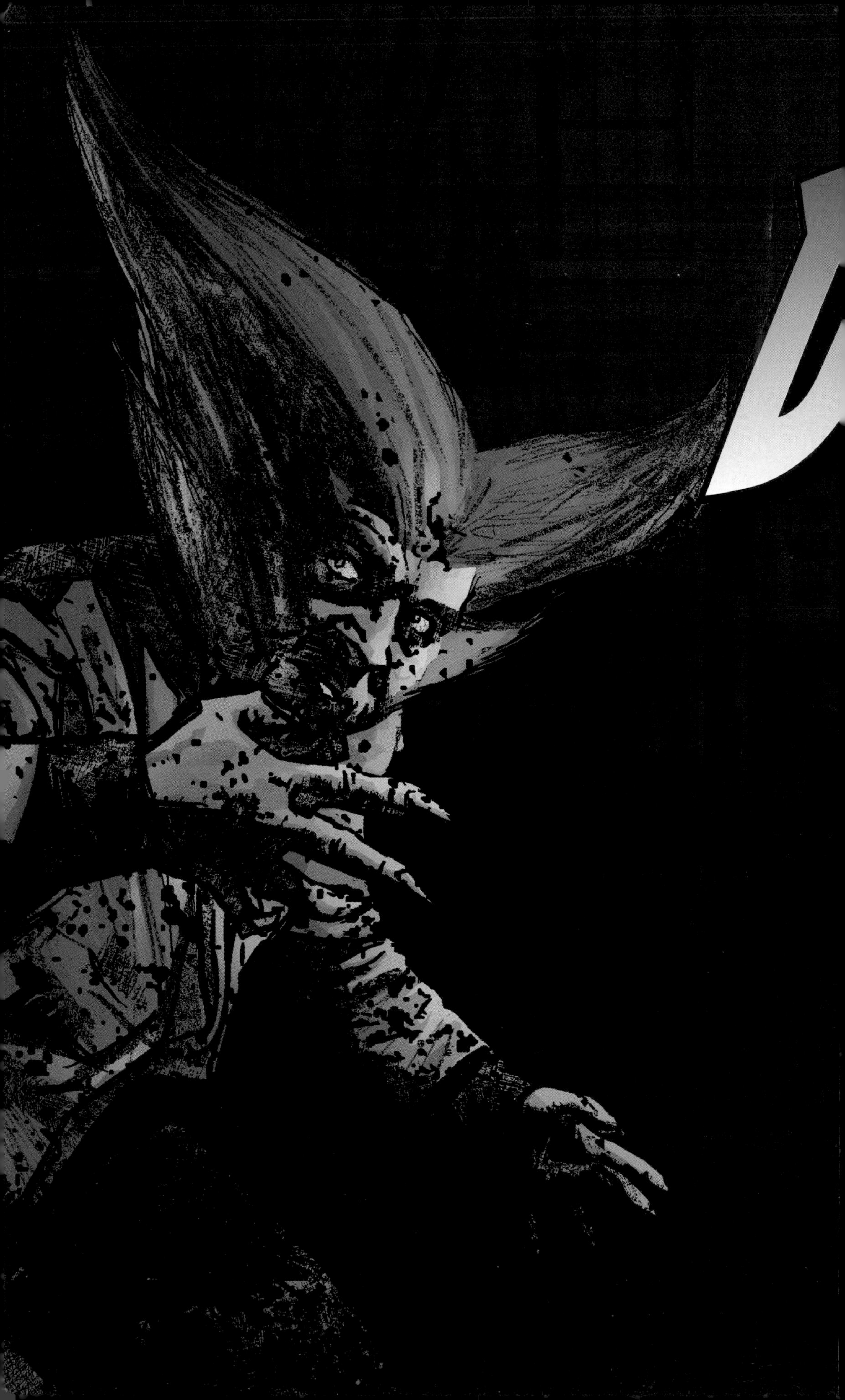

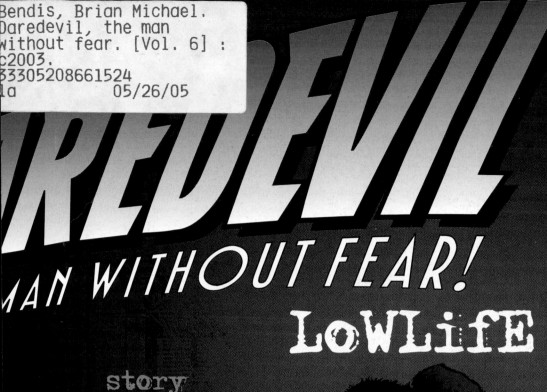

REDEVIL

MAN WITHOUT FEAR!

LoWLifE

story
BriAn
mIcHAel Bendis
art
AleX MaLeEv

colors
MaTT hoLLinGSworTh
letters
CorY pEtit
RS & ComiCrAft's
Wes aBBott
assistant editor
NicK 1OWe
editor
joE queSaDa
associate managing editor
kElly LamY
managing editor
NanCi daKEsIan

collections editor
jEfF yOUngqUiST
assistant editor
JennIFEr GrünWaLD
book designer
jeOF ViTA

editor in ch
JoE QUesaD
publisher
DaN buCKley

ATTORNEY MATT MURDOCK IS BLIND, BUT HIS OTHER FOUR SENSES FUNCTION WITH SUPERHUMAN SHARPNESS AND A RADAR SENSE. WITH AMAZING FIGHTING SKILLS HE STALKS THE STREETS AT NIGHT, A RELENTLESS AVENGER OF JUSTICE: DAREDEVIL, THE MAN WITHOUT FEAR!

DAREDEVIL
THE MAN WITHOUT FEAR!

Previously in Daredevil:

Mr. Silke was a new memb of the Kingpin's crew. Wh his coup attempt against the Kingpin failed, he turned himself into th FBI.

Wilson Fisk survive the assassination attempt but was wounded severely. Vanessa, his wife, shipped Wilson out the country to save his life from other attempts. Vanessa sold the Fisk Towers and all of Wilson's organized crime businesses, dismantli the empire and leaving America forever.

The FBI refuse Silke's request for protection from t Kingpin's wife, so he gives the the one piece of information that the Kingpin had -- that Daredevil is really a blind lawyer named Matt Murdo

The FBI decide not to follow up on the Daredevil information. But the next day, on the cover of the biggest tabloid in the city, the headline reads: Daredevil's Secret Identity Revealed!

The secret is out.

Matt Murdock files a 400 million dollar lawsuit against th Daily Globe for printing the story. Mr. Rosenthal, the owner of the paper, vows to go the distance with Murdock because he know the story is true.

Matt's public struggle against the newspaper makes his alter ego more popular with the people than ever before.

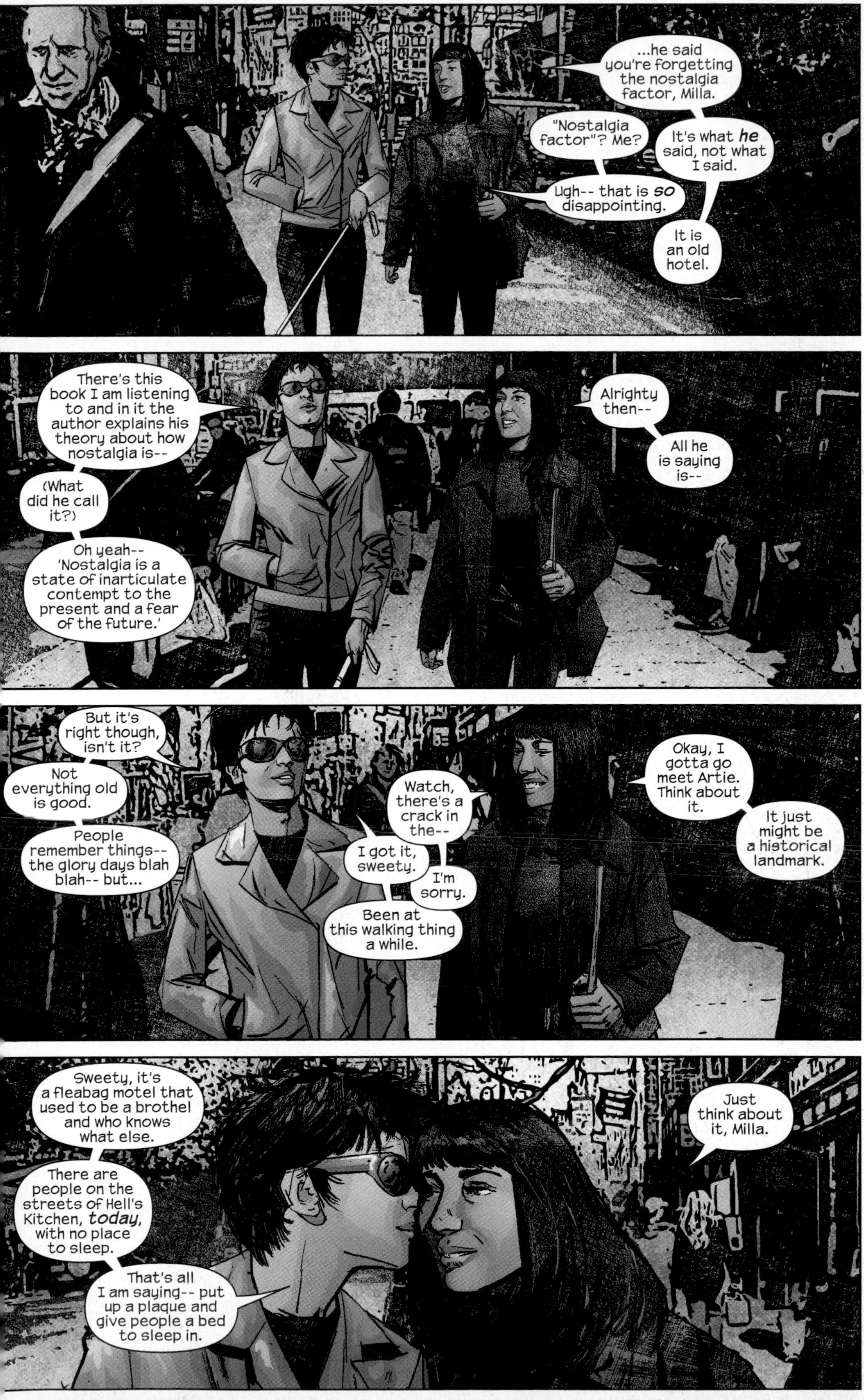
...he said you're forgetting the nostalgia factor, Milla.
"Nostalgia factor"? Me?
It's what he said, not what I said.
Ugh-- that is so disappointing.
It is an old hotel.
There's this book I am listening to and in it the author explains his theory about how nostalgia is--
(What did he call it?)
Oh yeah-- 'Nostalgia is a state of inarticulate contempt to the present and a fear of the future.'
Alrighty then--
All he is saying is--
But it's right though, isn't it?
Not everything old is good.
People remember things-- the glory days blah blah-- but...
Watch, there's a crack in the--
I got it, sweety.
I'm sorry.
Been at this walking thing a while.
Okay, I gotta go meet Artie. Think about it.
It just might be a historical landmark.
Sweety, it's a fleabag motel that used to be a brothel and who knows what else.
There are people on the streets of Hell's Kitchen, today, with no place to sleep.
That's all I am saying-- put up a plaque and give people a bed to sleep in.
Just think about it, Milla.

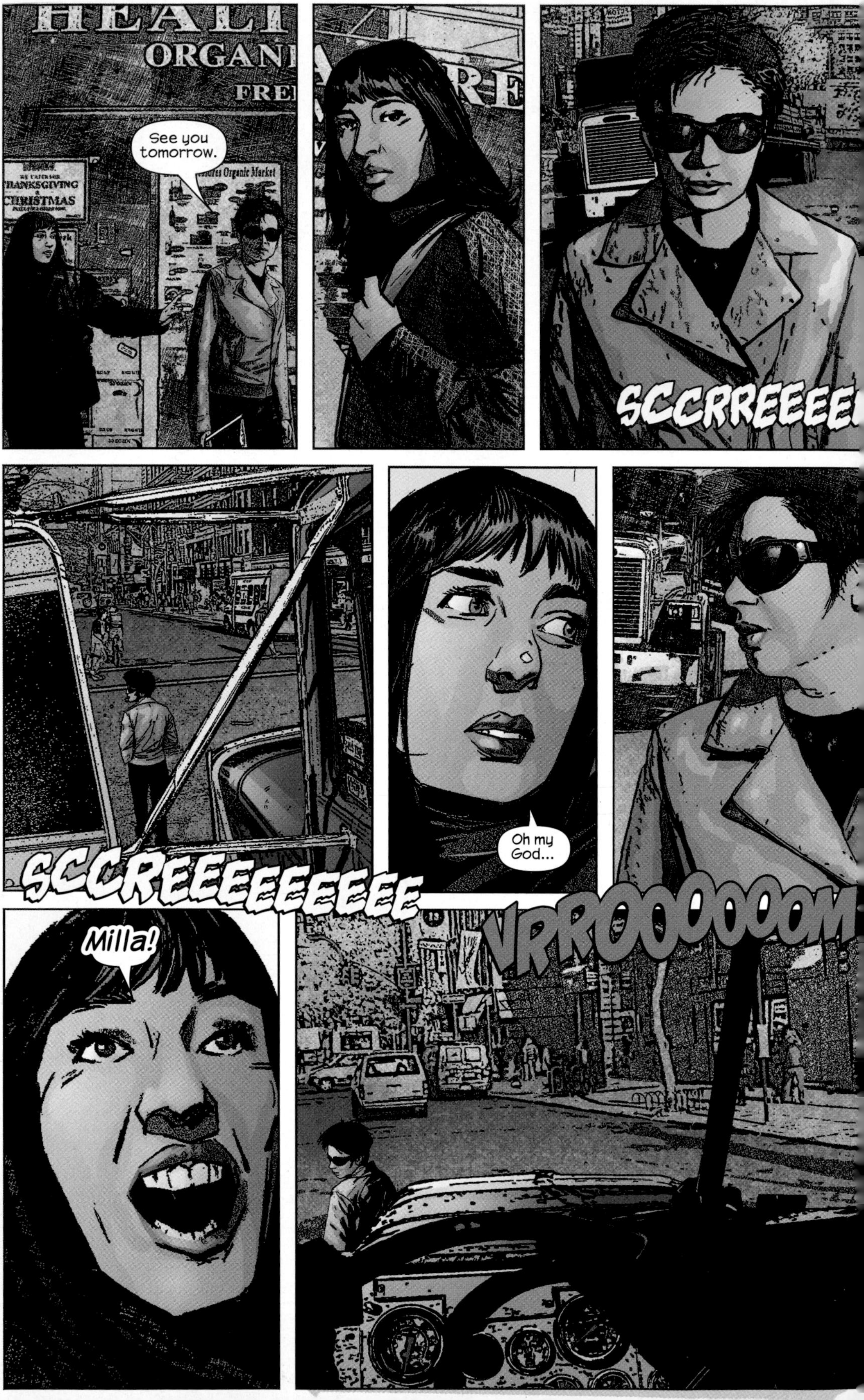
HEALT
ORGANI
FRE
WE CATER FOR
THANKSGIVING
&
CHRISTMAS
See you
tomorrow.
SCCRREEEEE
SCCREEEEEEEEEE
Oh my
God...
VRROOOOOOM
Milla!

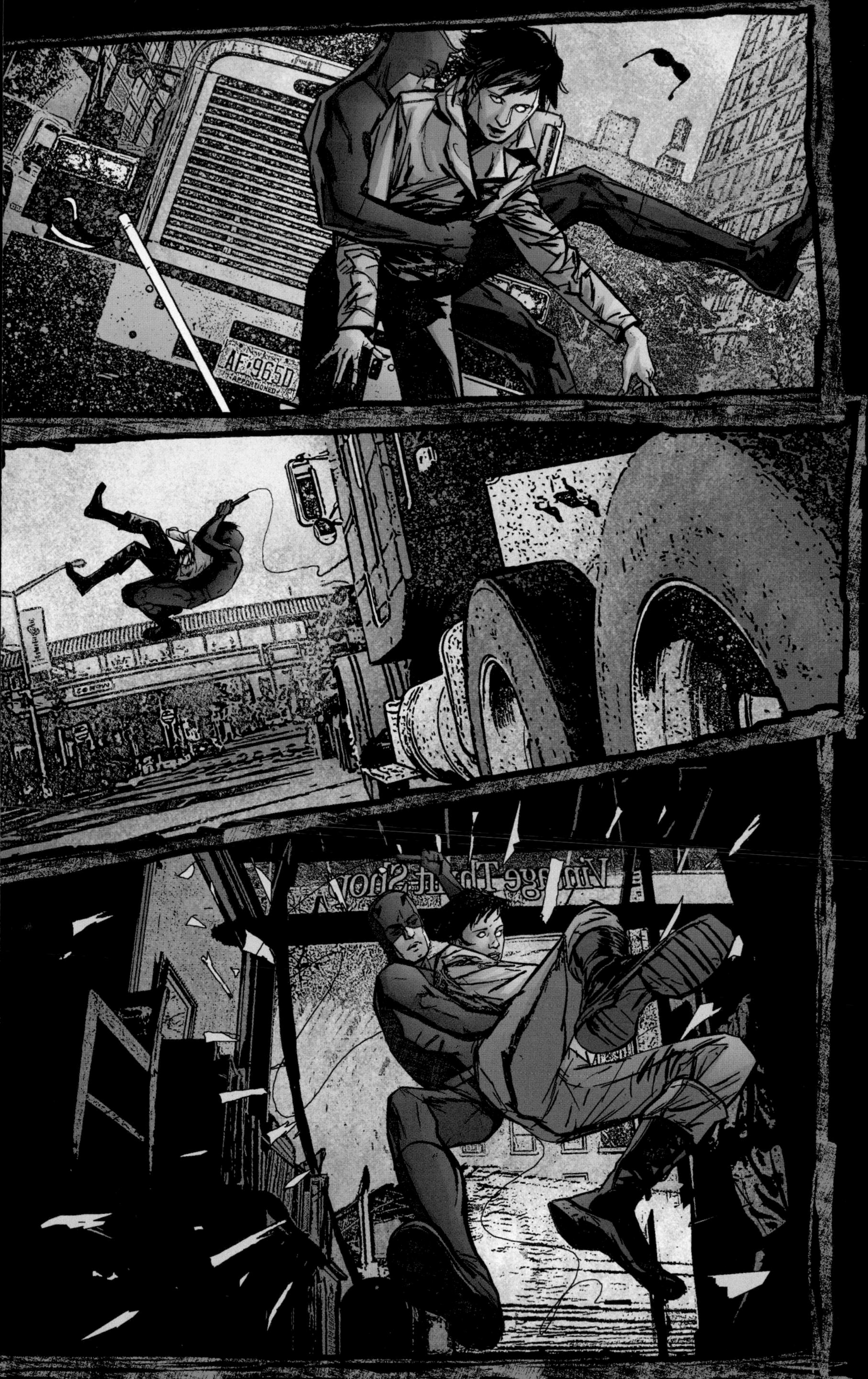
AF 965D
APPORTIONED

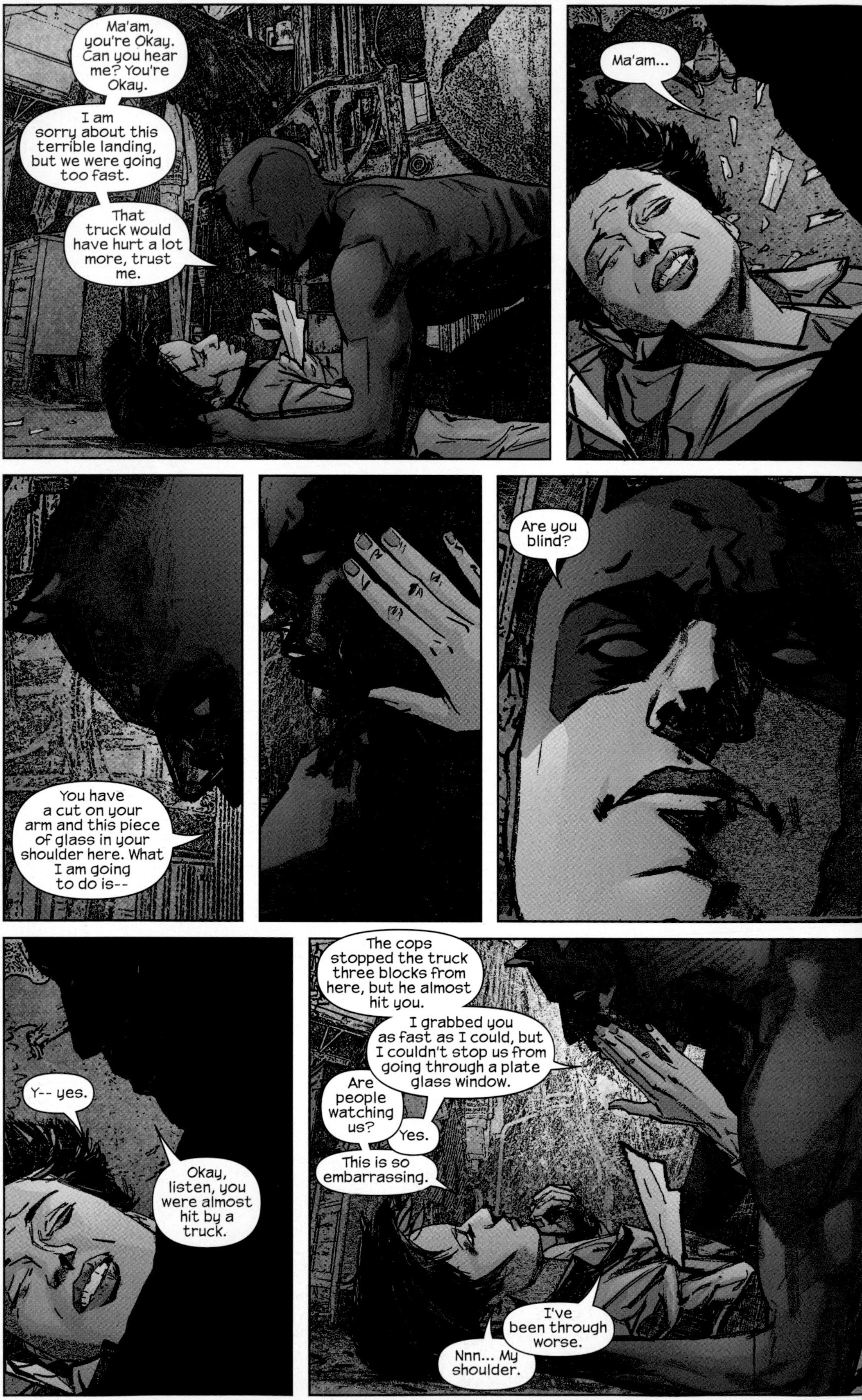

Ma'am, you're Okay. Can you hear me? You're Okay.
I am sorry about this terrible landing, but we were going too fast.
That truck would have hurt a lot more, trust me.
Ma'am...
You have a cut on your arm and this piece of glass in your shoulder here. What I am going to do is--
Are you blind?
Y-- yes.
Okay, listen, you were almost hit by a truck.
The cops stopped the truck three blocks from here, but he almost hit you.
I grabbed you as fast as I could, but I couldn't stop us from going through a plate glass window.
Are people watching us?
Yes.
This is so embarrassing.
I've been through worse.
Nnn... My shoulder.

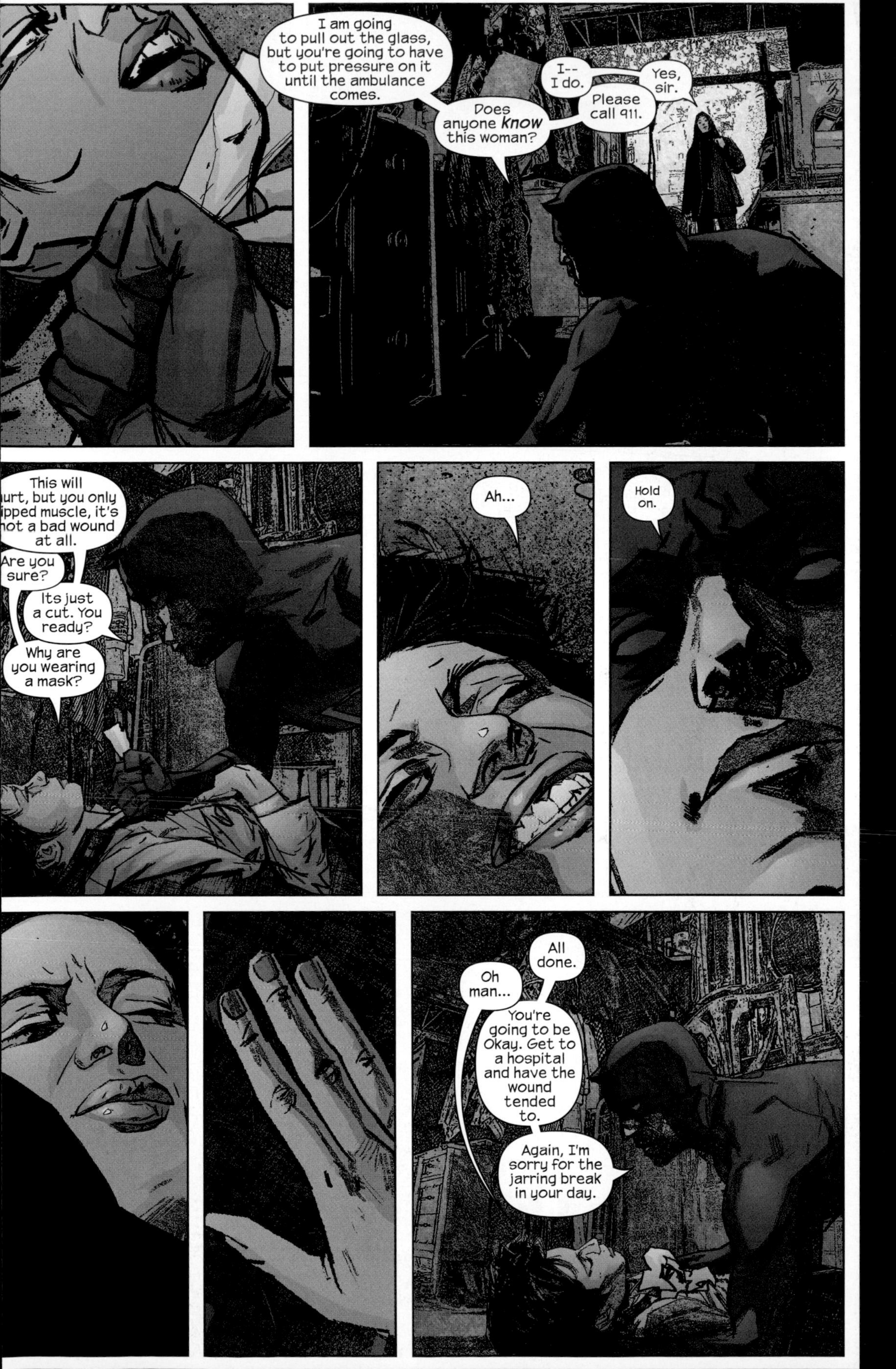
I am going to pull out the glass, but you're going to have to put pressure on it until the ambulance comes.
Does anyone *know* this woman?
I-- I do.
Yes, sir.
Please call 911.
This will urt, but you only ipped muscle, it's not a bad wound at all.
Are you sure?
Its just a cut. You ready?
Why are you wearing a mask?
Ah...
Hold on.
All done.
Oh man...
You're going to be Okay. Get to a hospital and have the wound tended to.
Again, I'm sorry for the jarring break in your day.

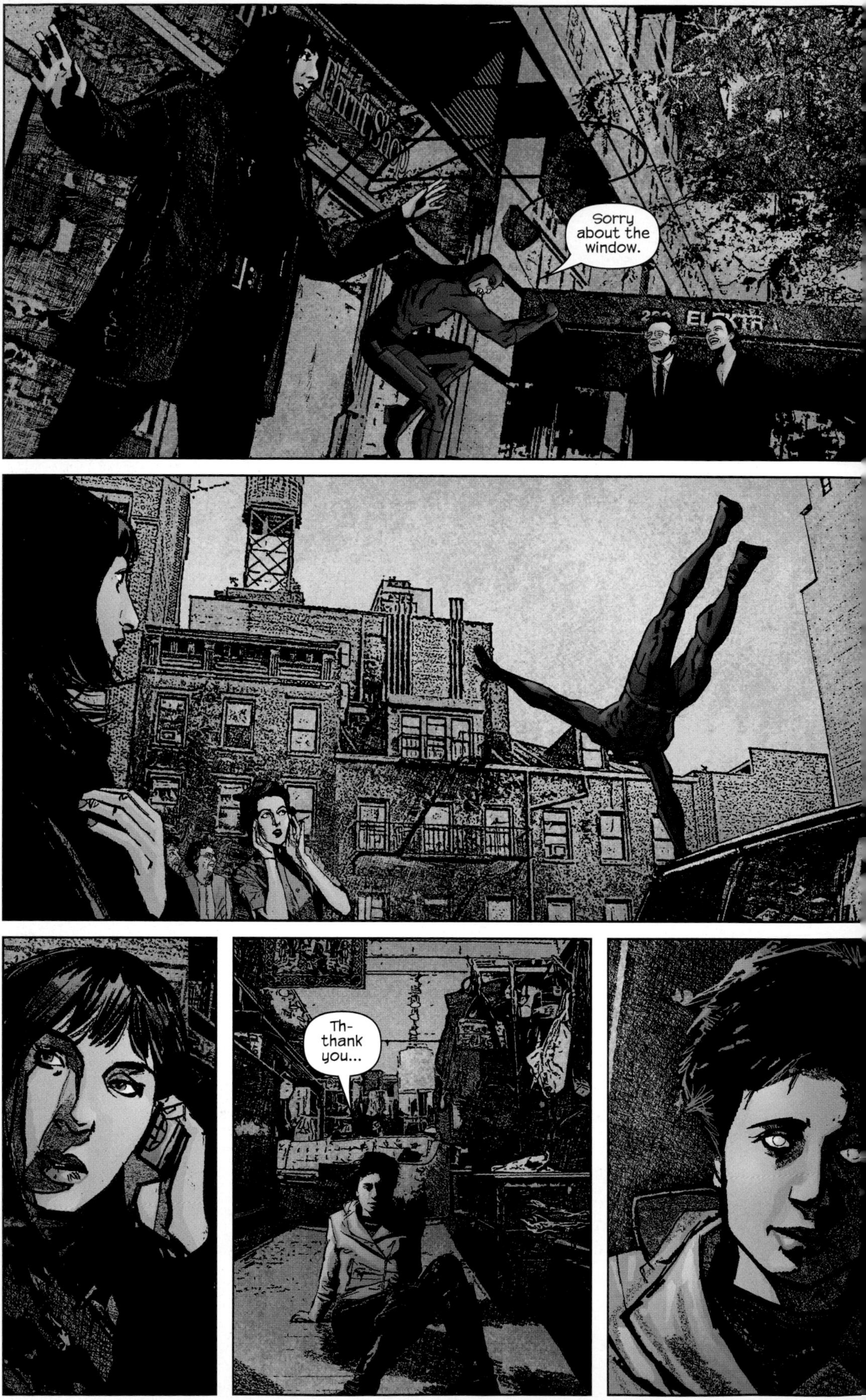
Sorry about the window.
Th- thank you...

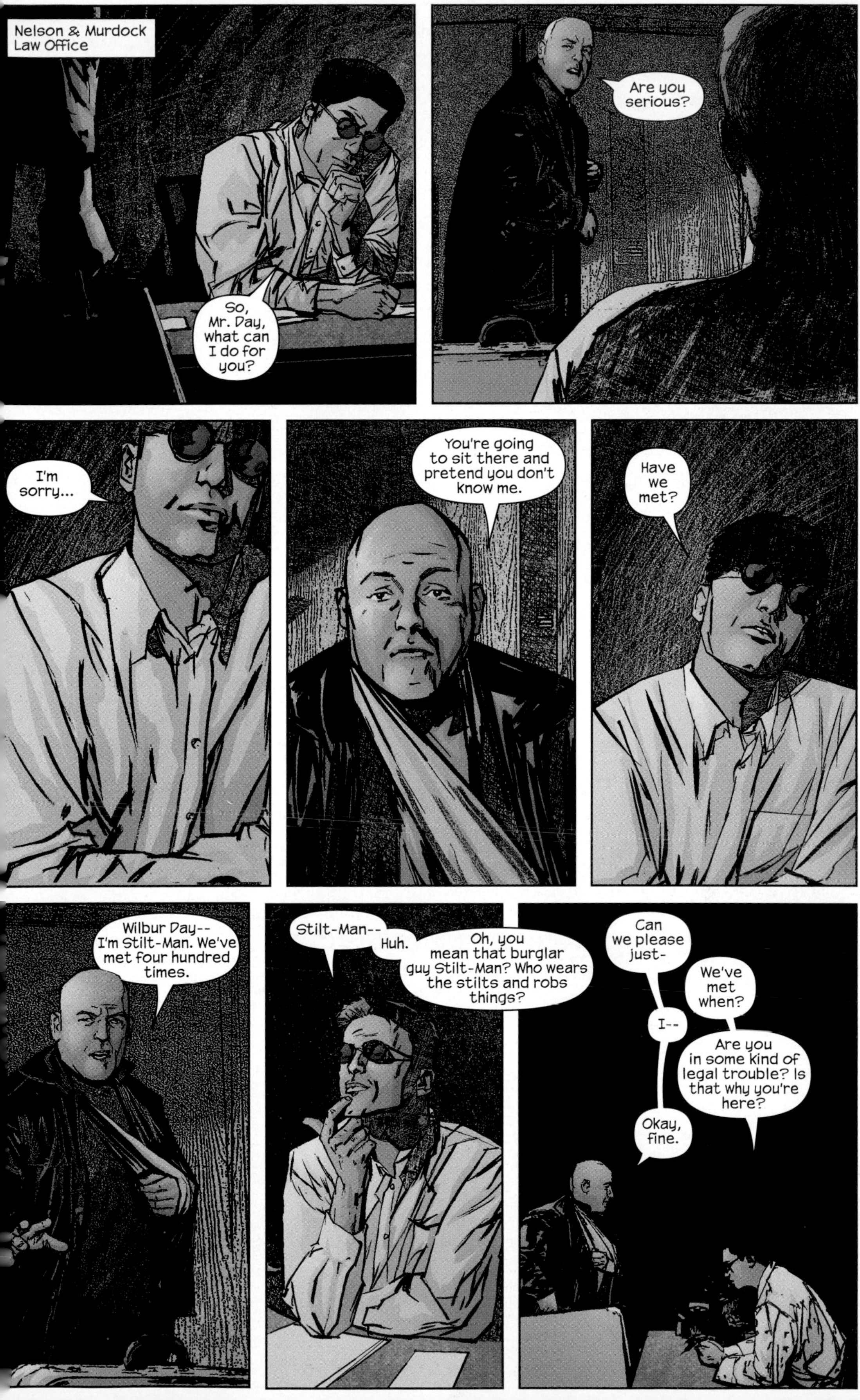
Nelson & Murdock
Law Office
So, Mr. Day, what can I do for you?
Are you serious?
I'm sorry...
You're going to sit there and pretend you don't know me.
Have we met?
Wilbur Day-- I'm Stilt-Man. We've met four hundred times.
Stilt-Man--
Huh.
Oh, you mean that burglar guy Stilt-Man? Who wears the stilts and robs things?
Can we please just-
We've met when?
I--
Are you in some kind of legal trouble? Is that why you're here?
Okay, fine.

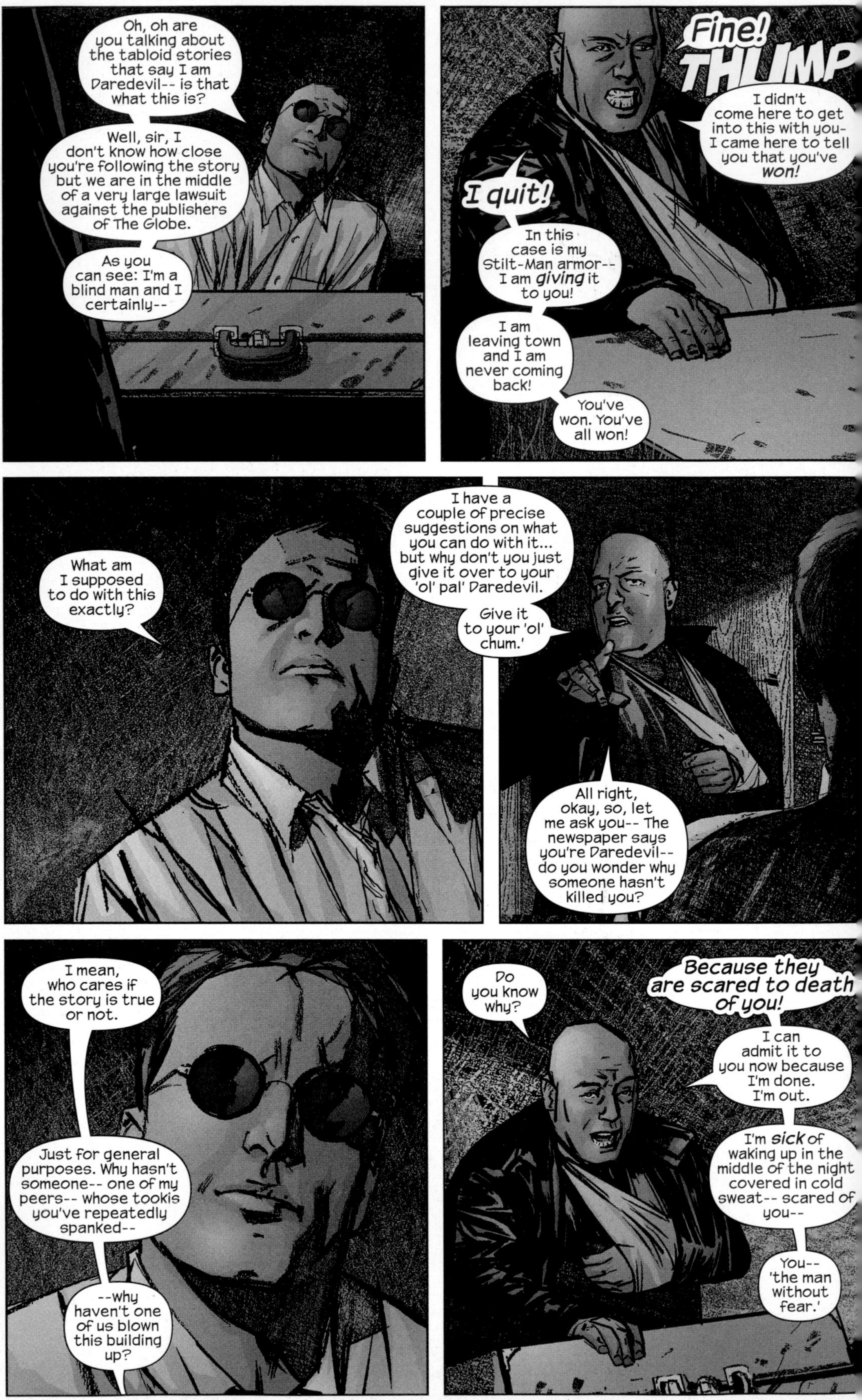

Oh, oh are you talking about the tabloid stories that say I am Daredevil-- is that what this is?
Well, sir, I don't know how close you're following the story but we are in the middle of a very large lawsuit against the publishers of The Globe.
As you can see: I'm a blind man and I certainly--
Fine!
THUMP
I didn't come here to get into this with you-- I came here to tell you that you've won!
I quit!
In this case is my Stilt-Man armor-- I am giving it to you!
I am leaving town and I am never coming back!
You've won. You've all won!
What am I supposed to do with this exactly?
I have a couple of precise suggestions on what you can do with it... but why don't you just give it over to your 'ol' pal' Daredevil.
Give it to your 'ol' chum.'
All right, okay, so, let me ask you-- The newspaper says you're Daredevil-- do you wonder why someone hasn't killed you?
I mean, who cares if the story is true or not.
Just for general purposes. Why hasn't someone-- one of my peers-- whose tookis you've repeatedly spanked--
--why haven't one of us blown this building up?
Do you know why?
Because they are scared to death of you!
I can admit it to you now because I'm done. I'm out.
I'm sick of waking up in the middle of the night covered in cold sweat-- scared of you--
You-- 'the man without fear.'

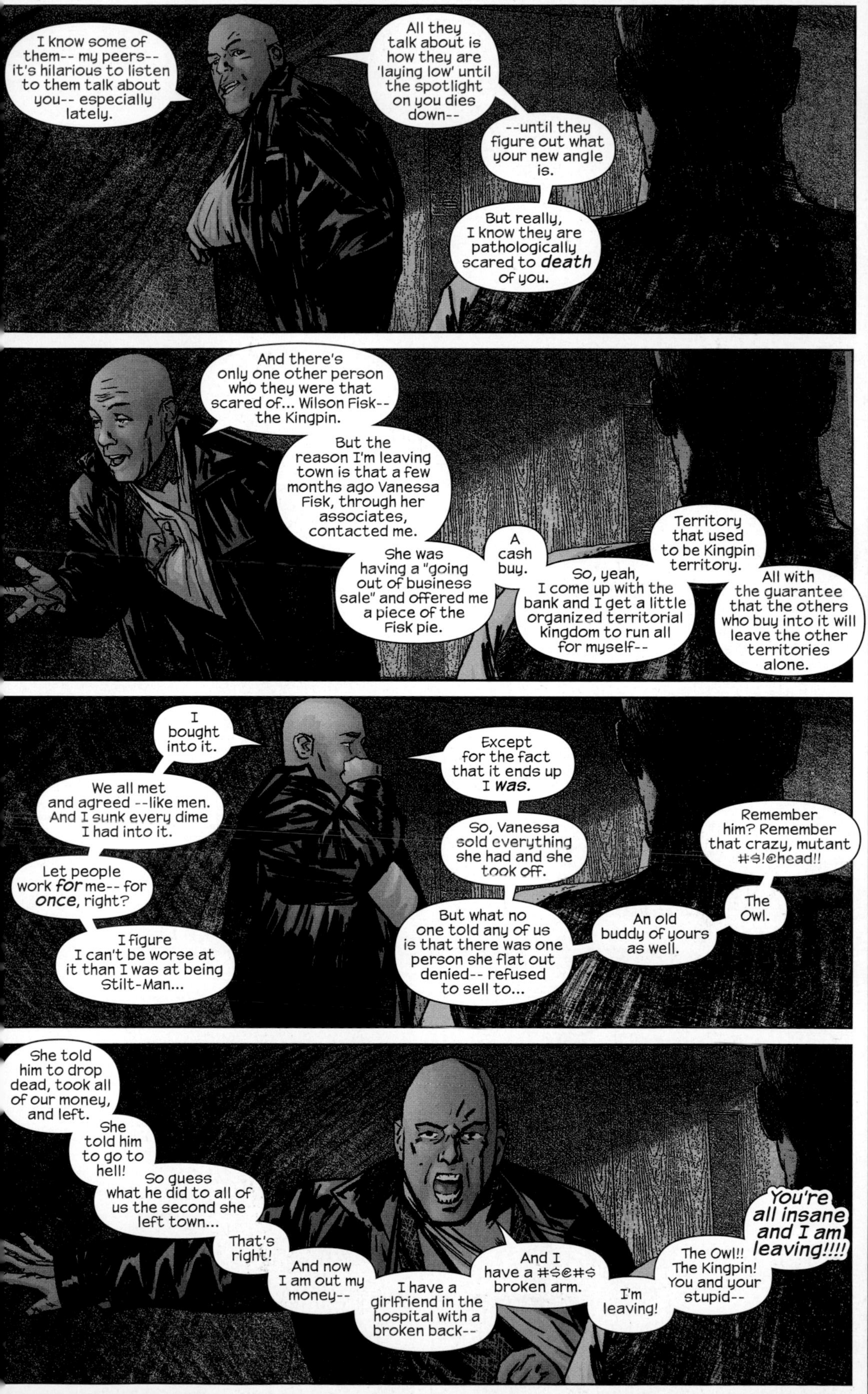
I know some of them-- my peers-- it's hilarious to listen to them talk about you-- especially lately.
All they talk about is how they are 'laying low' until the spotlight on you dies down--
--until they figure out what your new angle is.
But really, I know they are pathologically scared to death of you.
And there's only one other person who they were that scared of... Wilson Fisk-- the Kingpin.
But the reason I'm leaving town is that a few months ago Vanessa Fisk, through her associates, contacted me.
She was having a "going out of business sale" and offered me a piece of the Fisk pie.
A cash buy.
Territory that used to be Kingpin territory.
So, yeah, I come up with the bank and I get a little organized territorial kingdom to run all for myself--
All with the guarantee that the others who buy into it will leave the other territories alone.
I bought into it.
We all met and agreed --like men. And I sunk every dime I had into it.
Let people work for me-- for once, right?
I figure I can't be worse at it than I was at being Stilt-Man...
Except for the fact that it ends up I was.
So, Vanessa sold everything she had and she took off.
But what no one told any of us is that there was one person she flat out denied-- refused to sell to...
An old buddy of yours as well.
The Owl.
Remember him? Remember that crazy, mutant #$!@head!!
She told him to drop dead, took all of our money, and left.
She told him to go to hell!
So guess what he did to all of us the second she left town...
That's right!
And now I am out my money--
I have a girlfriend in the hospital with a broken back--
And I have a #$@#$ broken arm.
I'm leaving!
The Owl!! The Kingpin! You and your stupid--
You're all insane and I am leaving!!!!

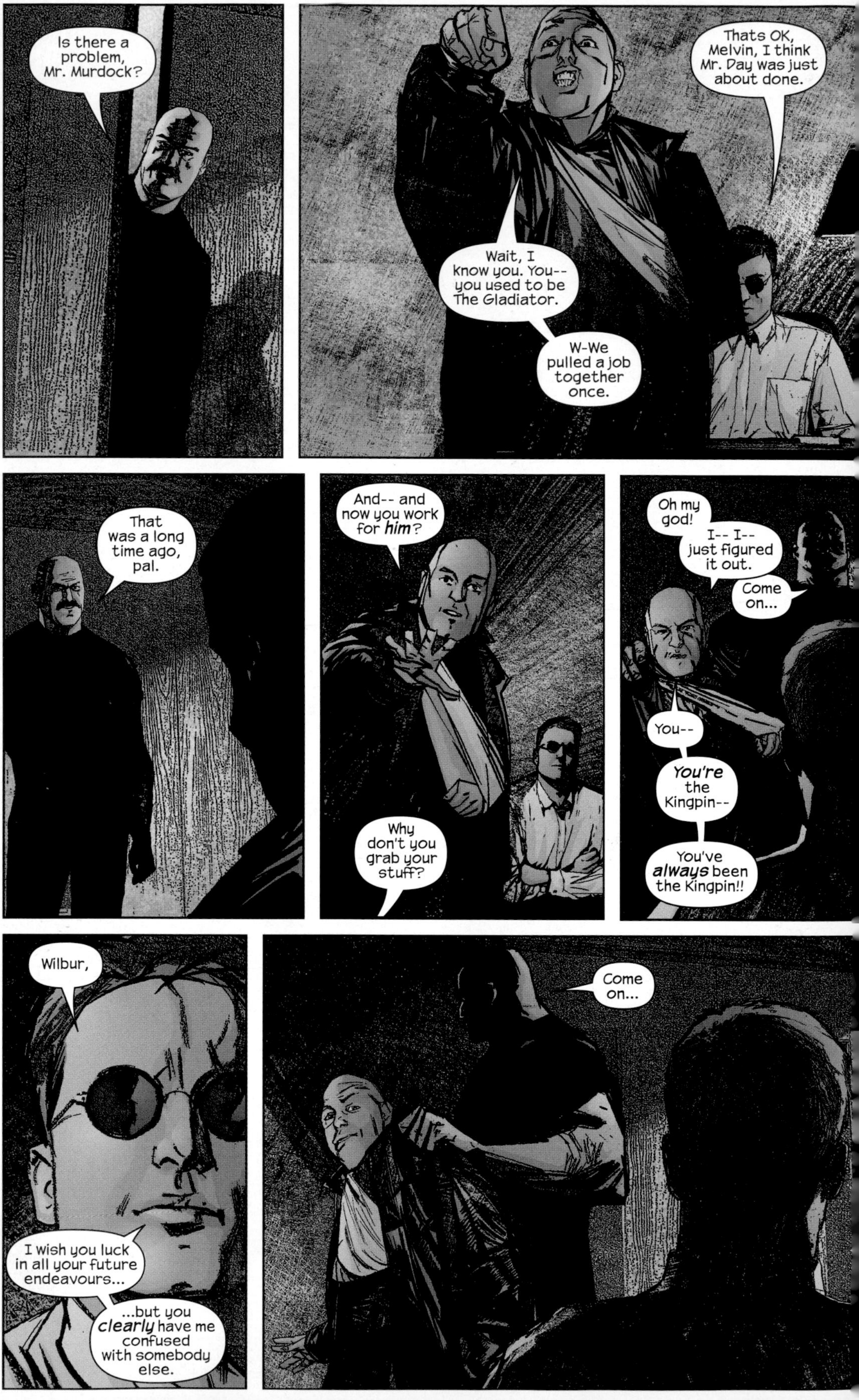
Is there a problem, Mr. Murdock?
Thats OK, Melvin, I think Mr. Day was just about done.
Wait, I know you. You-- you used to be The Gladiator.
W-We pulled a job together once.
That was a long time ago, pal.
And-- and now you work for *him*?
Why don't you grab your stuff?
Oh my god!
I-- I-- just figured it out.
Come on...
You--
You're the Kingpin--
You've *always* been the Kingpin!!
Wilbur,
I wish you luck in all your future endeavours...
...but you *clearly* have me confused with somebody else.
Come on...

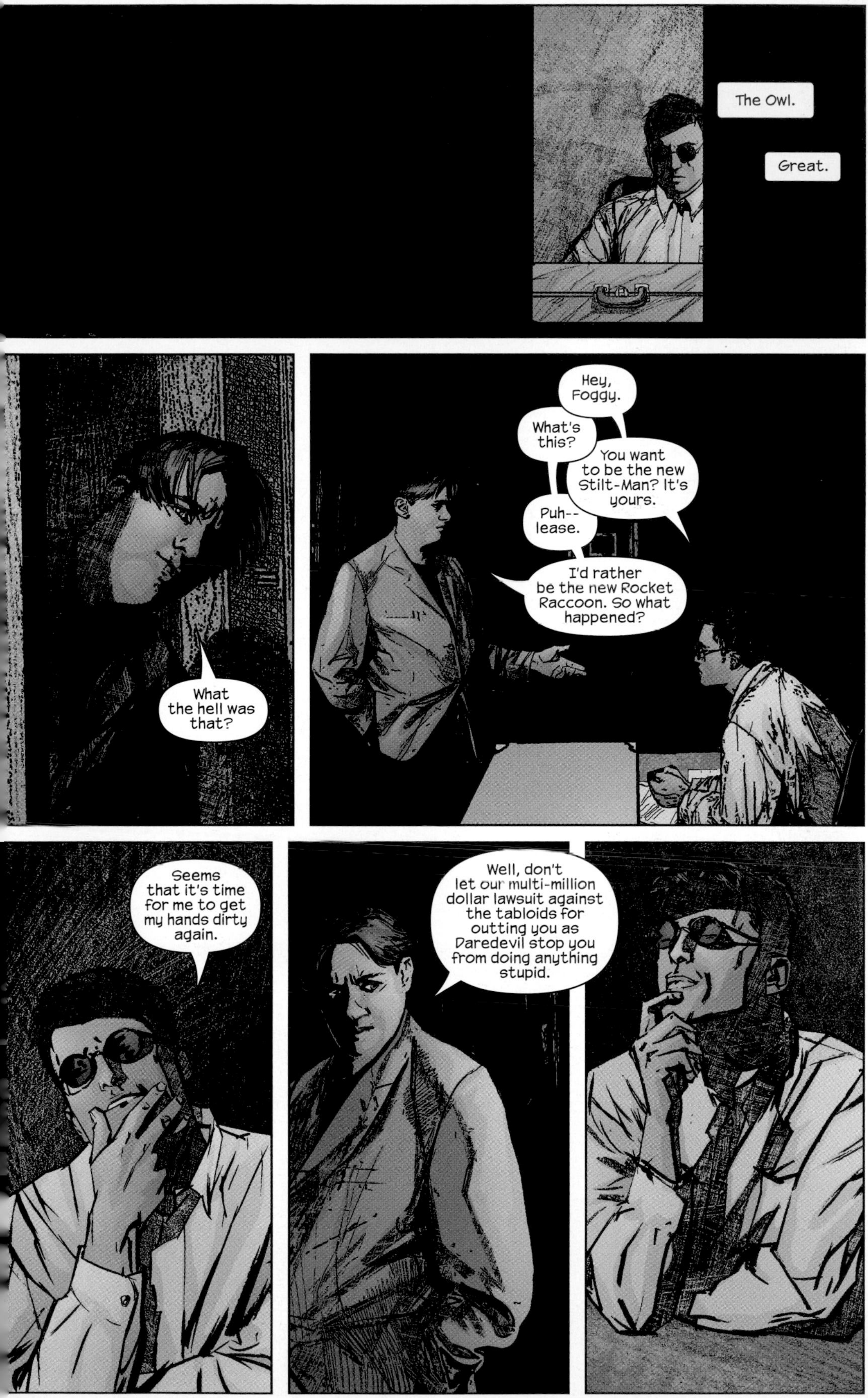
The Owl.
Great.
What the hell was that?
Hey, Foggy.
What's this?
You want to be the new Stilt-Man? It's yours.
Puh-- lease.
I'd rather be the new Rocket Raccoon. So what happened?
Seems that it's time for me to get my hands dirty again.
Well, don't let our multi-million dollar lawsuit against the tabloids for outting you as Daredevil stop you from doing anything stupid.

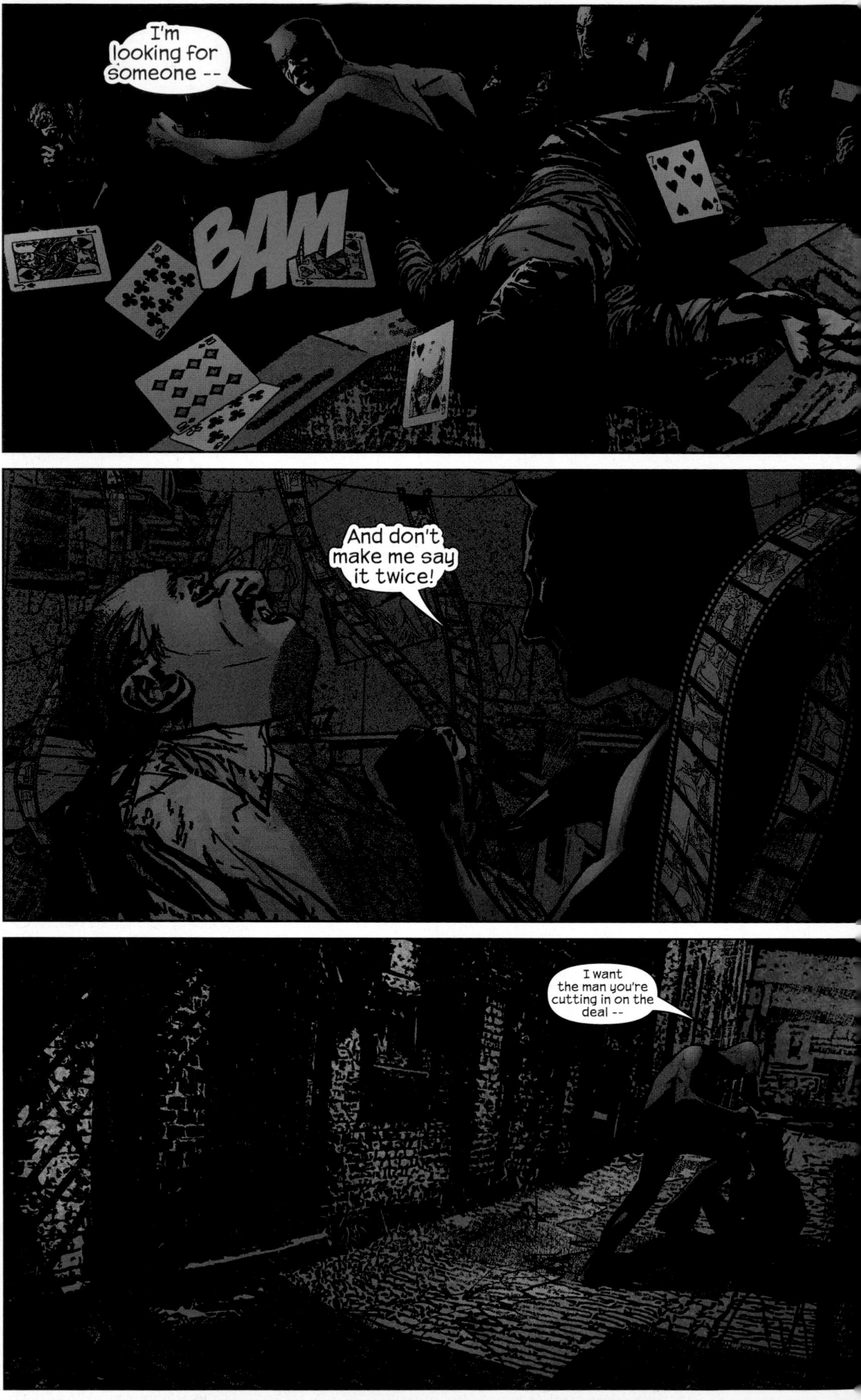
I'm looking for someone --
BAM
And don't make me say it twice!
I want the man you're cutting in on the deal --

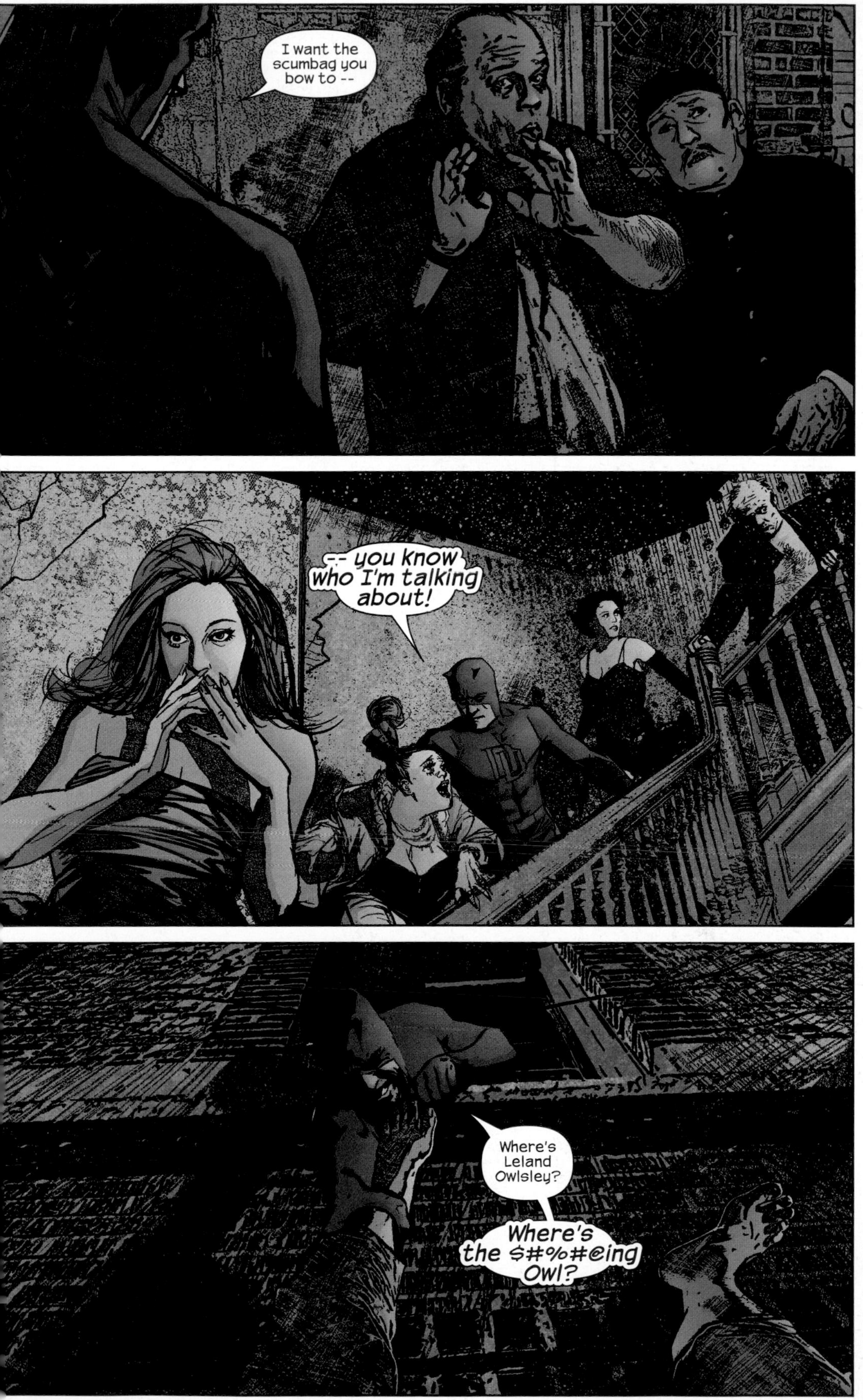
I want the scumbag you bow to --
-- you know who I'm talking about!
Where's Leland Owlsley?
Where's the $#%#@ing Owl?

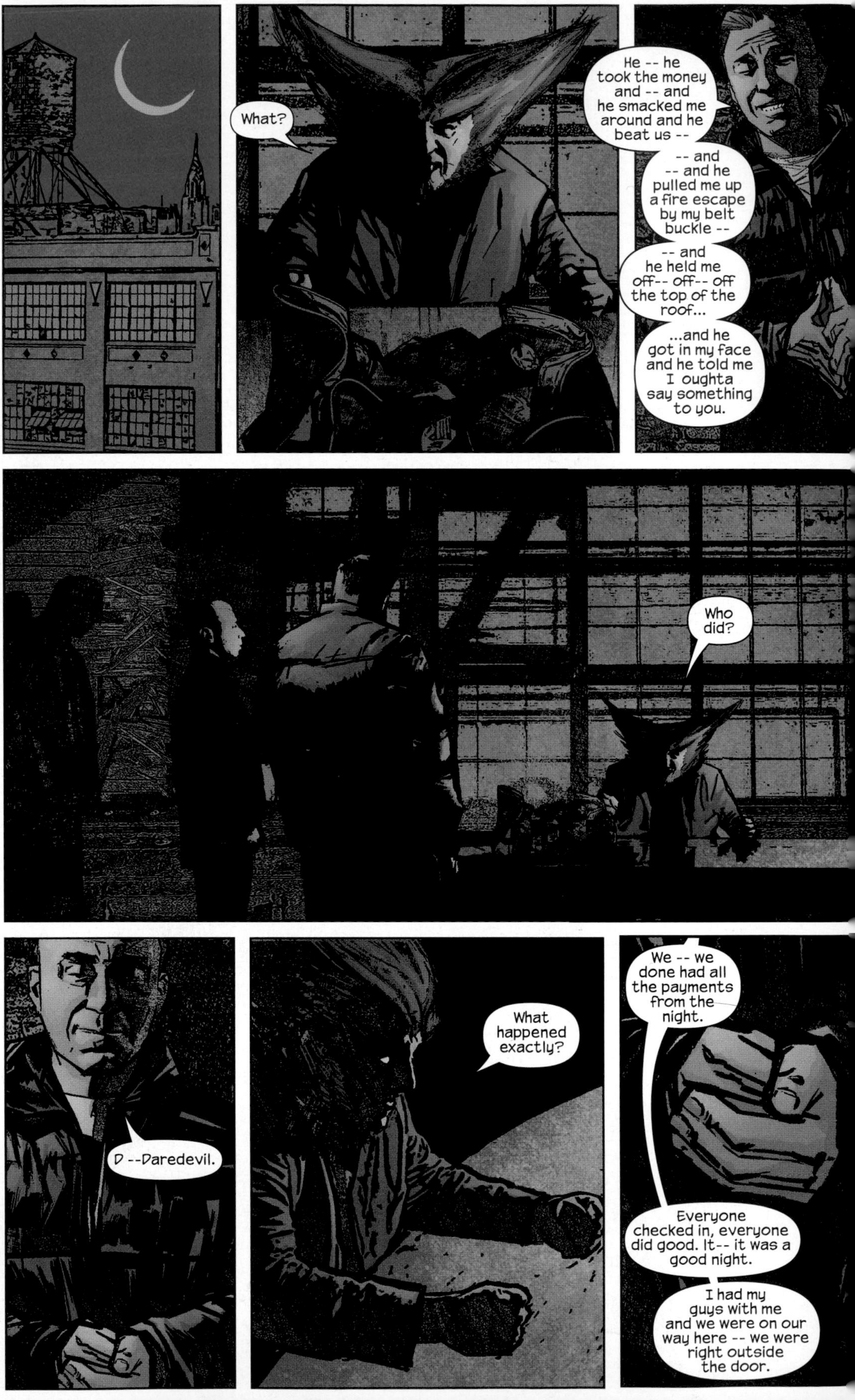
What?
He -- he took the money and -- and he smacked me around and he beat us --
-- and -- and he pulled me up a fire escape by my belt buckle --
-- and he held me off-- off-- off the top of the roof...
...and he got in my face and he told me I oughta say something to you.
Who did?
D --Daredevil.
What happened exactly?
We -- we done had all the payments from the night.
Everyone checked in, everyone did good. It-- it was a good night.
I had my guys with me and we were on our way here -- we were right outside the door.

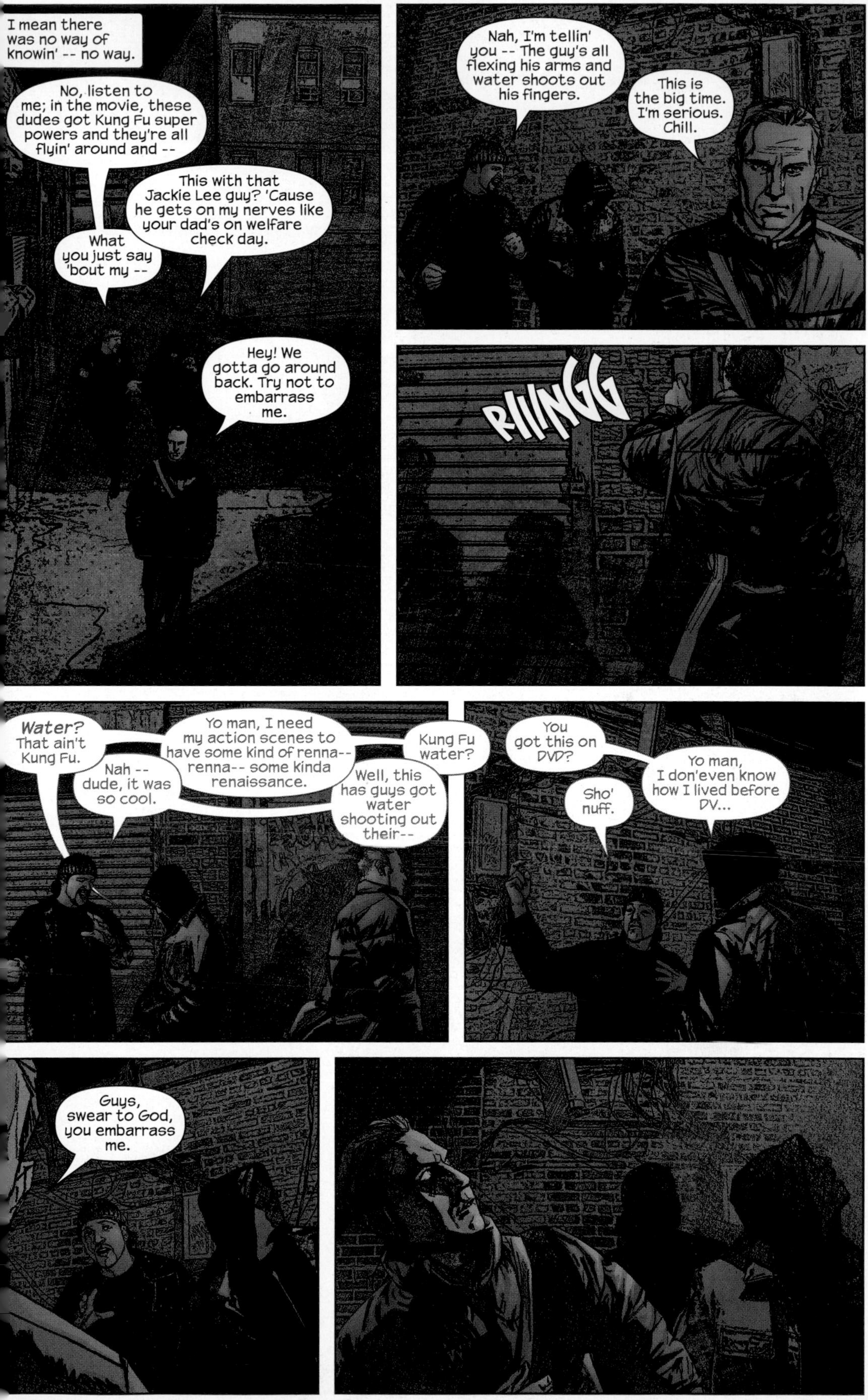
I mean there was no way of knowin' -- no way.
No, listen to me; in the movie, these dudes got Kung Fu super powers and they're all flyin' around and --
This with that Jackie Lee guy? 'Cause he gets on my nerves like your dad's on welfare check day.
What you just say 'bout my --
Hey! We gotta go around back. Try not to embarrass me.
Nah, I'm tellin' you -- The guy's all flexing his arms and water shoots out his fingers.
This is the big time. I'm serious. Chill.
RIIINGG
Water? That ain't Kung Fu.
Yo man, I need my action scenes to have some kind of renna-- renna-- some kinda renaissance.
Kung Fu water?
Nah -- dude, it was so cool.
Well, this has guys got water shooting out their--
You got this on DVD?
Yo man, I don'even know how I lived before DV...
Sho' nuff.
Guys, swear to God, you embarrass me.

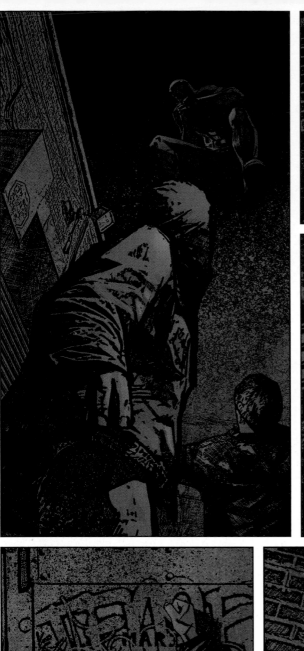

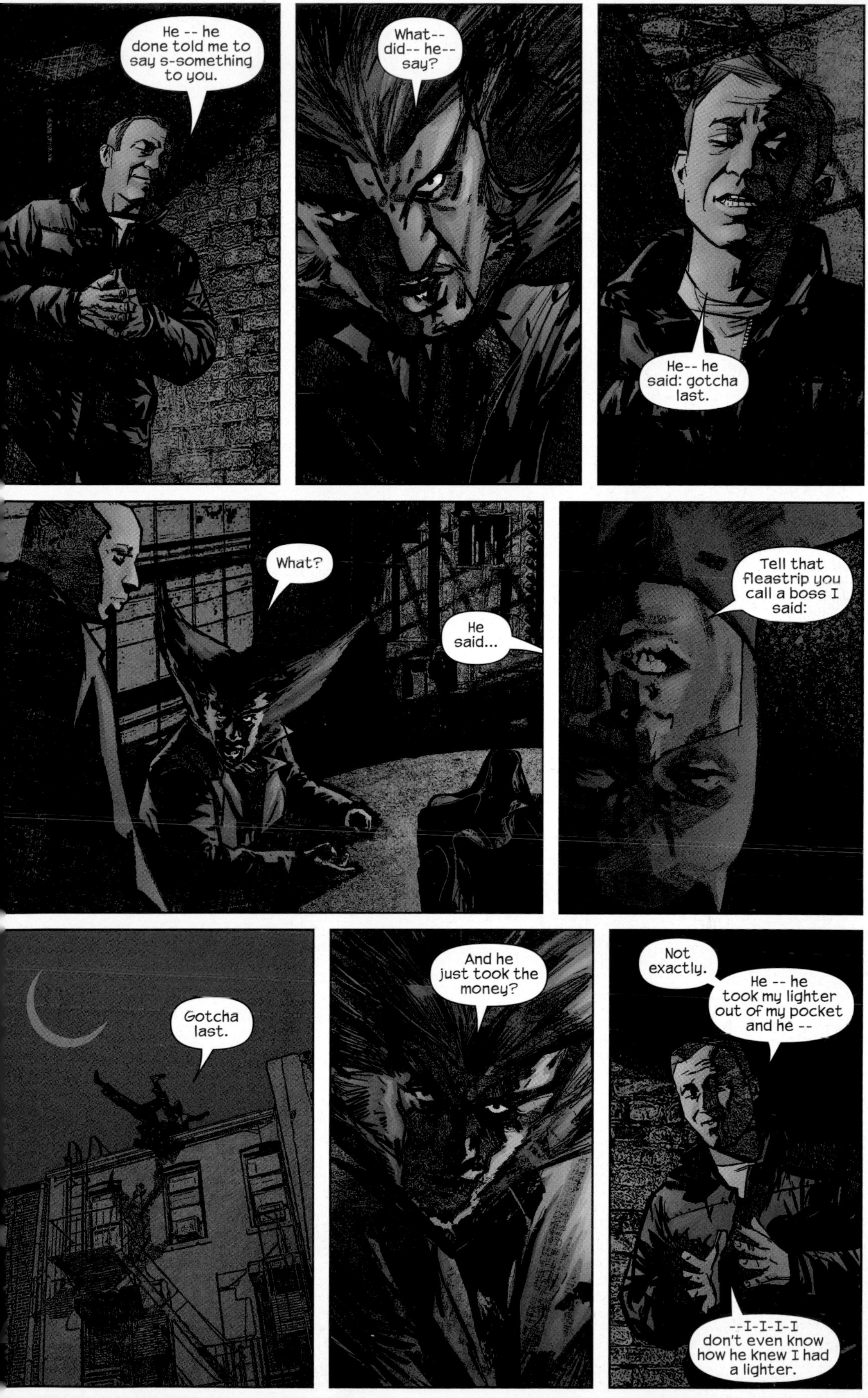
He -- he done told me to say s-something to you.
What-- did-- he-- say?
He-- he said: gotcha last.
What?
He said...
Tell that fleastrip you call a boss I said:
Gotcha last.
And he just took the money?
Not exactly.
He -- he took my lighter out of my pocket and he --
--I-I-I-I don't even know how he knew I had a lighter.

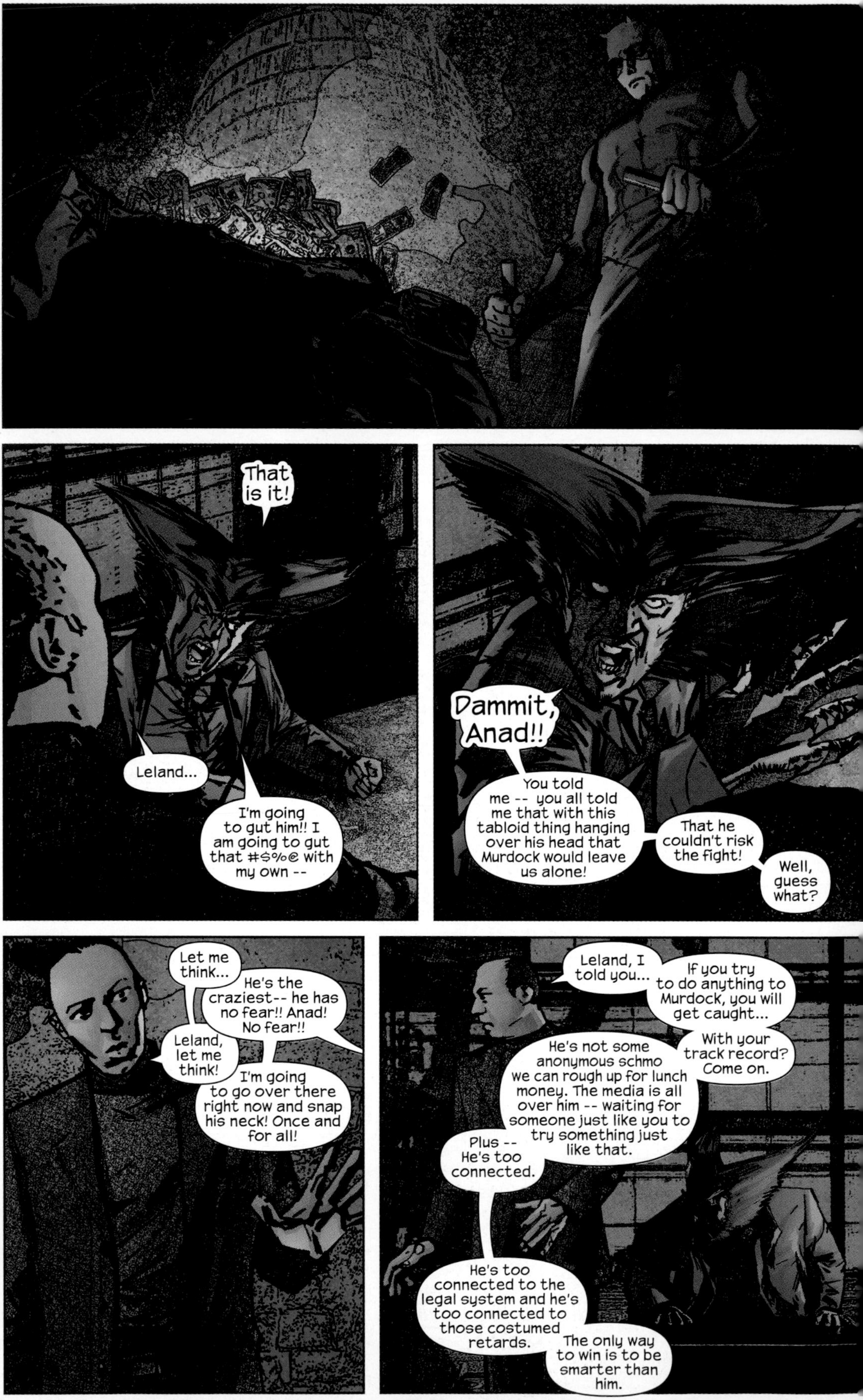
That is it!
Leland...
I'm going to gut him!! I am going to gut that #$%@ with my own --
Dammit, Anad!!
You told me -- you all told me that with this tabloid thing hanging over his head that Murdock would leave us alone!
That he couldn't risk the fight!
Well, guess what?
Let me think...
He's the craziest-- he has no fear!! Anad! No fear!!
Leland, let me think!
I'm going to go over there right now and snap his neck! Once and for all!
Leland, I told you...
If you try to do anything to Murdock, you will get caught...
With your track record? Come on.
He's not some anonymous schmo we can rough up for lunch money. The media is all over him -- waiting for someone just like you to try something just like that.
Plus -- He's too connected.
He's too connected to the legal system and he's too connected to those costumed retards.
The only way to win is to be smarter than him.

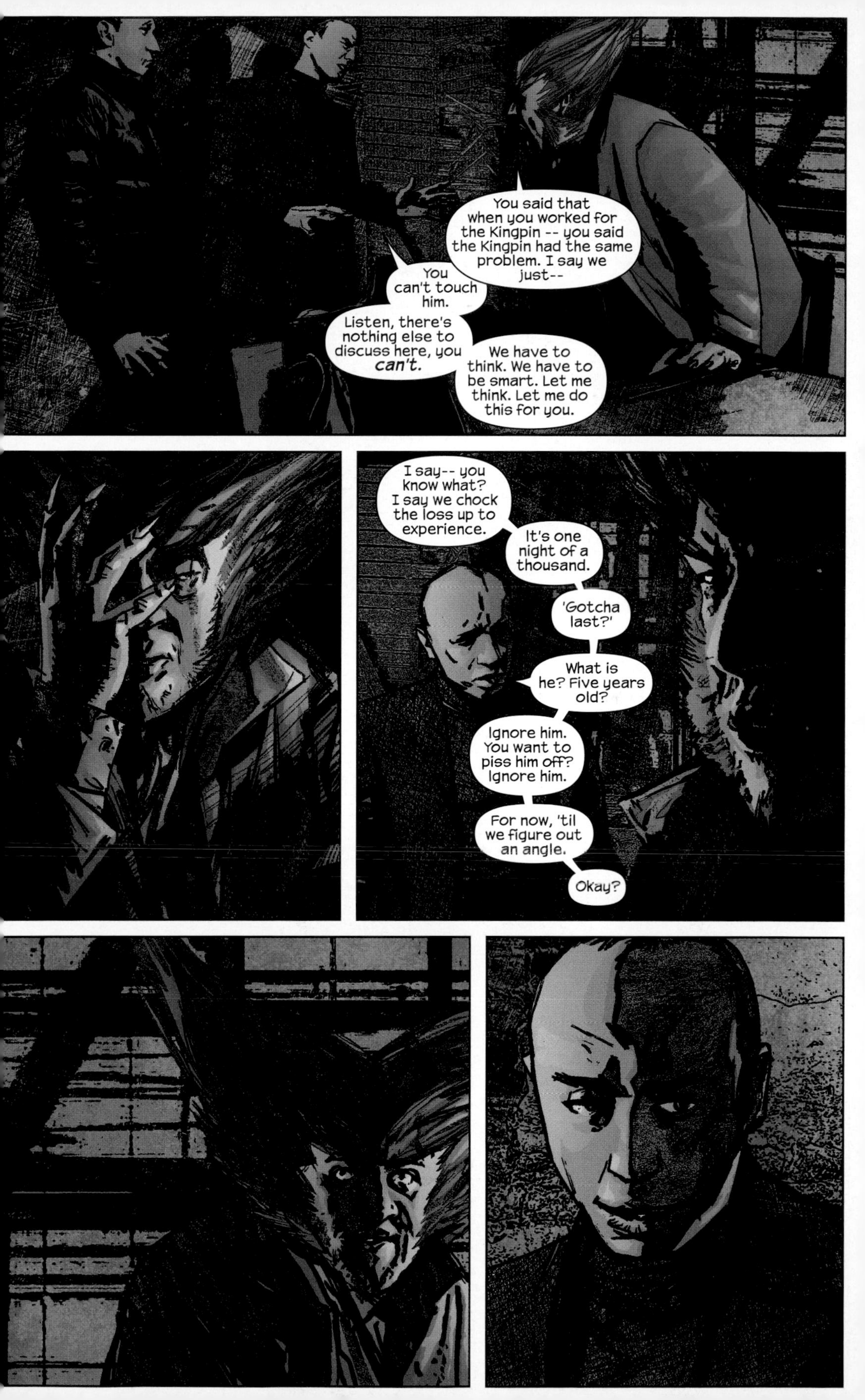
You said that when you worked for the Kingpin -- you said the Kingpin had the same problem. I say we just--
You can't touch him.
Listen, there's nothing else to discuss here, you *can't.*
We have to think. We have to be smart. Let me think. Let me do this for you.
I say-- you know what? I say we chock the loss up to experience.
It's one night of a thousand.
'Gotcha last?'
What is he? Five years old?
Ignore him. You want to piss him off? Ignore him.
For now, 'til we figure out an angle.
Okay?

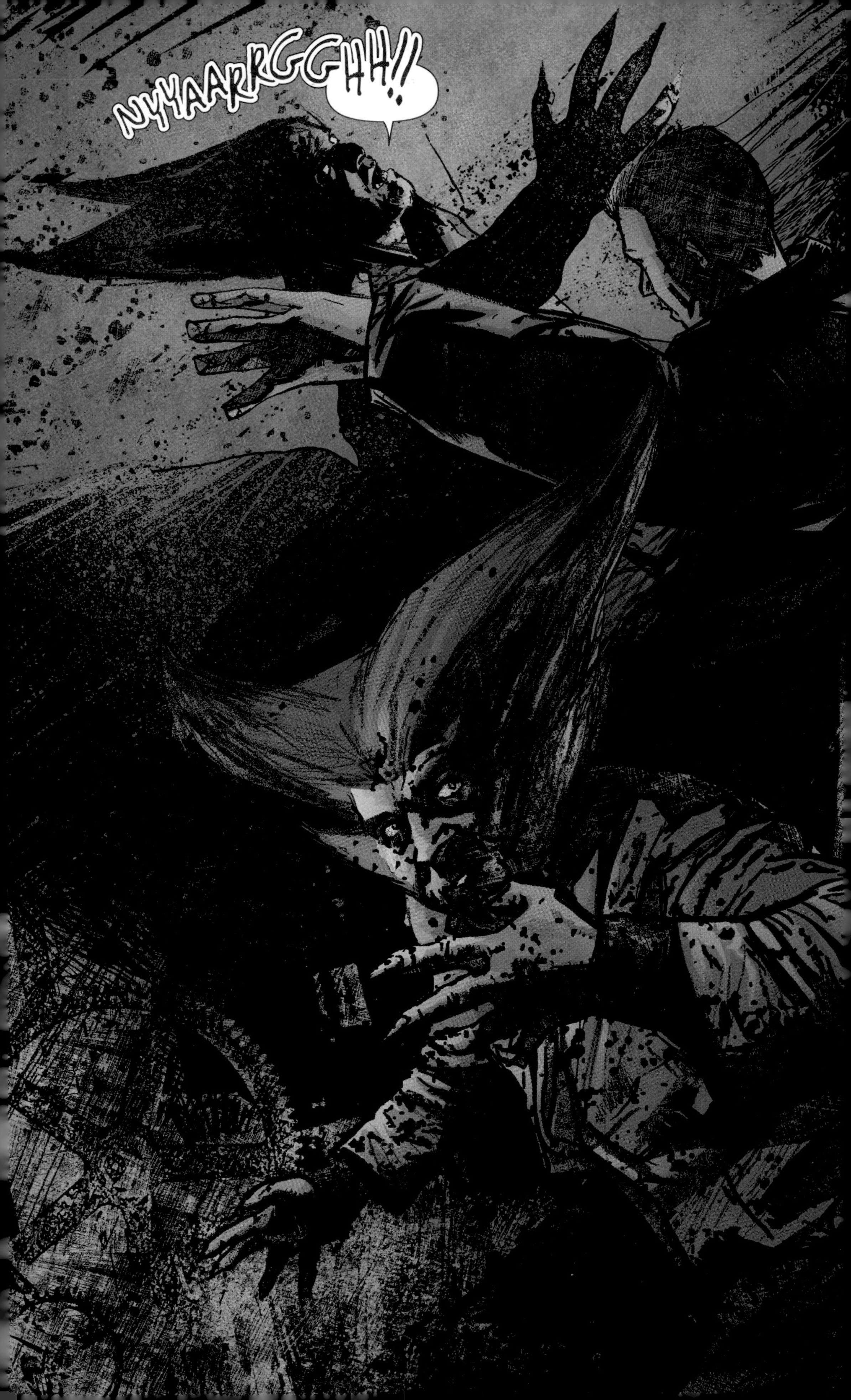
NYYAARRGGHH!!

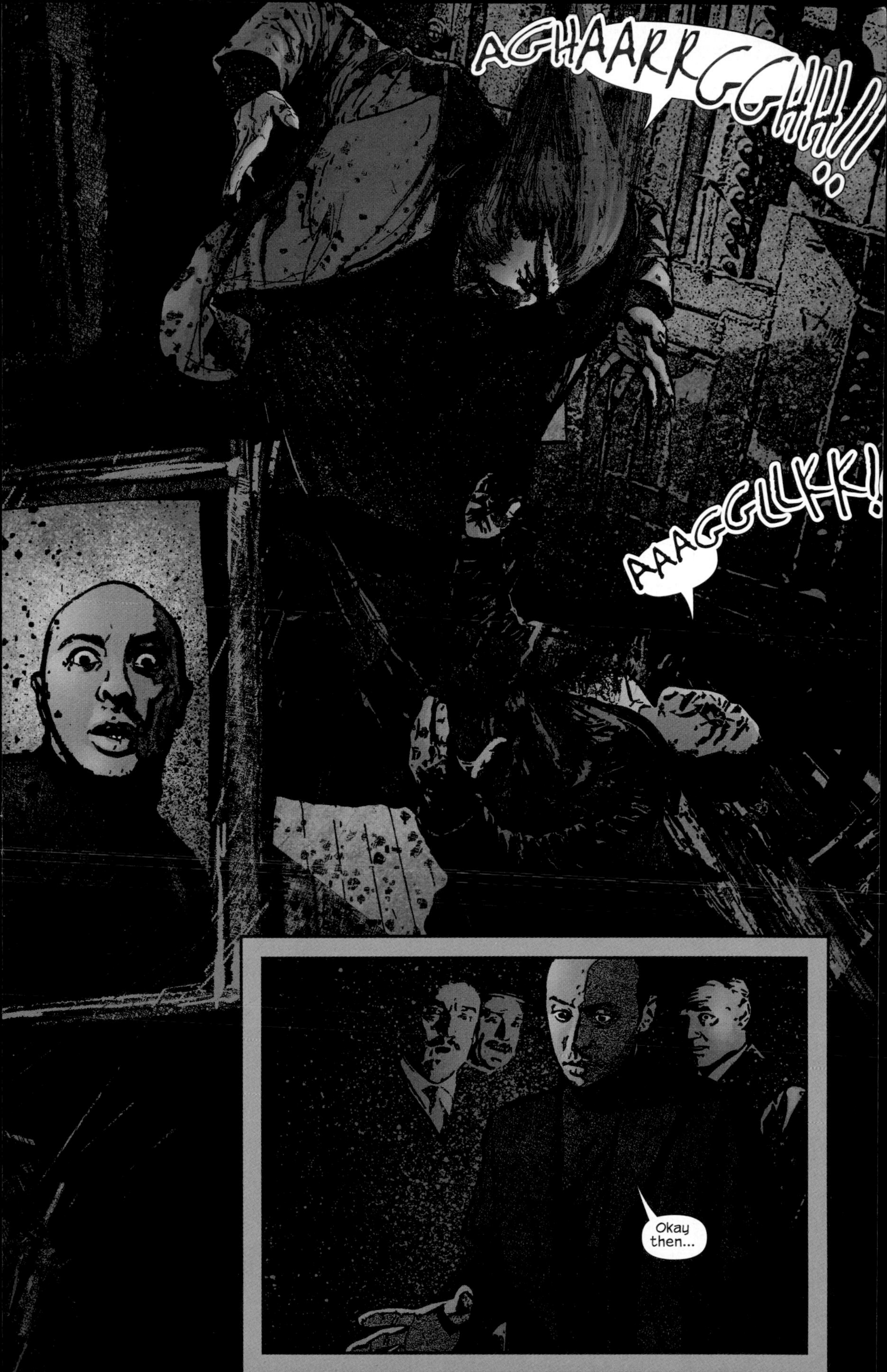
AGHAARRGGHH!!
AAAGGLLKK!
Okay then...

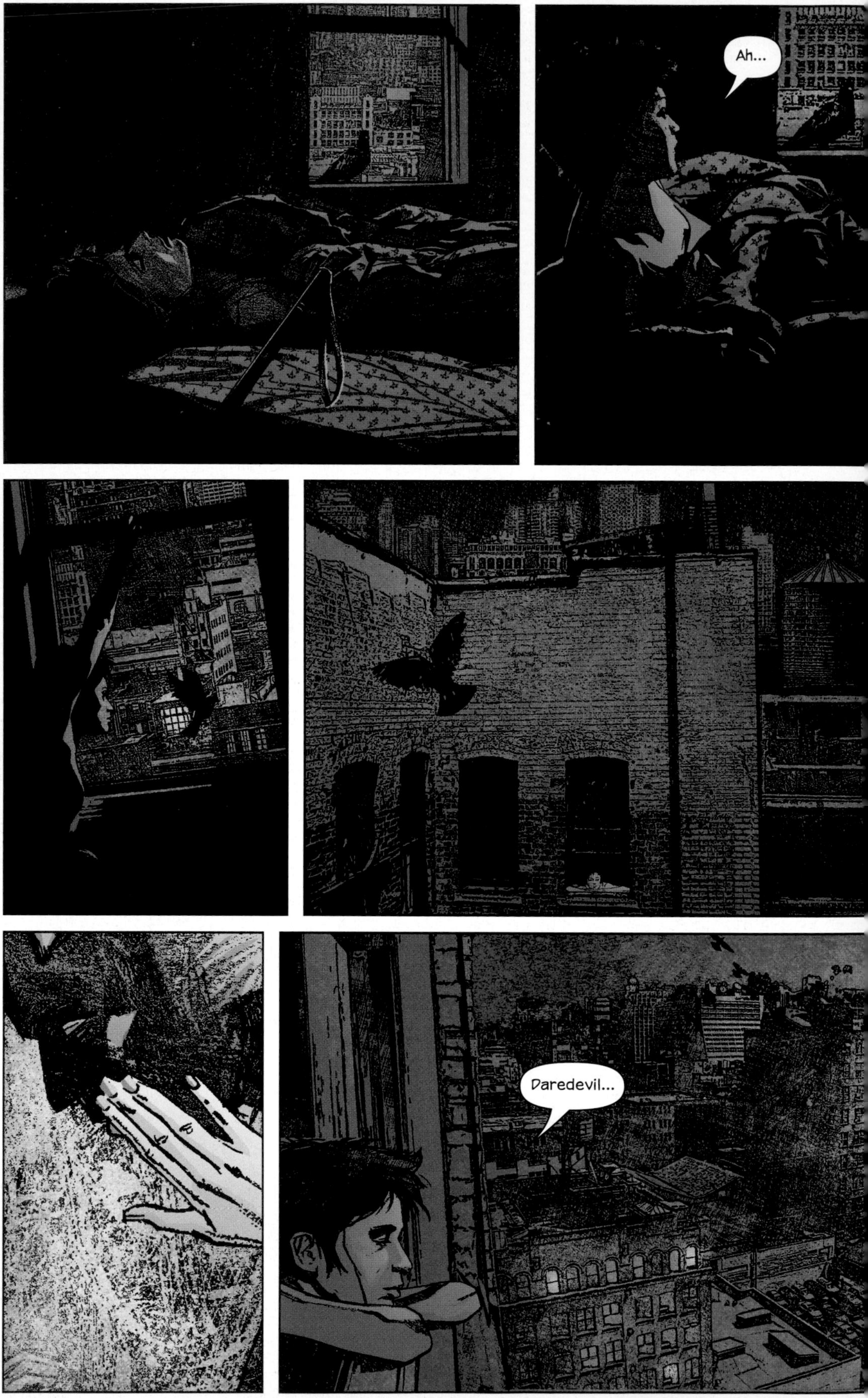
Ah...
Daredevil...

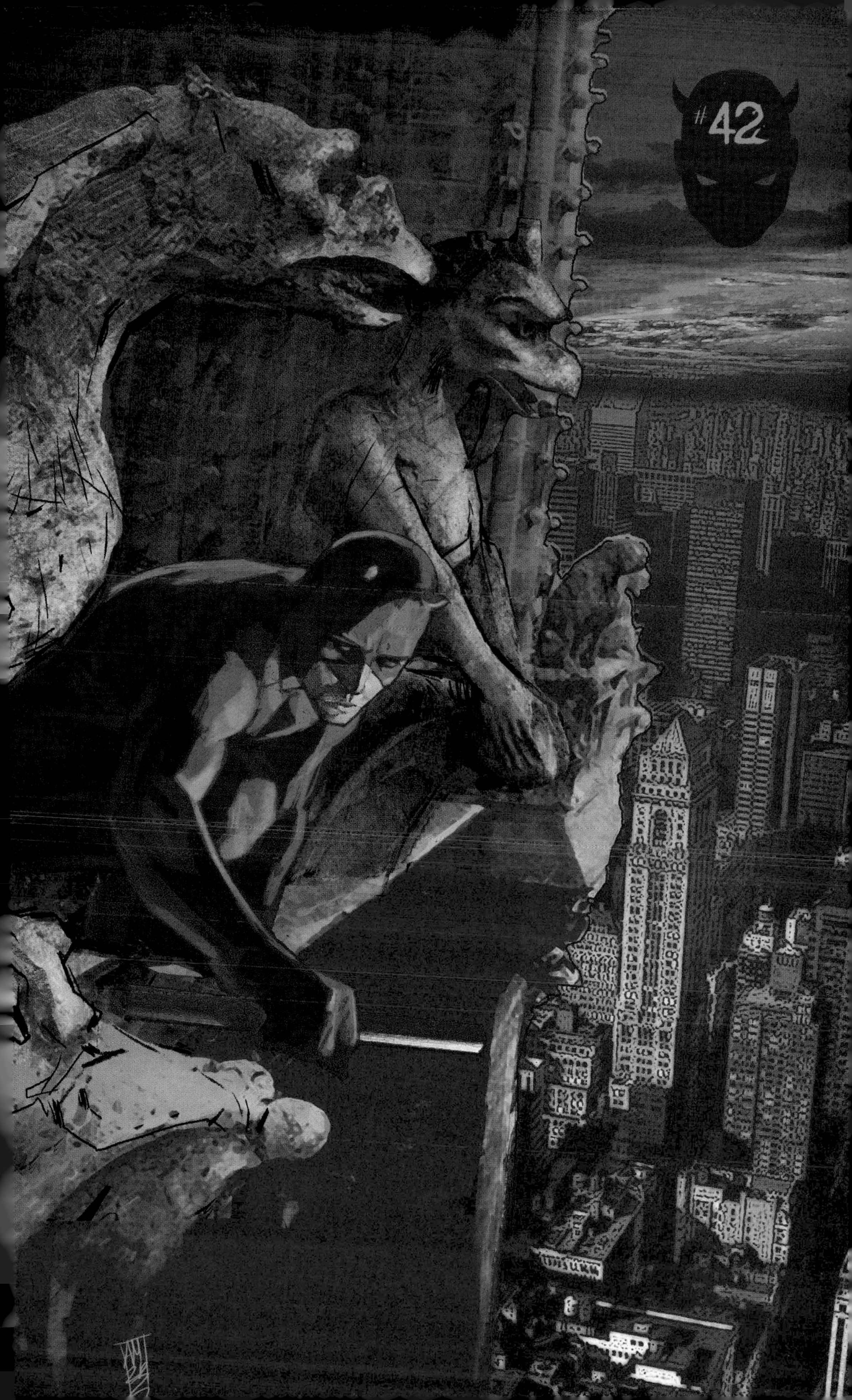
#42

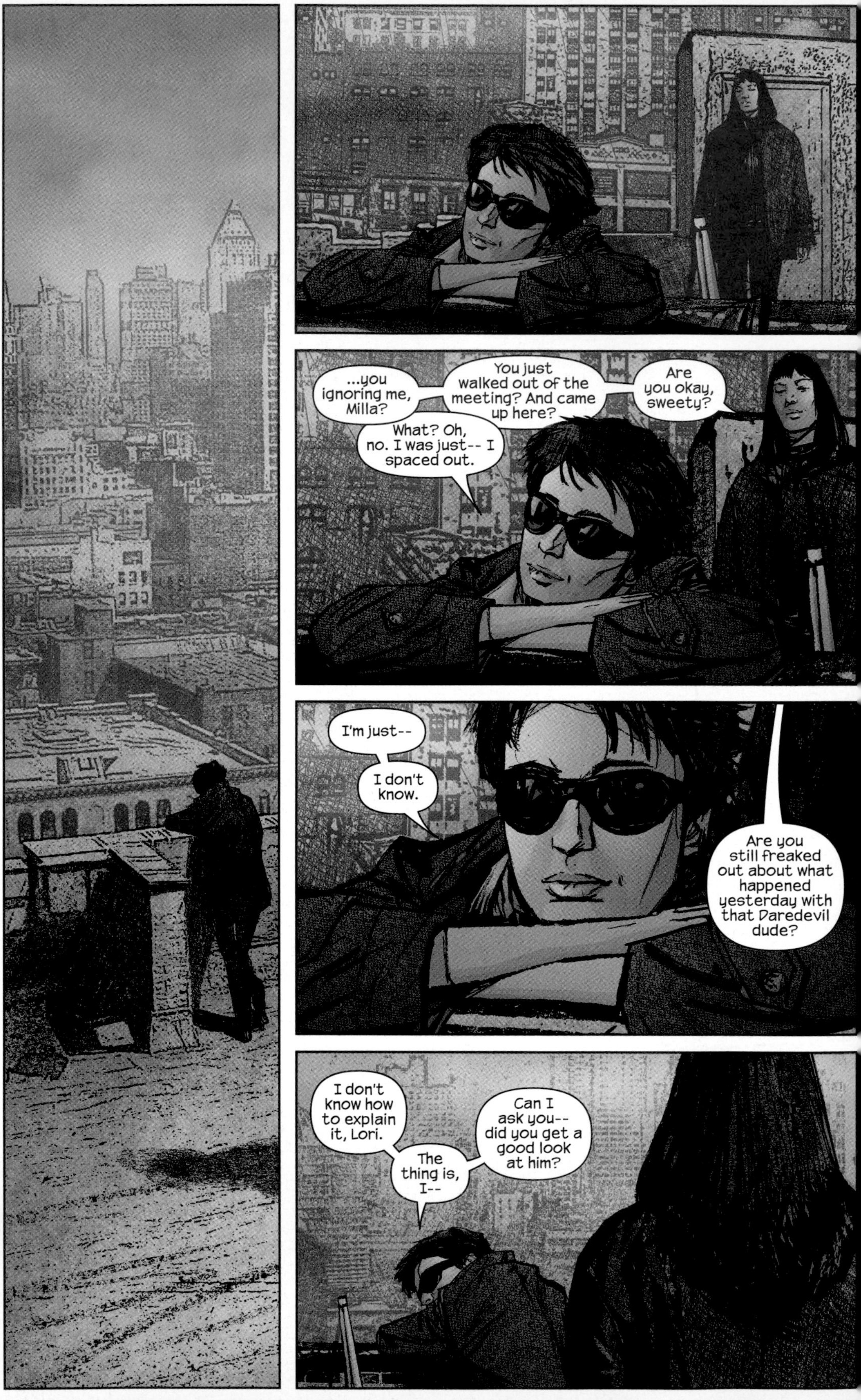
...you ignoring me, Milla?
You just walked out of the meeting? And came up here?
Are you okay, sweety?
What? Oh, no. I was just-- I spaced out.
I'm just--
I don't know.
Are you still freaked out about what happened yesterday with that Daredevil dude?
I don't know how to explain it, Lori.
The thing is, I--
Can I ask you-- did you get a good look at him?

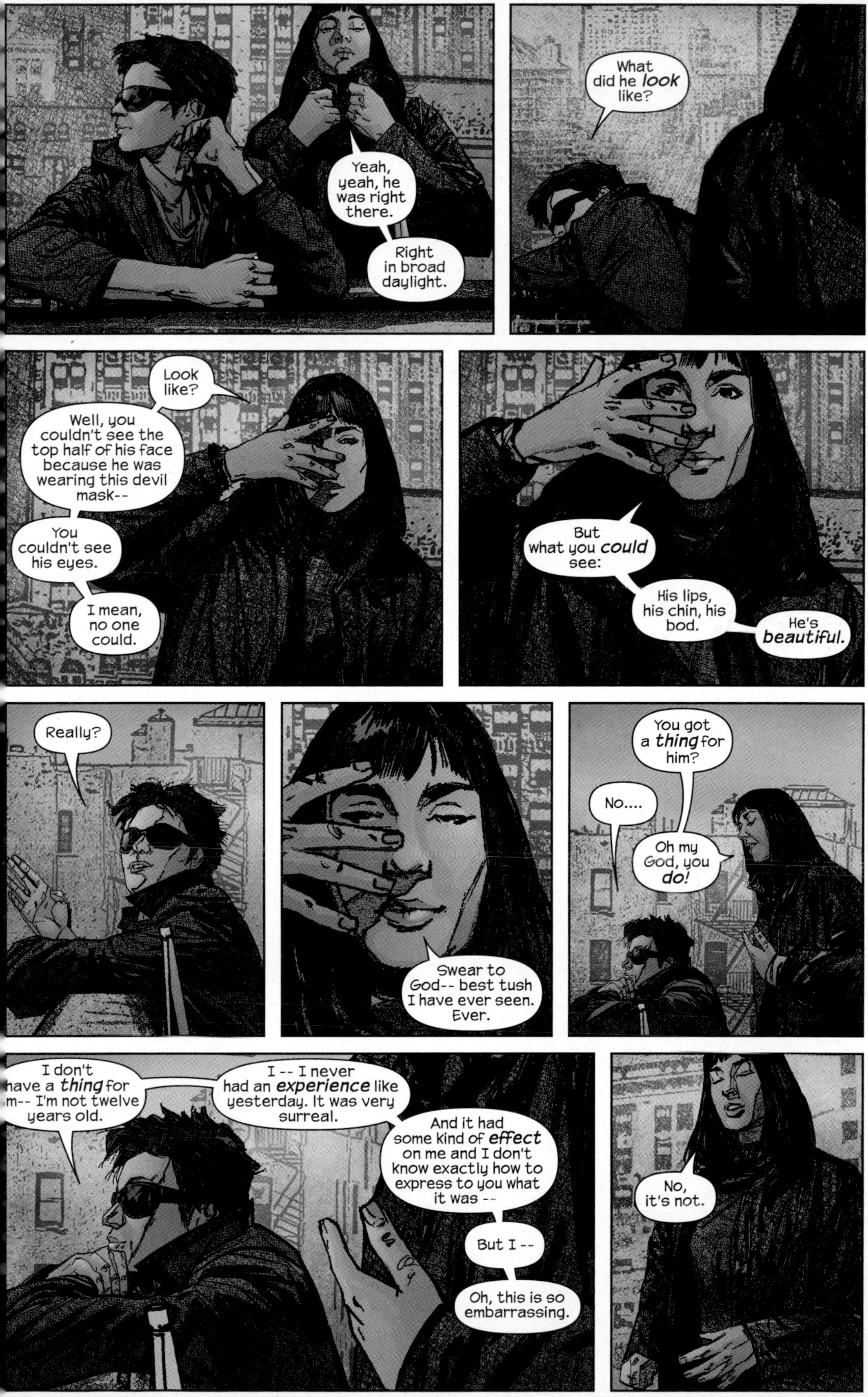
Yeah, yeah, he was right there.
Right in broad daylight.
What did he *look* like?
Look like?
Well, you couldn't see the top half of his face because he was wearing this devil mask--
You couldn't see his eyes.
I mean, no one could.
But what you *could* see:
His lips, his chin, his bod.
He's *beautiful.*
Really?
Swear to God-- best tush I have ever seen. Ever.
You got a *thing* for him?
No....
Oh my God, you *do!*
I don't have a *thing* for m-- I'm not twelve years old.
I -- I never had an *experience* like yesterday. It was very surreal.
And it had some kind of *effect* on me and I don't know exactly how to express to you what it was --
But I --
Oh, this is so embarrassing.
No, it's not.

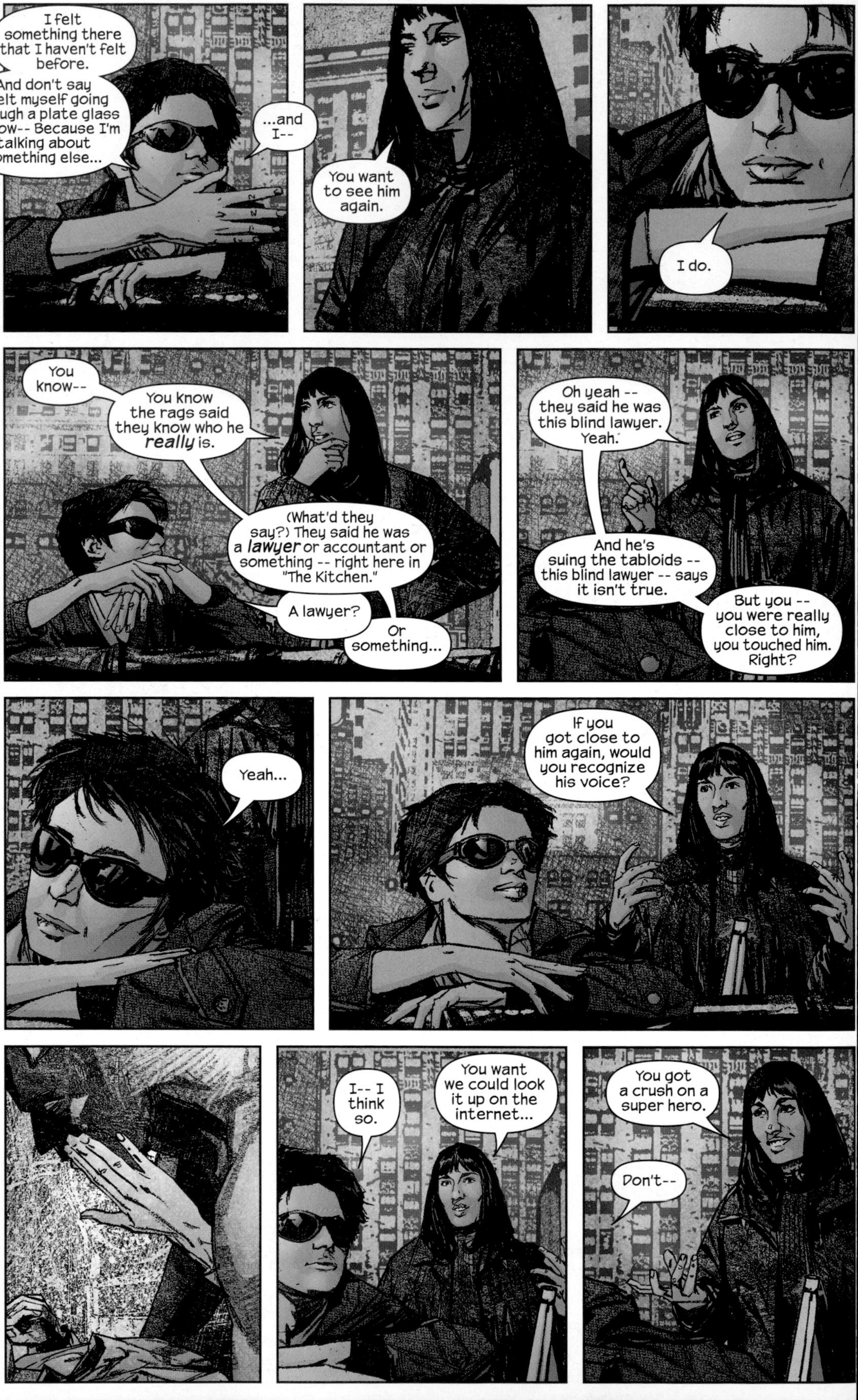
I felt something there that I haven't felt before.
And don't say I felt myself going through a plate glass window-- Because I'm talking about something else...
...and I--
You want to see him again.
I do.
You know--
You know the rags said they know who he *really* is.
(What'd they say?) They said he was a *lawyer* or accountant or something -- right here in "The Kitchen."
A lawyer?
Or something...
Oh yeah -- they said he was this blind lawyer. Yeah.
And he's suing the tabloids -- this blind lawyer -- says it isn't true.
But you -- you were really close to him, you touched him. Right?
Yeah...
If you got close to him again, would you recognize his voice?
I-- I think so.
You want we could look it up on the internet...
You got a crush on a super hero.
Don't--

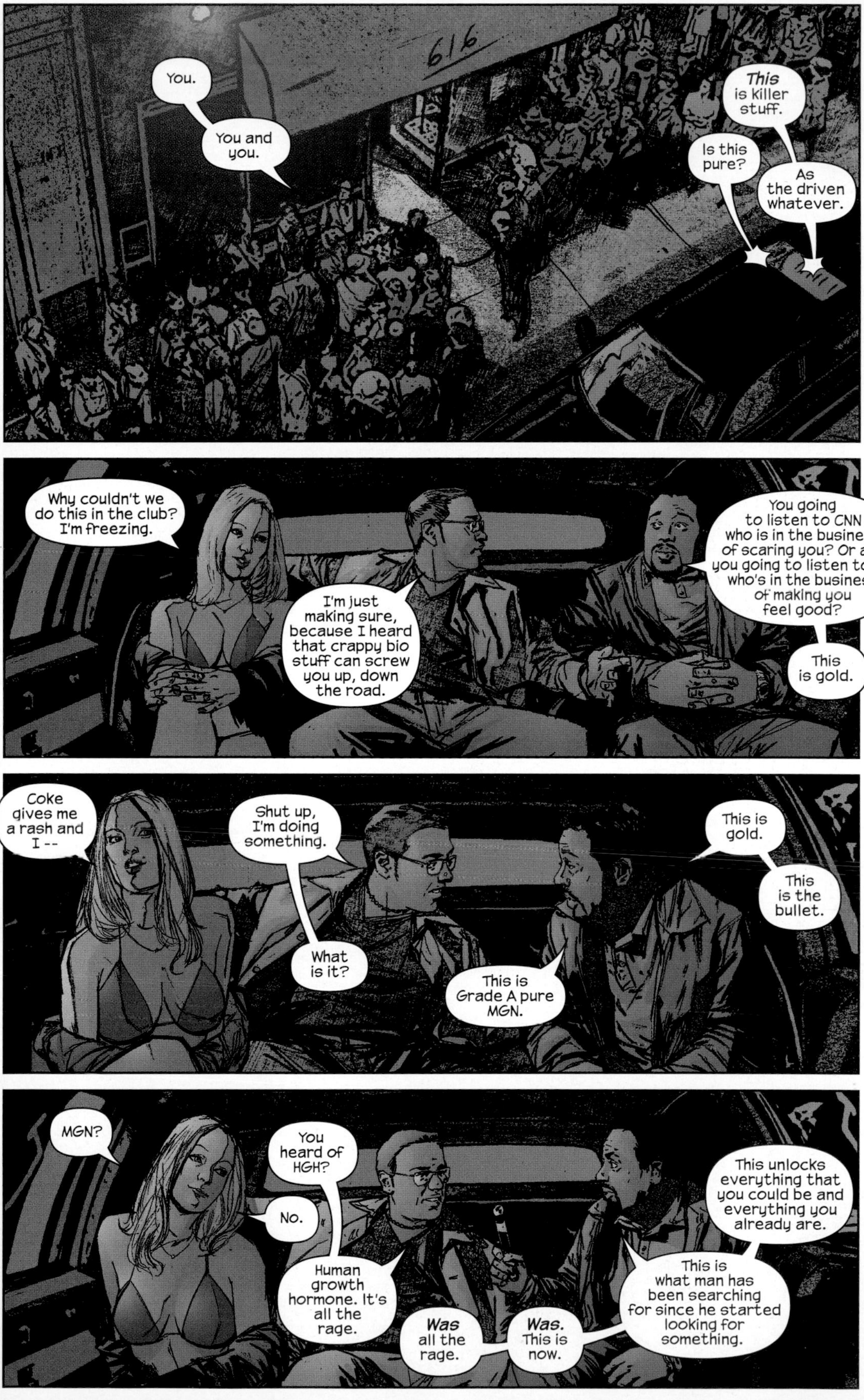
616
You.
You and you.
This is killer stuff.
Is this pure?
As the driven whatever.
Why couldn't we do this in the club? I'm freezing.
I'm just making sure, because I heard that crappy bio stuff can screw you up, down the road.
You going to listen to CNN who is in the business of scaring you? Or are you going to listen to me who's in the business of making you feel good?
This is gold.
Coke gives me a rash and I --
Shut up, I'm doing something.
This is gold.
This is the bullet.
What is it?
This is Grade A pure MGN.
MGN?
You heard of HGH?
No.
Human growth hormone. It's all the rage.
Was all the rage.
Was. This is now.
This unlocks everything that you could be and everything you already are.
This is what man has been searching for since he started looking for something.

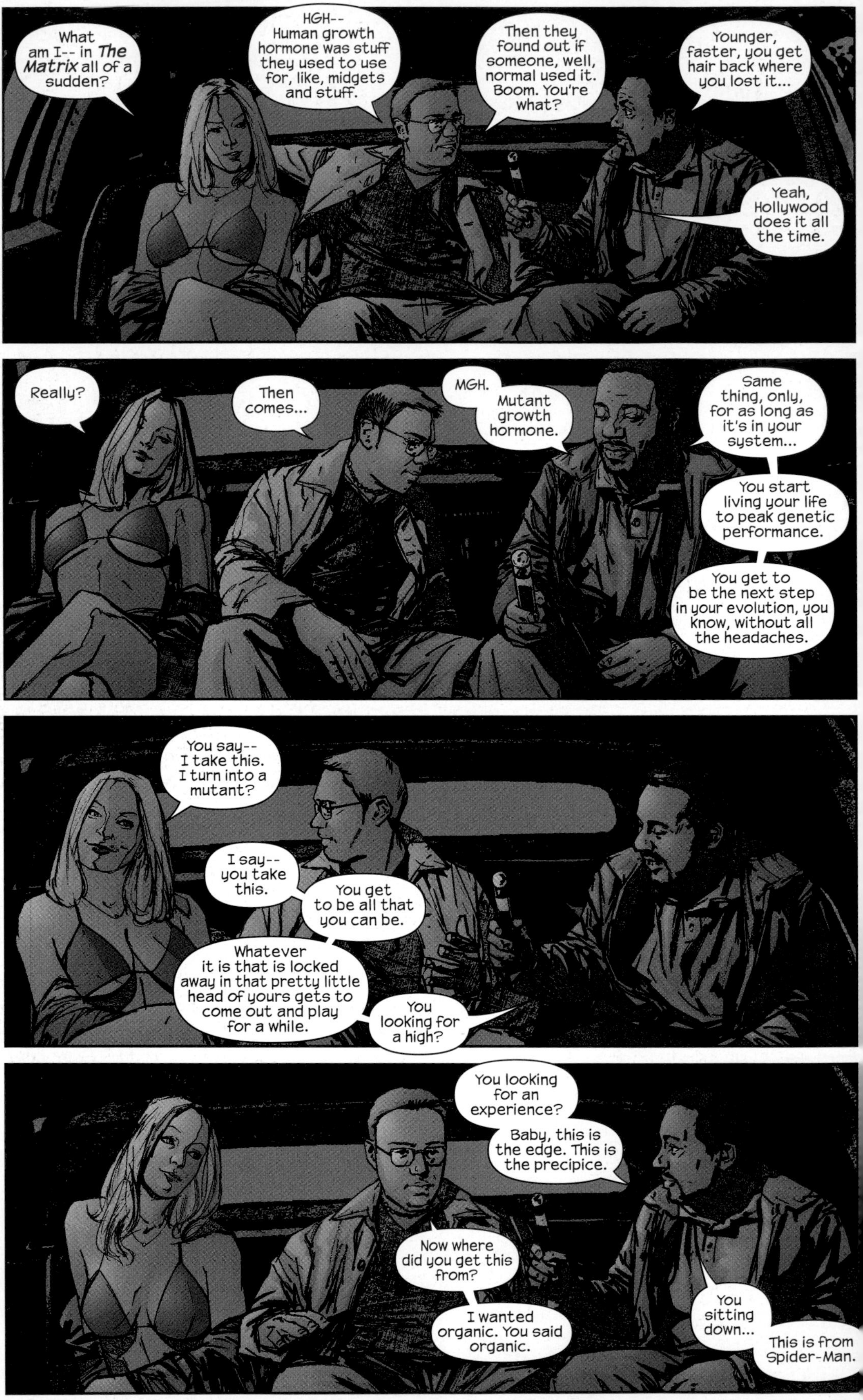
What am I-- in *The Matrix* all of a sudden?
HGH-- Human growth hormone was stuff they used to use for, like, midgets and stuff.
Then they found out if someone, well, normal used it. Boom. You're what?
Younger, faster, you get hair back where you lost it...
Yeah, Hollywood does it all the time.
Really?
Then comes...
MGH.
Mutant growth hormone.
Same thing, only, for as long as it's in your system...
You start living your life to peak genetic performance.
You get to be the next step in your evolution, you know, without all the headaches.
You say-- I take this. I turn into a mutant?
I say-- you take this.
You get to be all that you can be.
Whatever it is that is locked away in that pretty little head of yours gets to come out and play for a while.
You looking for a high?
You looking for an experience?
Baby, this is the edge. This is the precipice.
Now where did you get this from?
I wanted organic. You said organic.
You sitting down...
This is from Spider-Man.

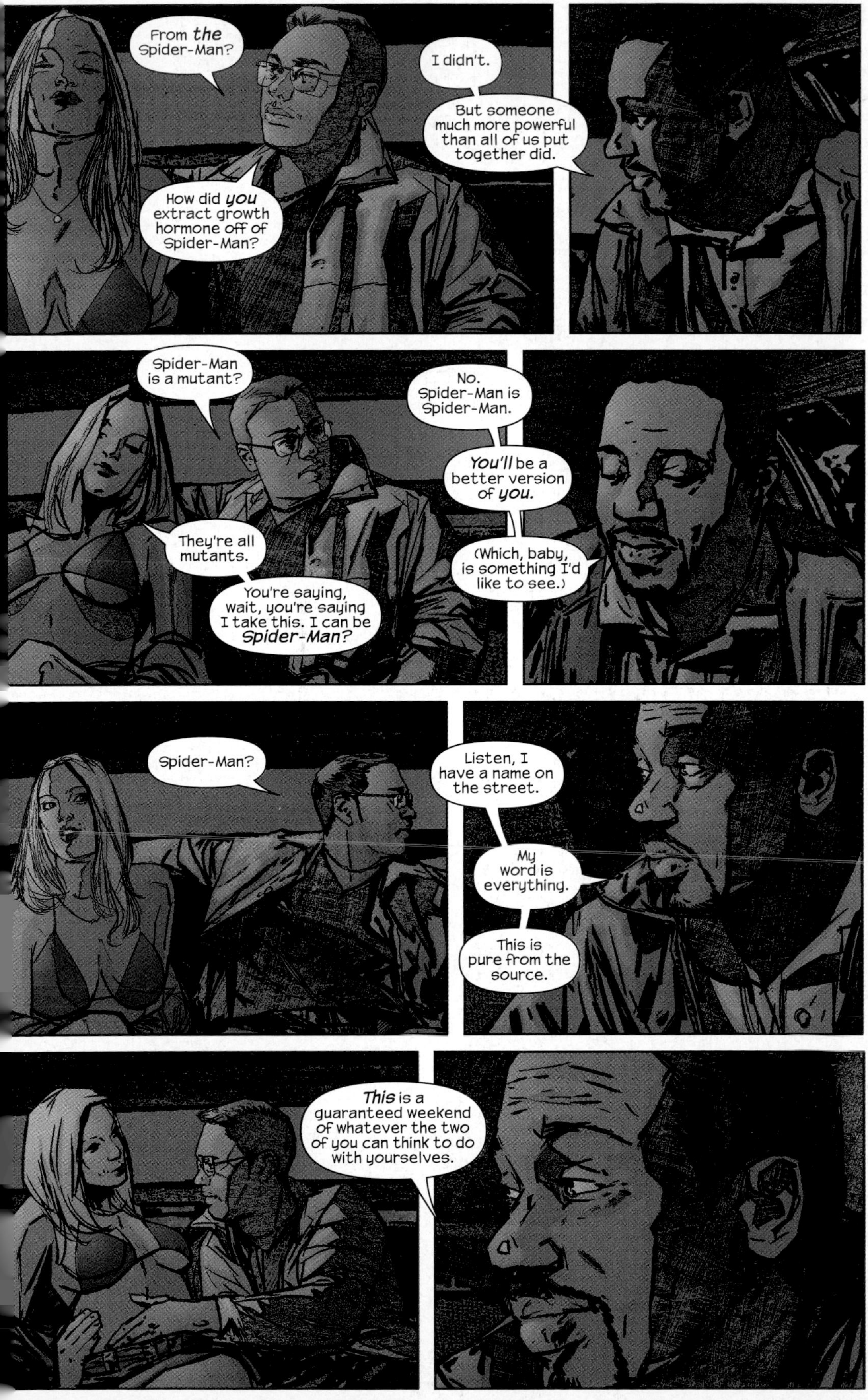
From the Spider-Man?
How did you extract growth hormone off of Spider-Man?
I didn't.
But someone much more powerful than all of us put together did.
Spider-Man is a mutant?
They're all mutants.
You're saying, wait, you're saying I take this. I can be Spider-Man?
No. Spider-Man is Spider-Man.
You'll be a better version of you.
(Which, baby, is something I'd like to see.)
Spider-Man?
Listen, I have a name on the street.
My word is everything.
This is pure from the source.
This is a guaranteed weekend of whatever the two of you can think to do with yourselves.

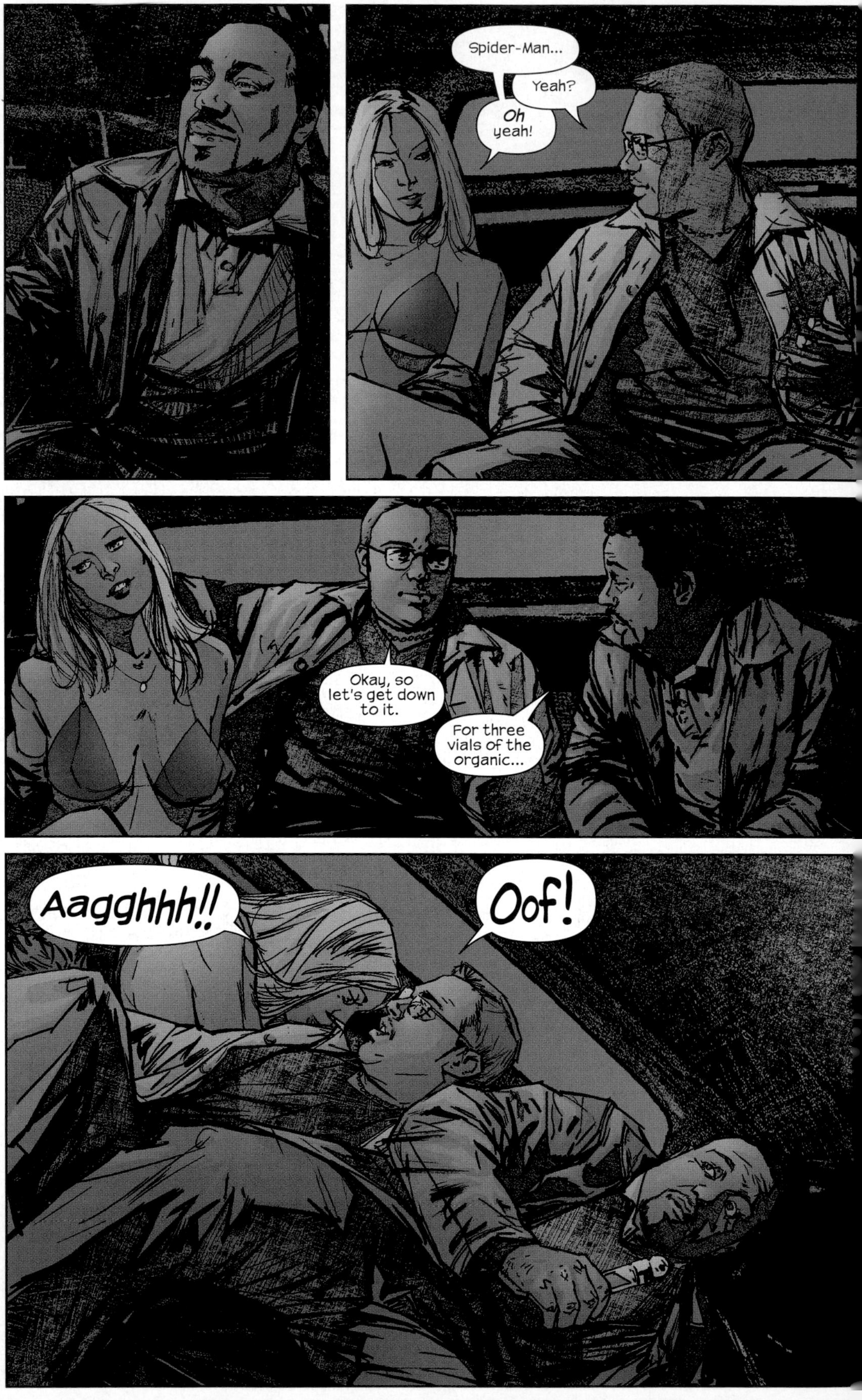
Spider-Man...
Yeah?
Oh yeah!
Okay, so let's get down to it.
For three vials of the organic...
Aagghhh!!
Oof!

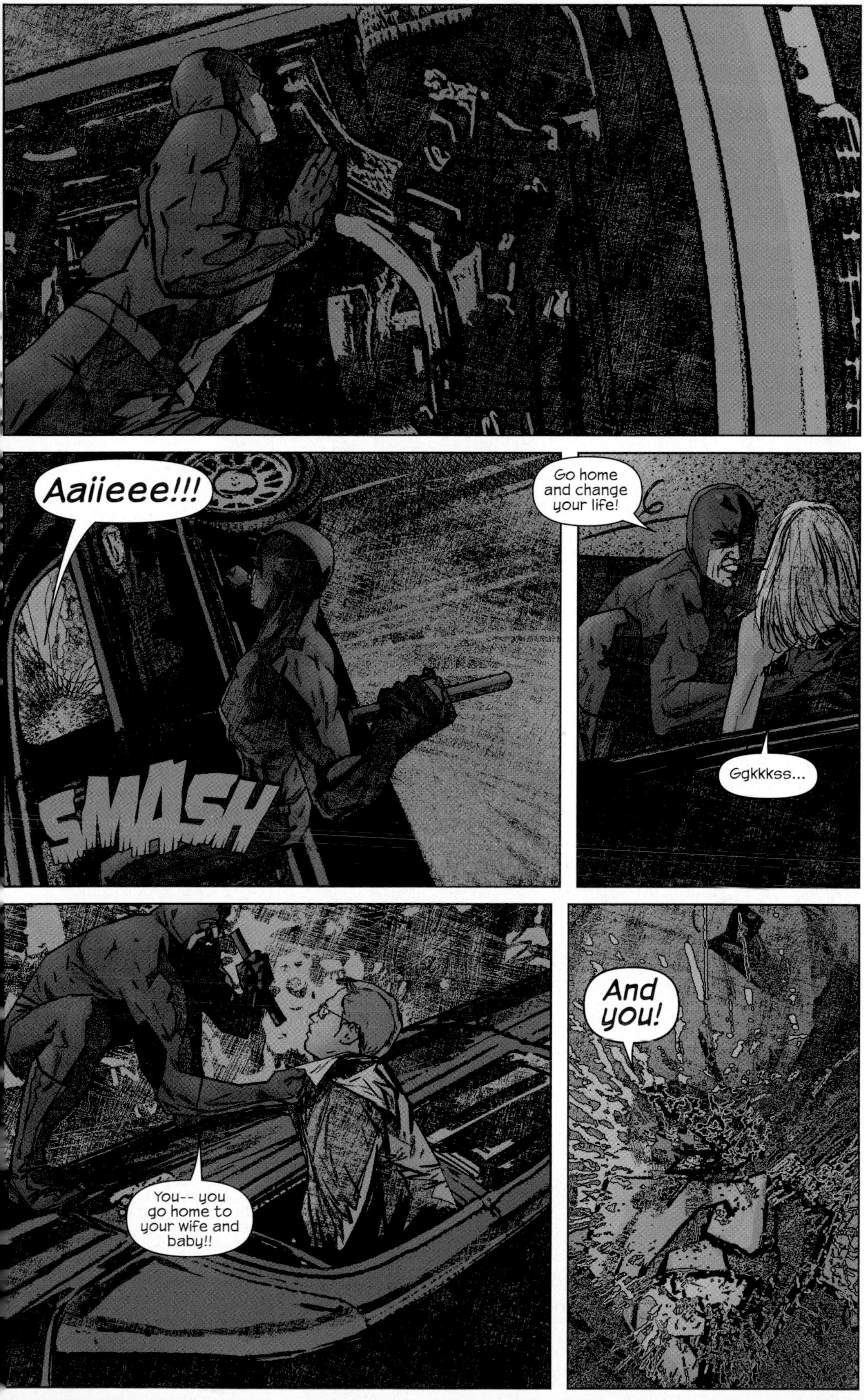
Aaiieee!!!
SMASH
Go home and change your life!
Ggkkkss...
You-- you go home to your wife and baby!!
And you!

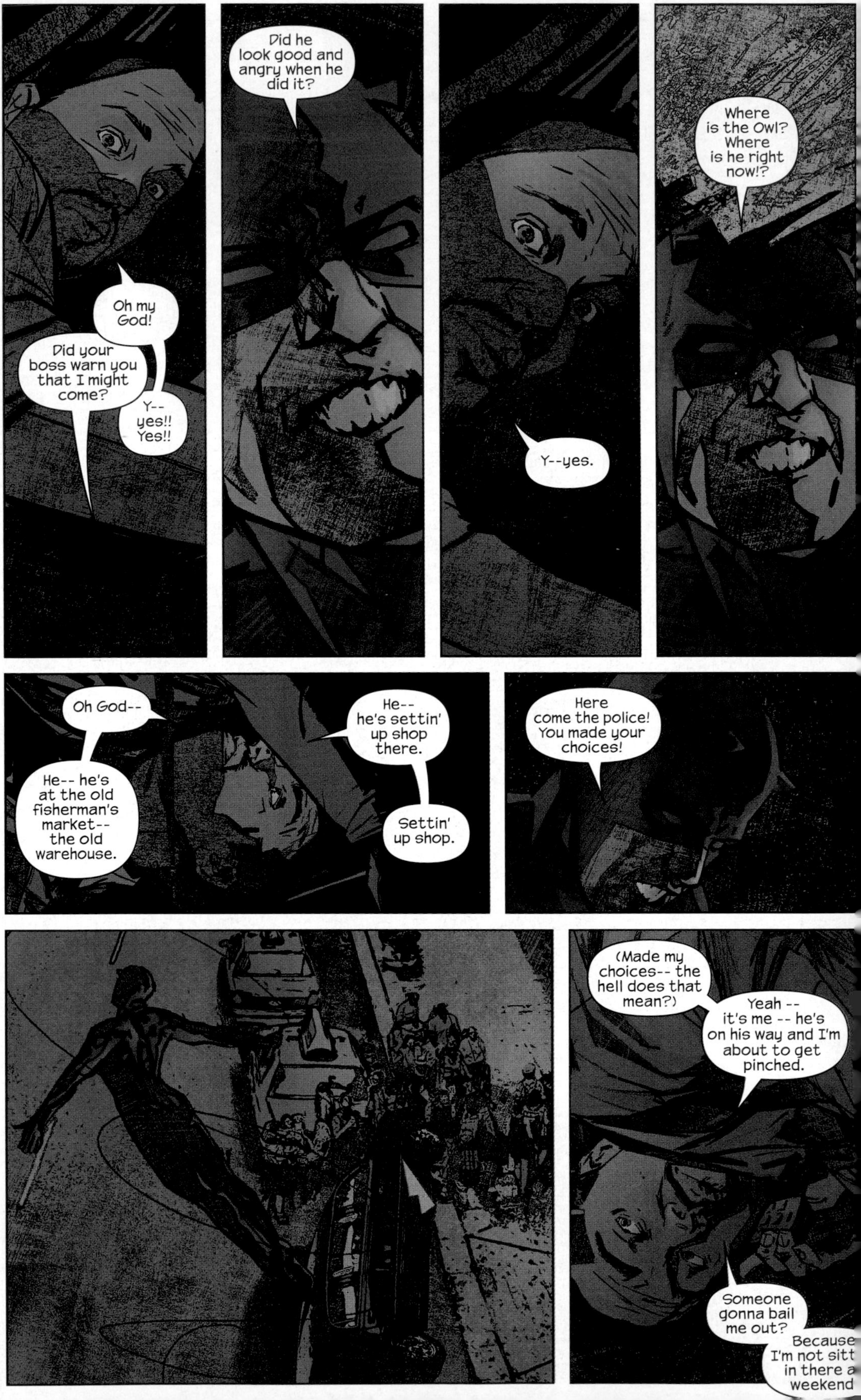
Oh my God!
Did your boss warn you that I might come?
Y-- yes!! Yes!!
Did he look good and angry when he did it?
Y--yes.
Where is the Owl? Where is he right now!?
Oh God--
He-- he's at the old fisherman's market-- the old warehouse.
He-- he's settin' up shop there.
Settin' up shop.
Here come the police! You made your choices!
(Made my choices-- the hell does that mean?)
Yeah -- it's me -- he's on his way and I'm about to get pinched.
Someone gonna bail me out?
Because I'm not sitt in there a weekend

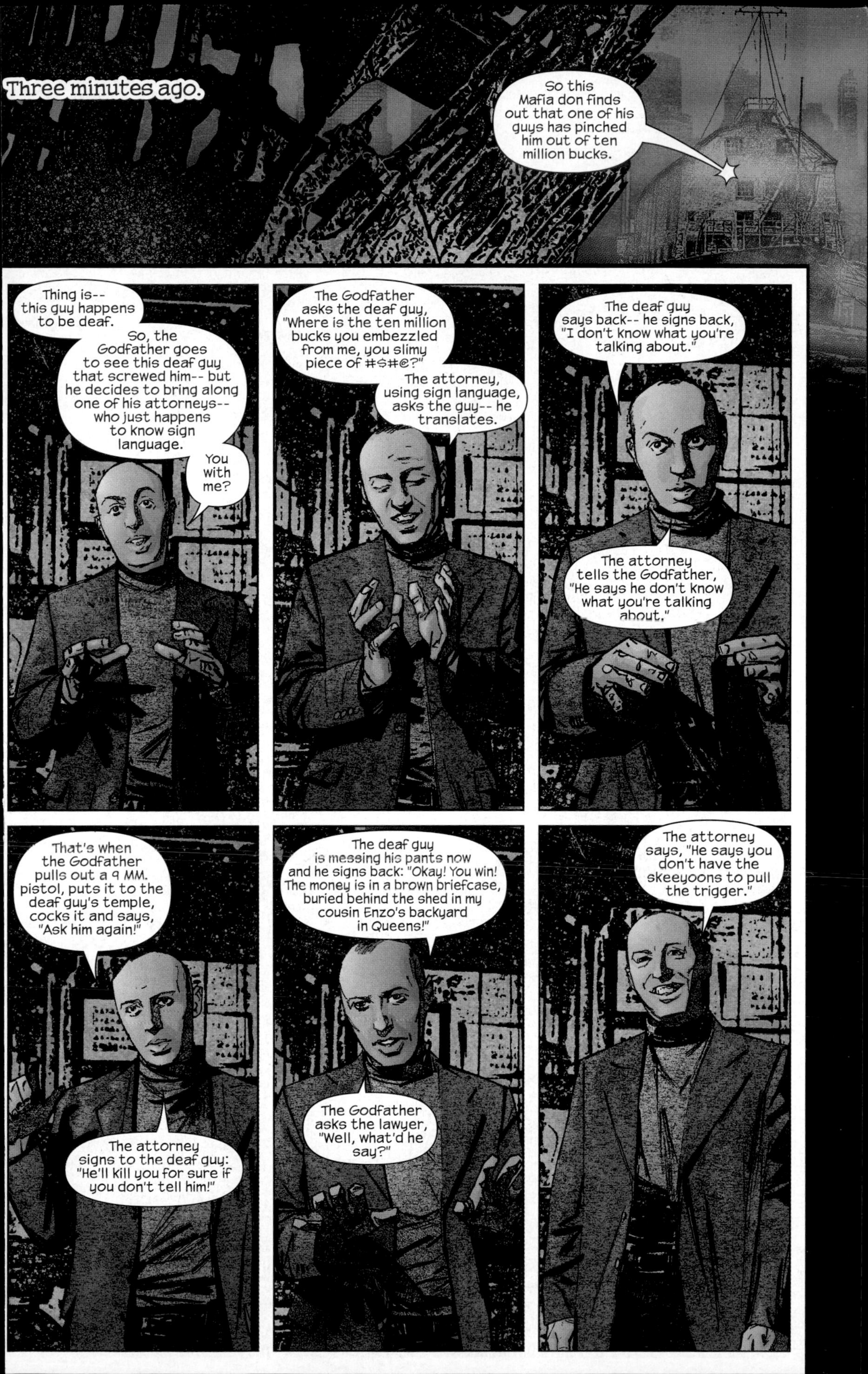
Three minutes ago.
So this Mafia don finds out that one of his guys has pinched him out of ten million bucks.
Thing is-- this guy happens to be deaf.
So, the Godfather goes to see this deaf guy that screwed him-- but he decides to bring along one of his attorneys-- who just happens to know sign language.
You with me?
The Godfather asks the deaf guy, "Where is the ten million bucks you embezzled from me, you slimy piece of #$#©?"
The attorney, using sign language, asks the guy-- he translates.
The deaf guy says back-- he signs back, "I don't know what you're talking about."
The attorney tells the Godfather, "He says he don't know what you're talking about."
That's when the Godfather pulls out a 9 MM. pistol, puts it to the deaf guy's temple, cocks it and says, "Ask him again!"
The attorney signs to the deaf guy: "He'll kill you for sure if you don't tell him!"
The deaf guy is messing his pants now and he signs back: "Okay! You win! The money is in a brown briefcase, buried behind the shed in my cousin Enzo's backyard in Queens!"
The Godfather asks the lawyer, "Well, what'd he say?"
The attorney says, "He says you don't have the skeeyoons to pull the trigger."

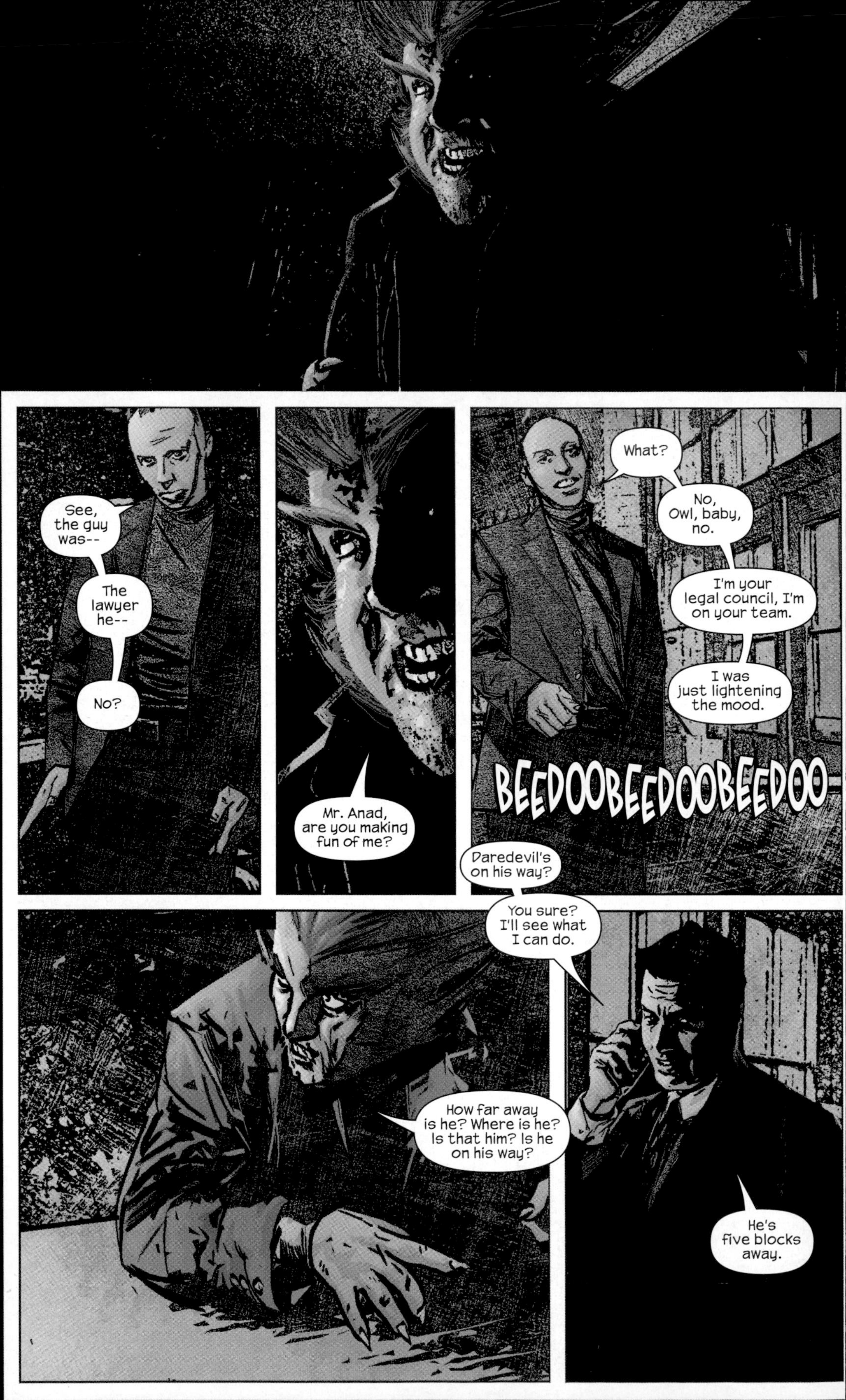
See, the guy was--
The lawyer he--
No?
Mr. Anad, are you making fun of me?
What?
No, Owl, baby, no.
I'm your legal council, I'm on your team.
I was just lightening the mood.
BEEDOOBEEDOOBEEDOO
Daredevil's on his way?
You sure? I'll see what I can do.
How far away is he? Where is he? Is that him? Is he on his way?
He's five blocks away.

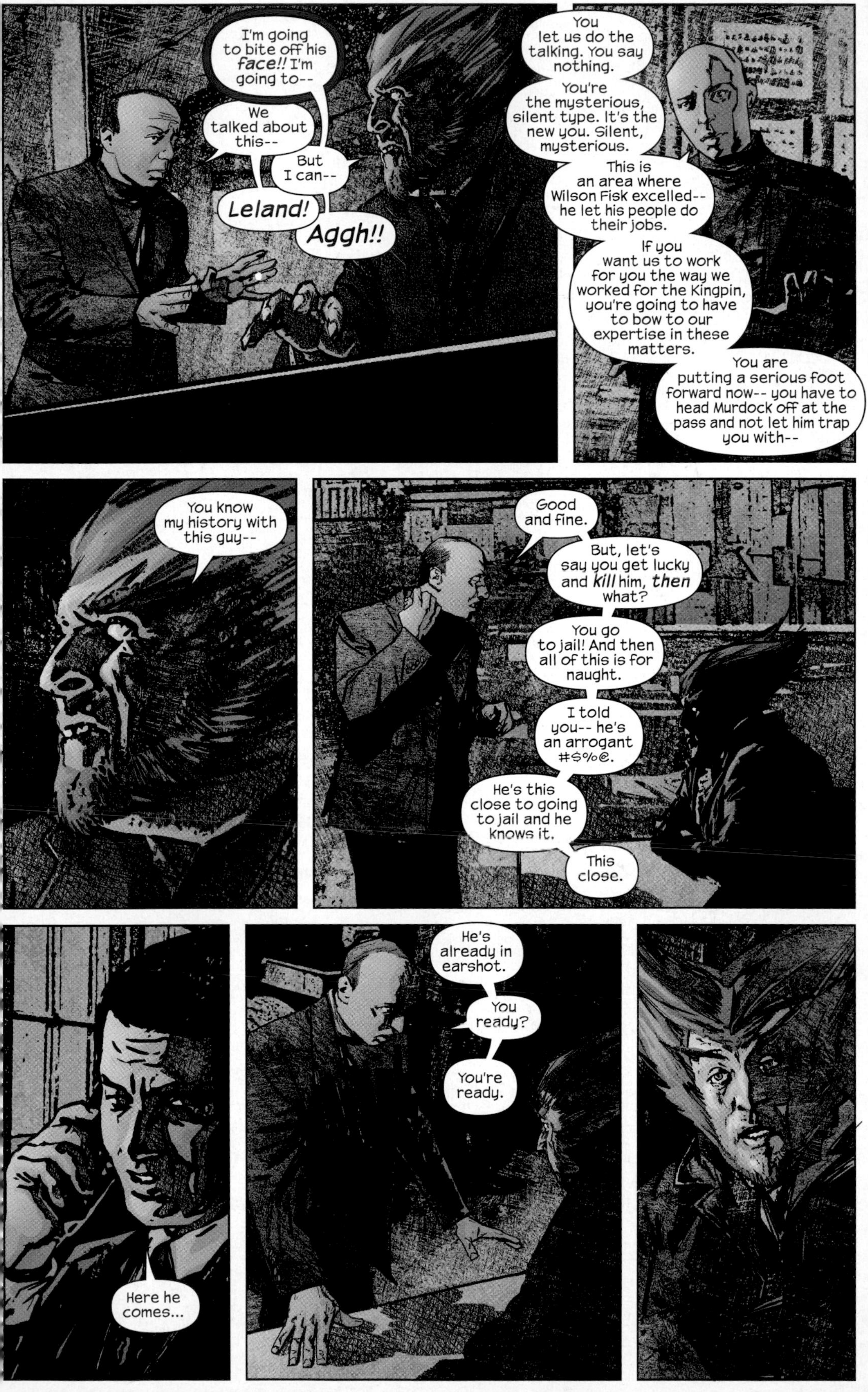
I'm going to bite off his *face!!* I'm going to--
We talked about this--
But I can--
Leland!
Aggh!!
You let us do the talking. You say nothing.
You're the mysterious, silent type. It's the new you. Silent, mysterious.
This is an area where Wilson Fisk excelled-- he let his people do their jobs.
If you want us to work for you the way we worked for the Kingpin, you're going to have to bow to our expertise in these matters.
You are putting a serious foot forward now-- you have to head Murdock off at the pass and not let him trap you with--
You know my history with this guy--
Good and fine.
But, let's say you get lucky and *kill* him, *then* what?
You go to jail! And then all of this is for naught.
I told you-- he's an arrogant #$%©.
He's this close to going to jail and he knows it.
This close.
He's already in earshot.
You ready?
You're ready.
Here he comes...

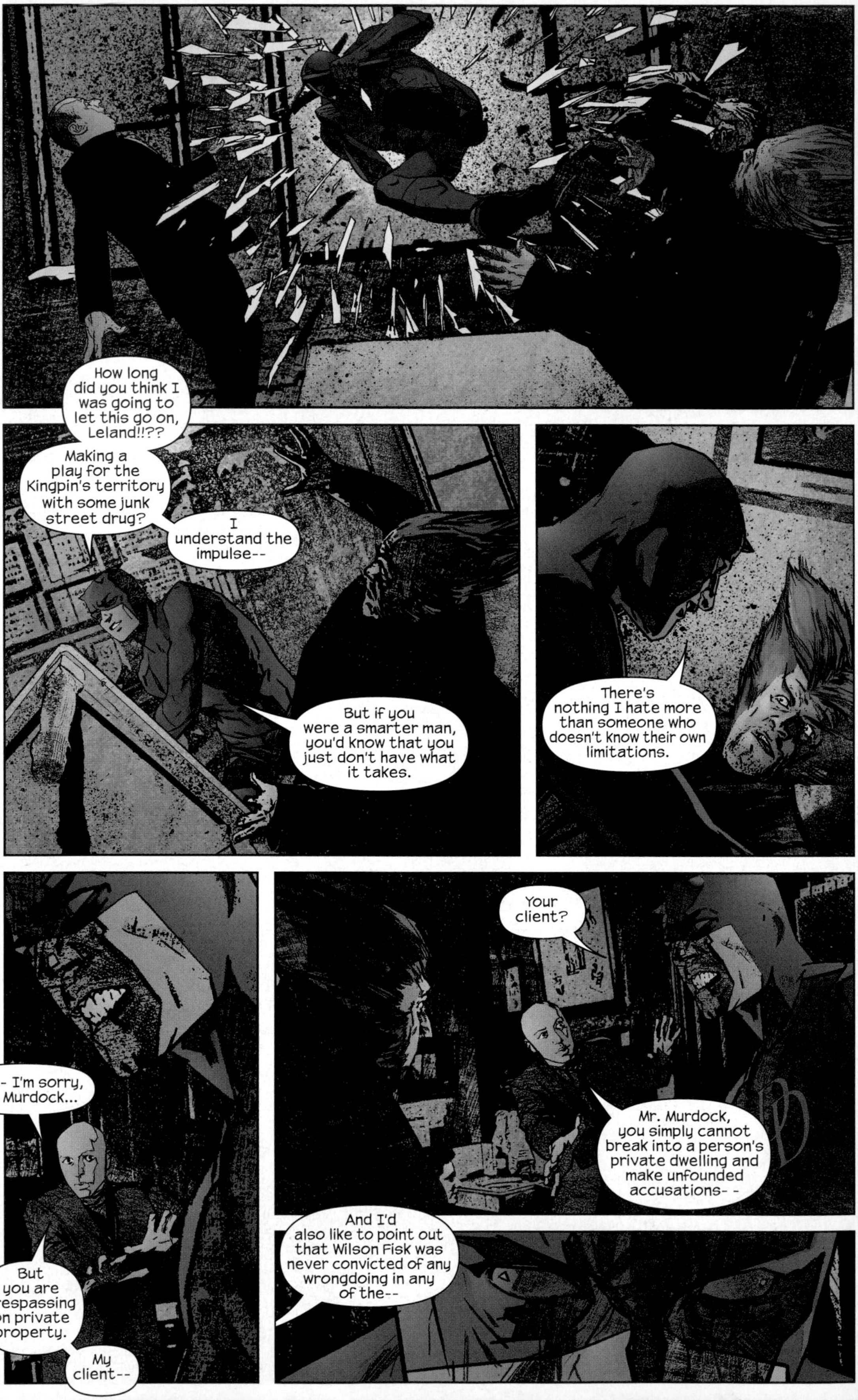
How long did you think I was going to let this go on, Leland!!??
Making a play for the Kingpin's territory with some junk street drug?
I understand the impulse--
But if you were a smarter man, you'd know that you just don't have what it takes.
There's nothing I hate more than someone who doesn't know their own limitations.
I'm-- I'm sorry, Mr. Murdock...
But you are trespassing on private property.
My client--
Your client?
Mr. Murdock, you simply cannot break into a person's private dwelling and make unfounded accusations- -
And I'd also like to point out that Wilson Fisk was never convicted of any wrongdoing in any of the--

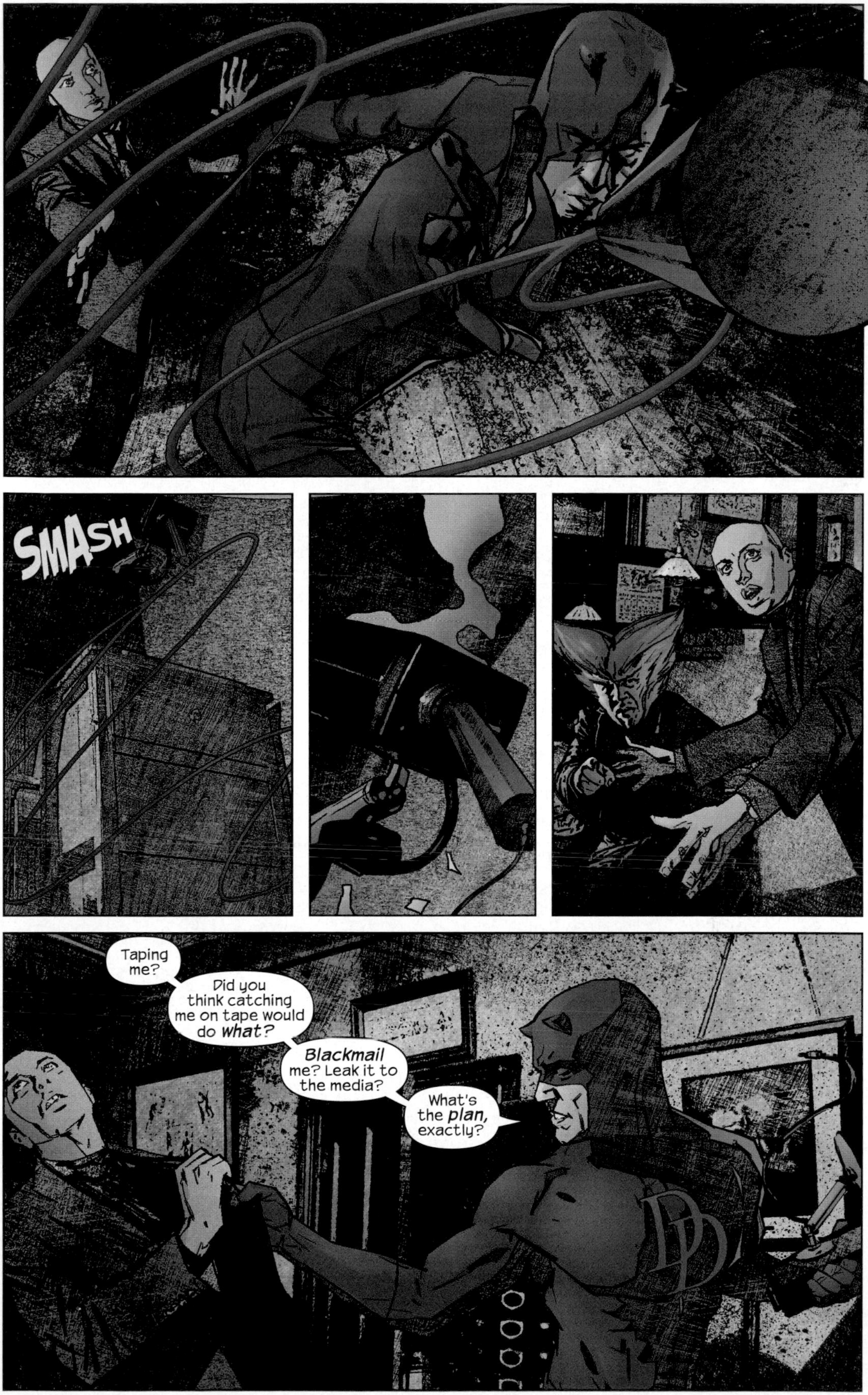

SMASH
Taping me?
Did you think catching me on tape would do *what?*
Blackmail me? Leak it to the media?
What's the *plan,* exactly?

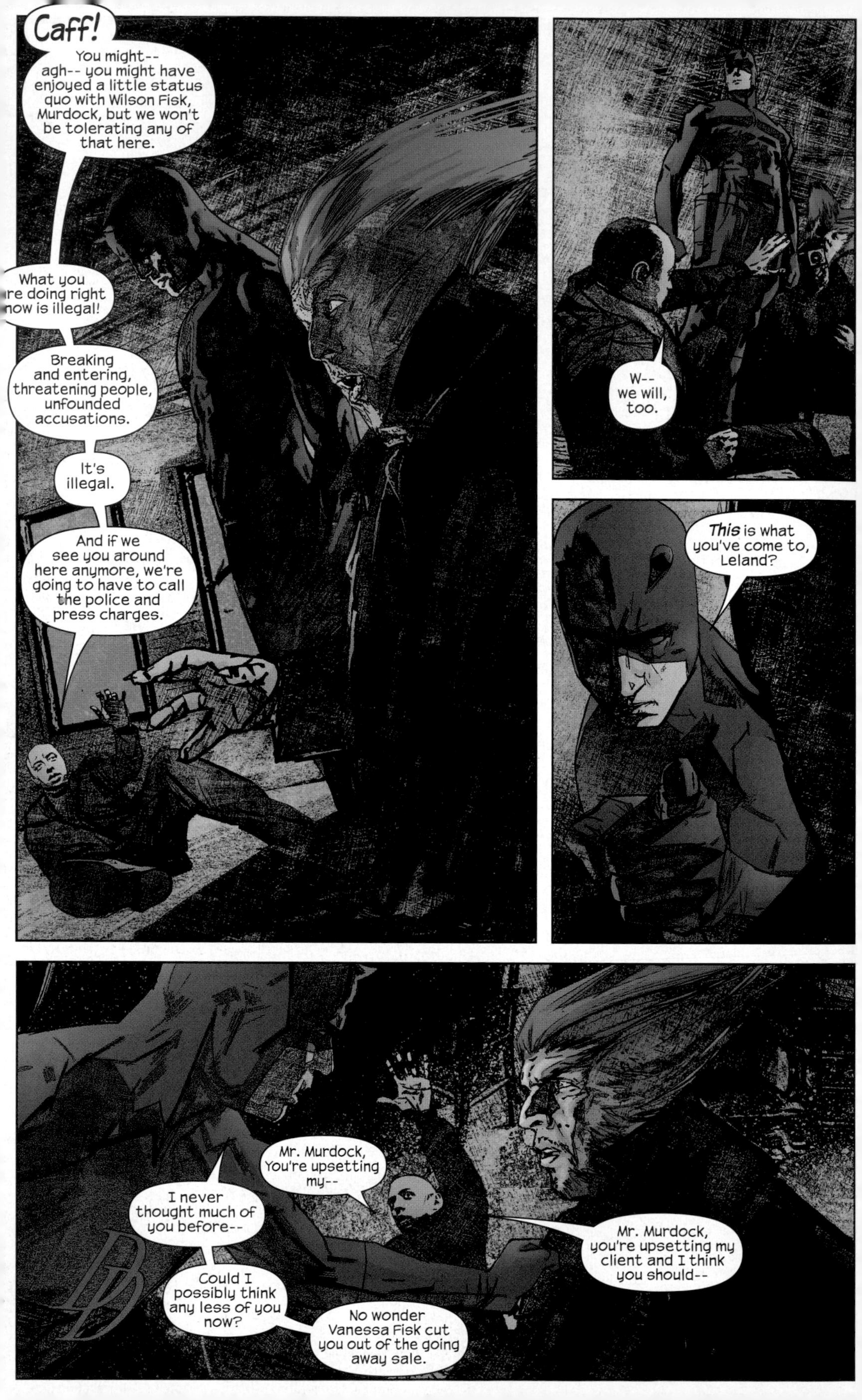
Caff!
You might-- agh-- you might have enjoyed a little status quo with Wilson Fisk, Murdock, but we won't be tolerating any of that here.
What you re doing right now is illegal!
Breaking and entering, threatening people, unfounded accusations.
It's illegal.
And if we see you around here anymore, we're going to have to call the police and press charges.
W-- we will, too.
This is what you've come to, Leland?
I never thought much of you before--
Mr. Murdock, You're upsetting my--
Could I possibly think any less of you now?
Mr. Murdock, you're upsetting my client and I think you should--
No wonder Vanessa Fisk cut you out of the going away sale.

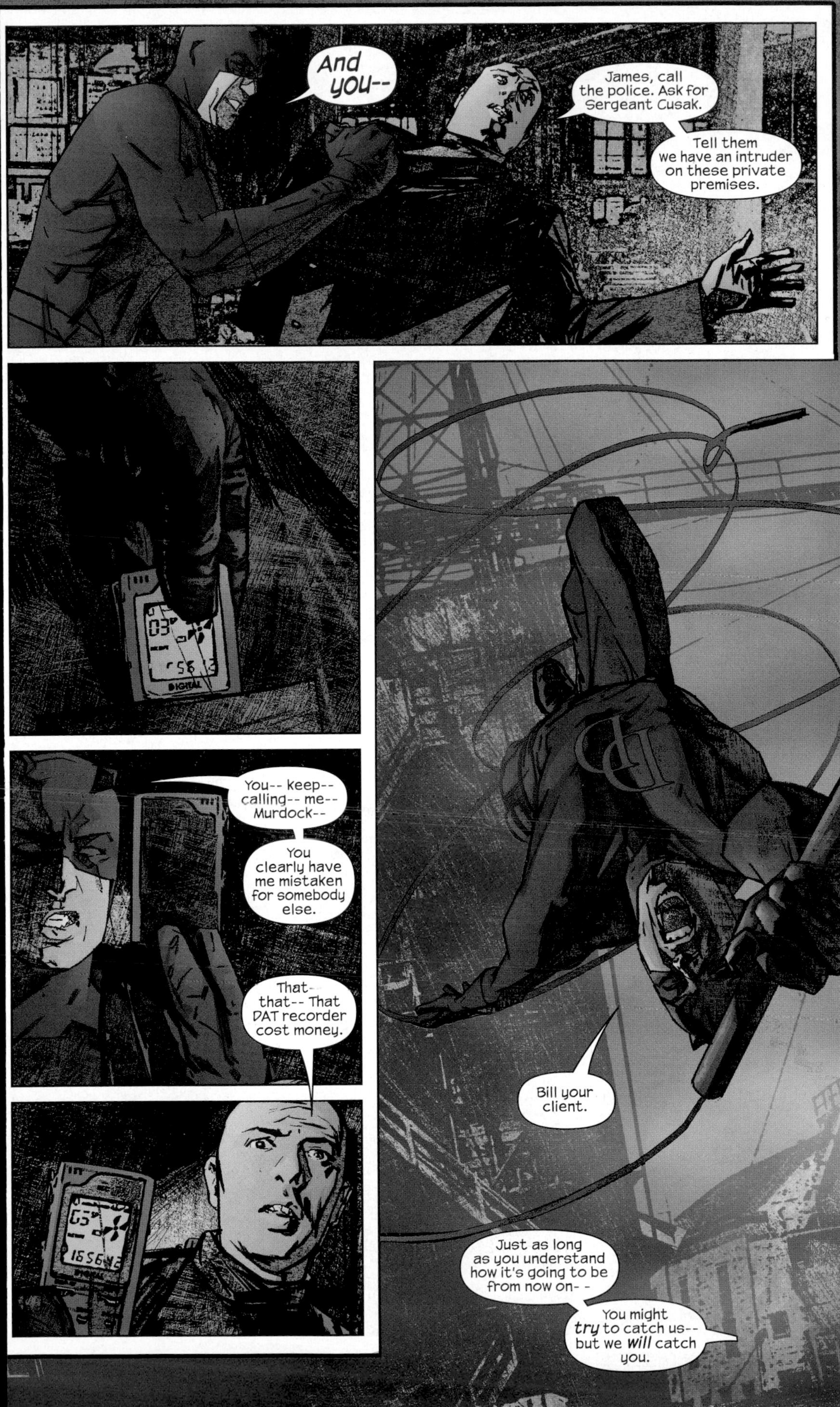
And you--
James, call the police. Ask for Sergeant Cusak.
Tell them we have an intruder on these private premises.
You-- keep-- calling-- me-- Murdock--
You clearly have me mistaken for somebody else.
That-- that-- That DAT recorder cost money.
Bill your client.
Just as long as you understand how it's going to be from now on- -
You might *try* to catch us-- but we *will* catch you.

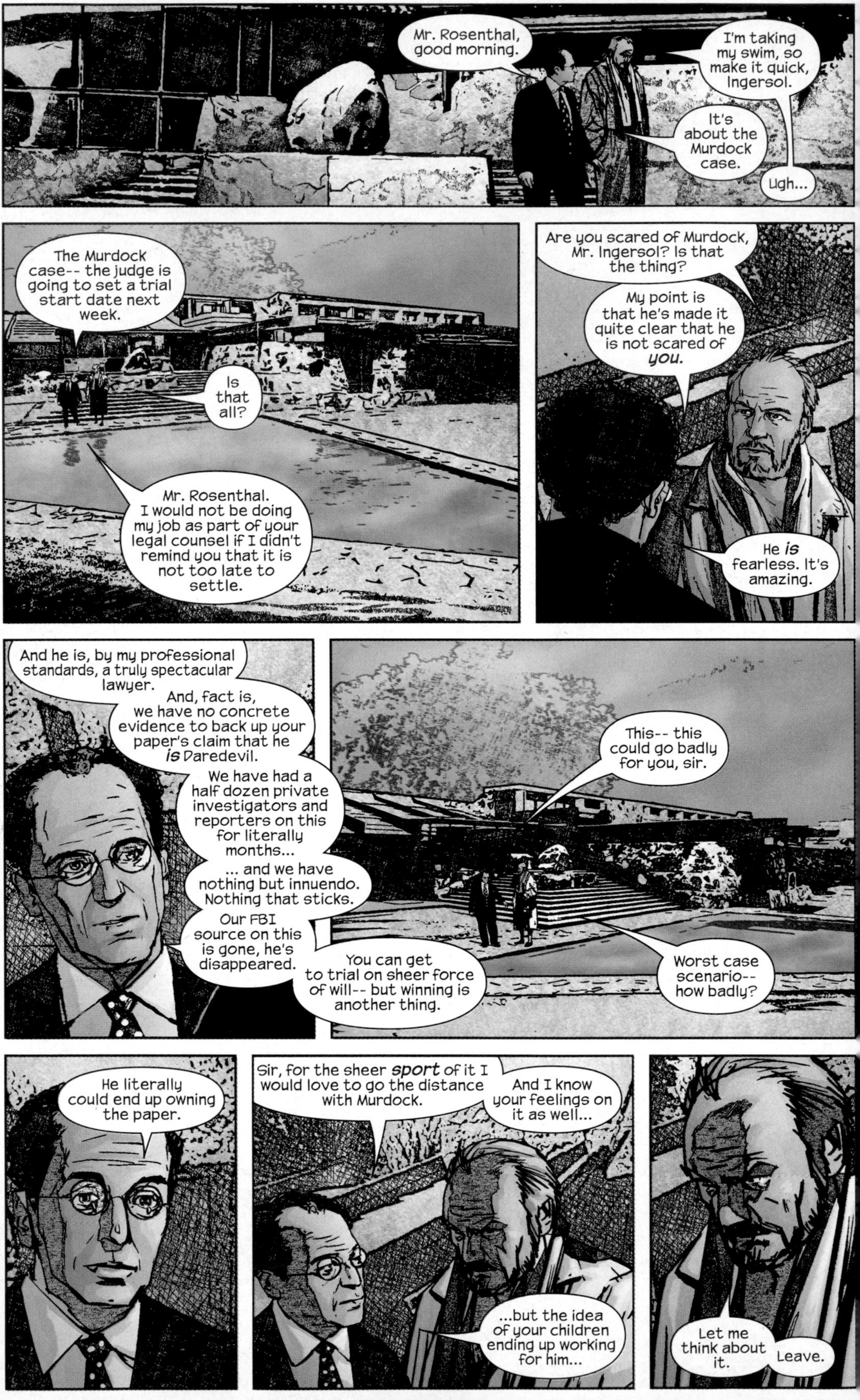
Mr. Rosenthal, good morning.
I'm taking my swim, so make it quick, Ingersol.
It's about the Murdock case.
Ugh...
The Murdock case-- the judge is going to set a trial start date next week.
Is that all?
Mr. Rosenthal. I would not be doing my job as part of your legal counsel if I didn't remind you that it is not too late to settle.
Are you scared of Murdock, Mr. Ingersol? Is that the thing?
My point is that he's made it quite clear that he is not scared of *you.*
He *is* fearless. It's amazing.
And he is, by my professional standards, a truly spectacular lawyer.
And, fact is, we have no concrete evidence to back up your paper's claim that he *is* Daredevil.
We have had a half dozen private investigators and reporters on this for literally months...
... and we have nothing but innuendo. Nothing that sticks.
Our FBI source on this is gone, he's disappeared.
You can get to trial on sheer force of will-- but winning is another thing.
This-- this could go badly for you, sir.
Worst case scenario-- how badly?
He literally could end up owning the paper.
Sir, for the sheer *sport* of it I would love to go the distance with Murdock.
And I know your feelings on it as well...
...but the idea of your children ending up working for him...
Let me think about it.
Leave.

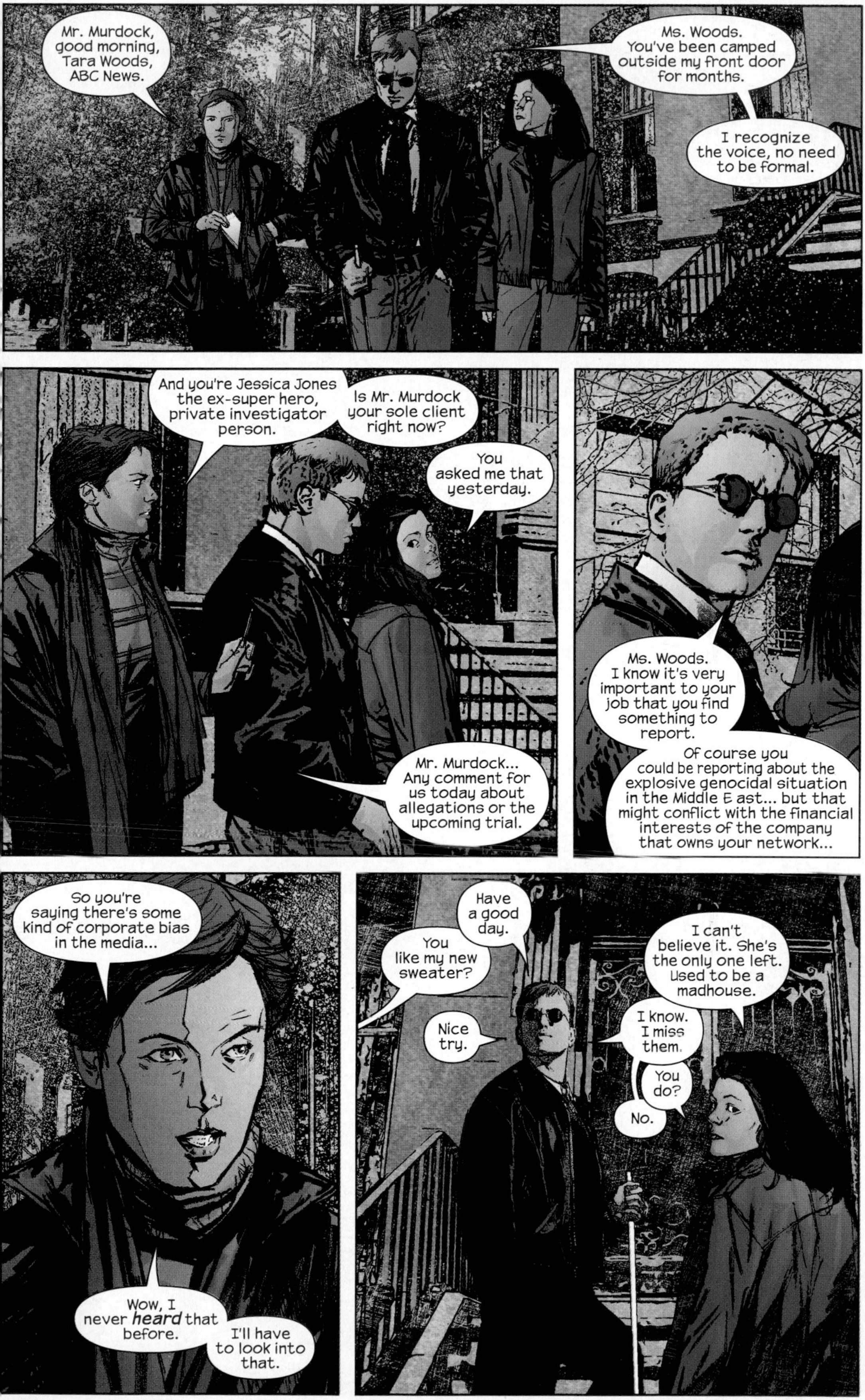
Mr. Murdock, good morning, Tara Woods, ABC News.
Ms. Woods. You've been camped outside my front door for months.
I recognize the voice, no need to be formal.
And you're Jessica Jones the ex-super hero, private investigator person.
Is Mr. Murdock your sole client right now?
You asked me that yesterday.
Mr. Murdock... Any comment for us today about allegations or the upcoming trial.
Ms. Woods. I know it's very important to your job that you find something to report.
Of course you could be reporting about the explosive genocidal situation in the Middle E ast... but that might conflict with the financial interests of the company that owns your network...
So you're saying there's some kind of corporate bias in the media...
Wow, I never *heard* that before.
I'll have to look into that.
Have a good day.
You like my new sweater?
Nice try.
I can't believe it. She's the only one left. Used to be a madhouse.
I know. I miss them.
You do?
No.

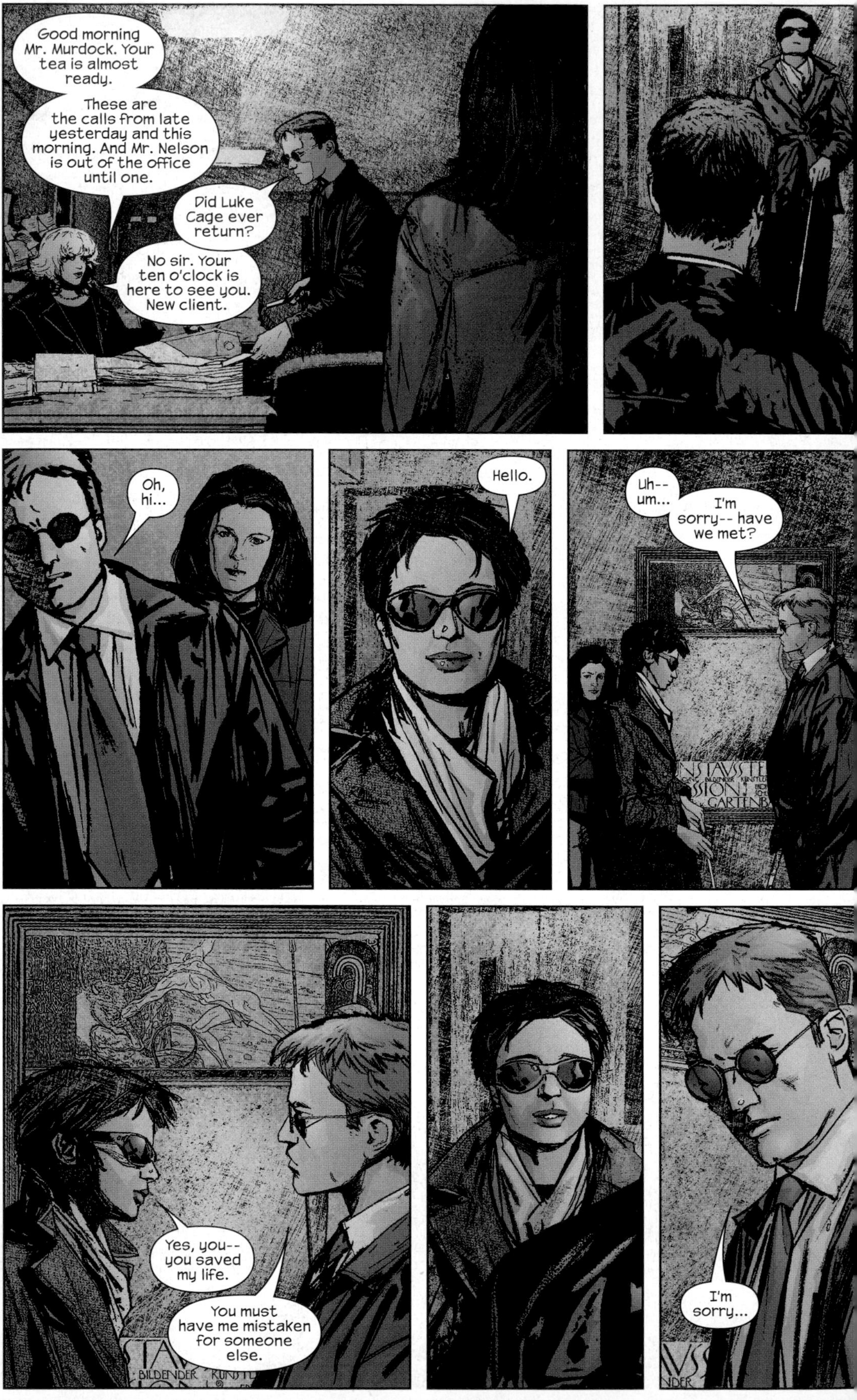
Good morning Mr. Murdock. Your tea is almost ready.
These are the calls from late yesterday and this morning. And Mr. Nelson is out of the office until one.
Did Luke Cage ever return?
No sir. Your ten o'clock is here to see you. New client.
Oh, hi...
Hello.
Uh-- um...
I'm sorry-- have we met?
Yes, you-- you saved my life.
You must have me mistaken for someone else.
I'm sorry...

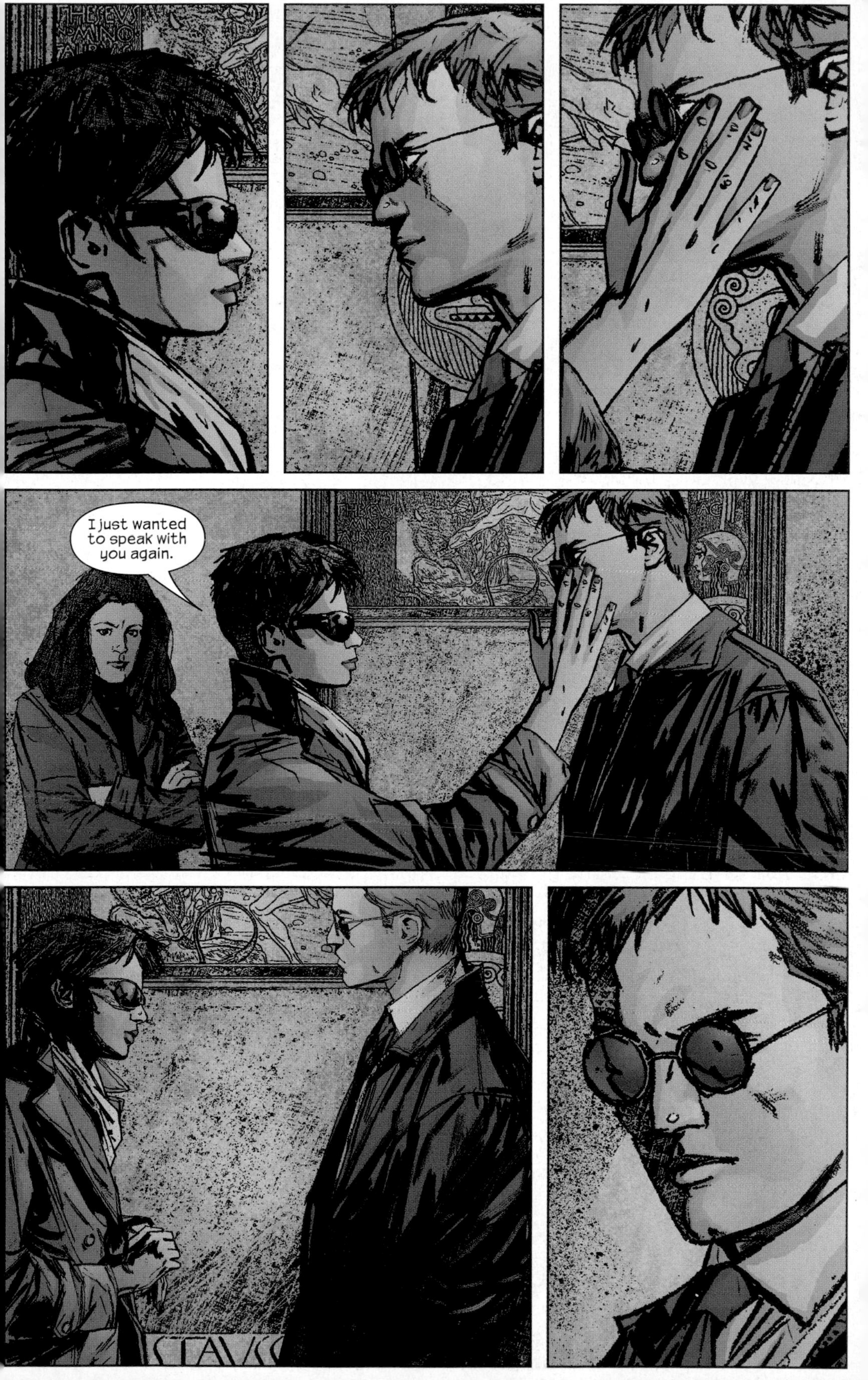
I just wanted to speak with you again.

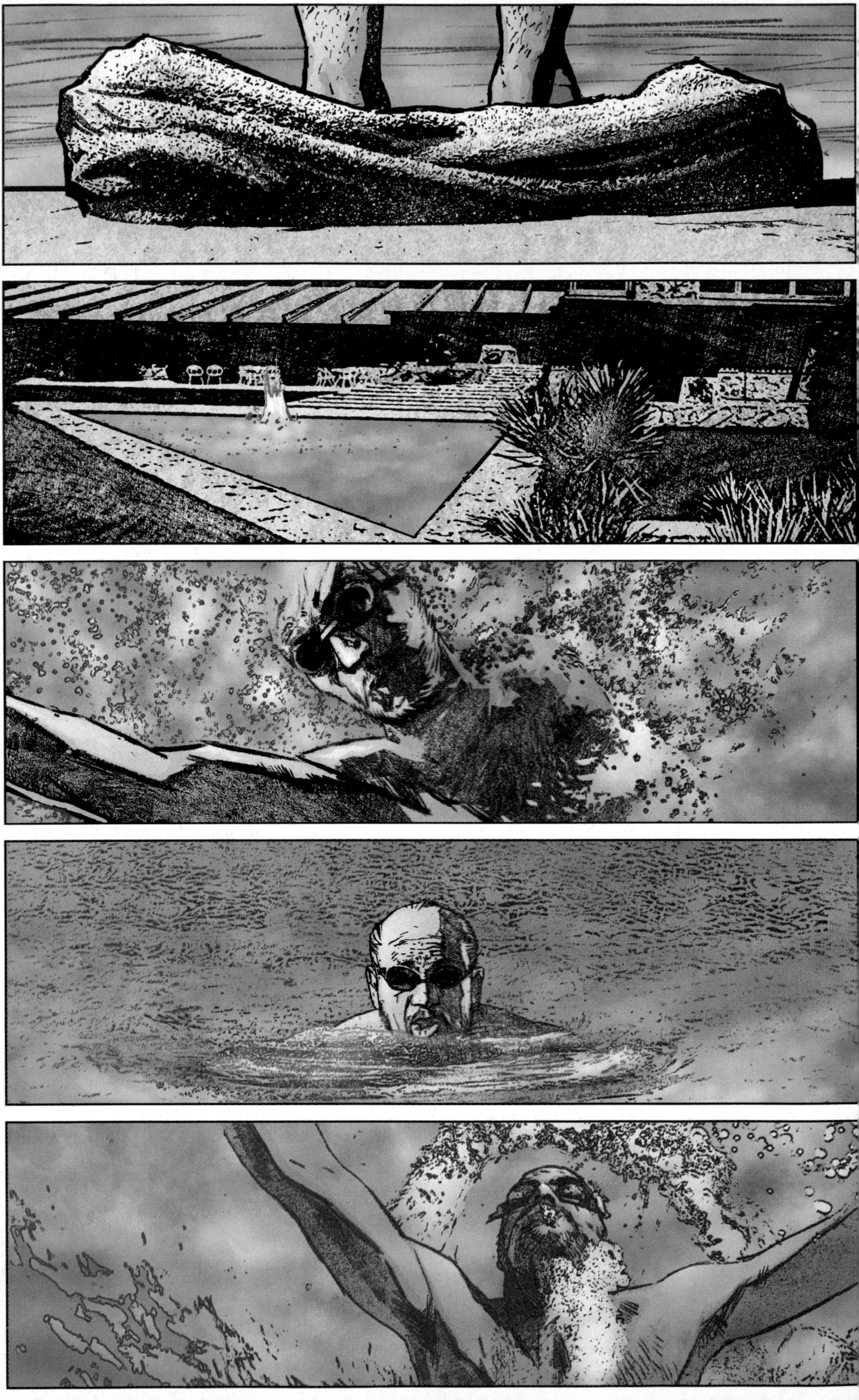

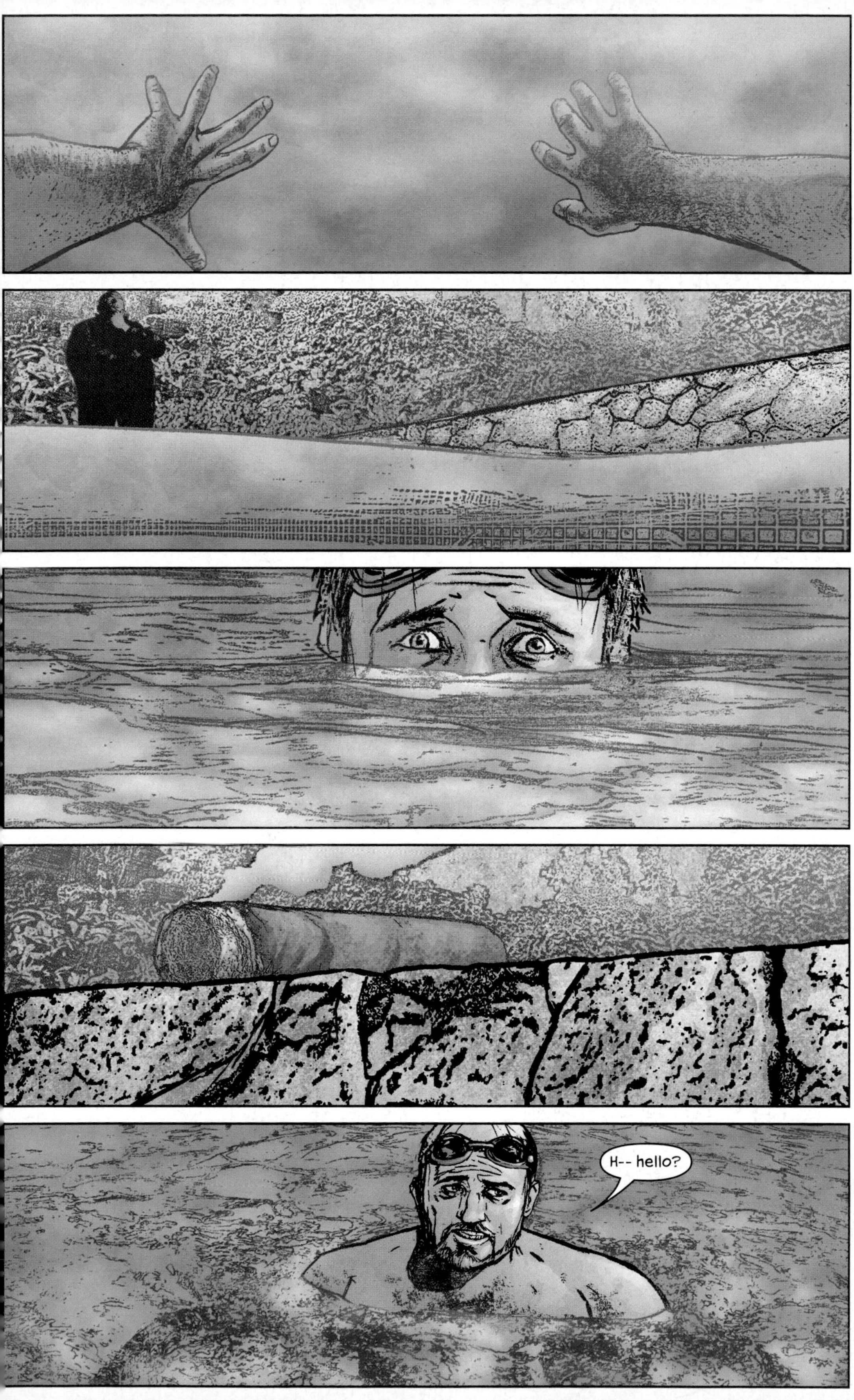
H-- hello?

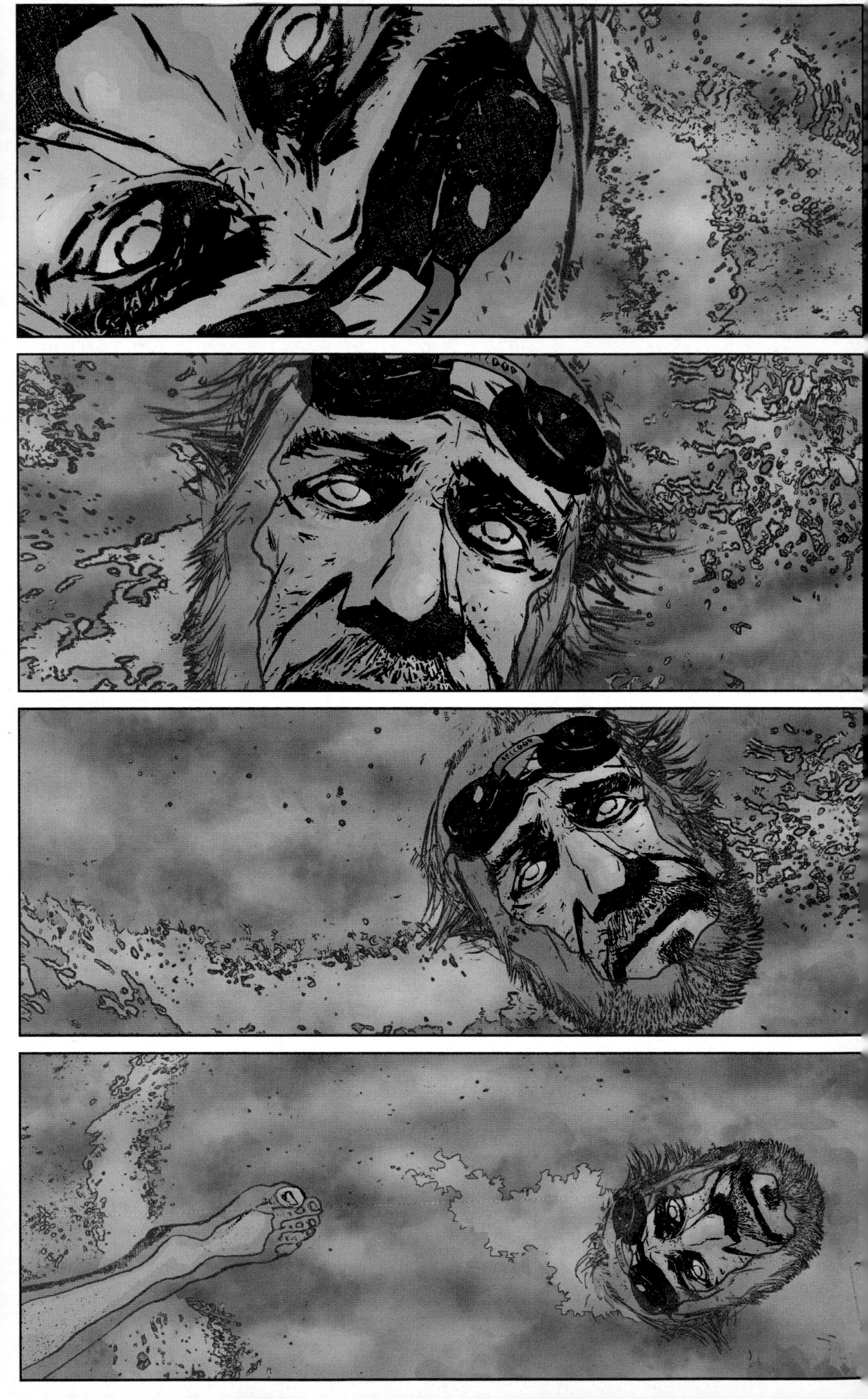

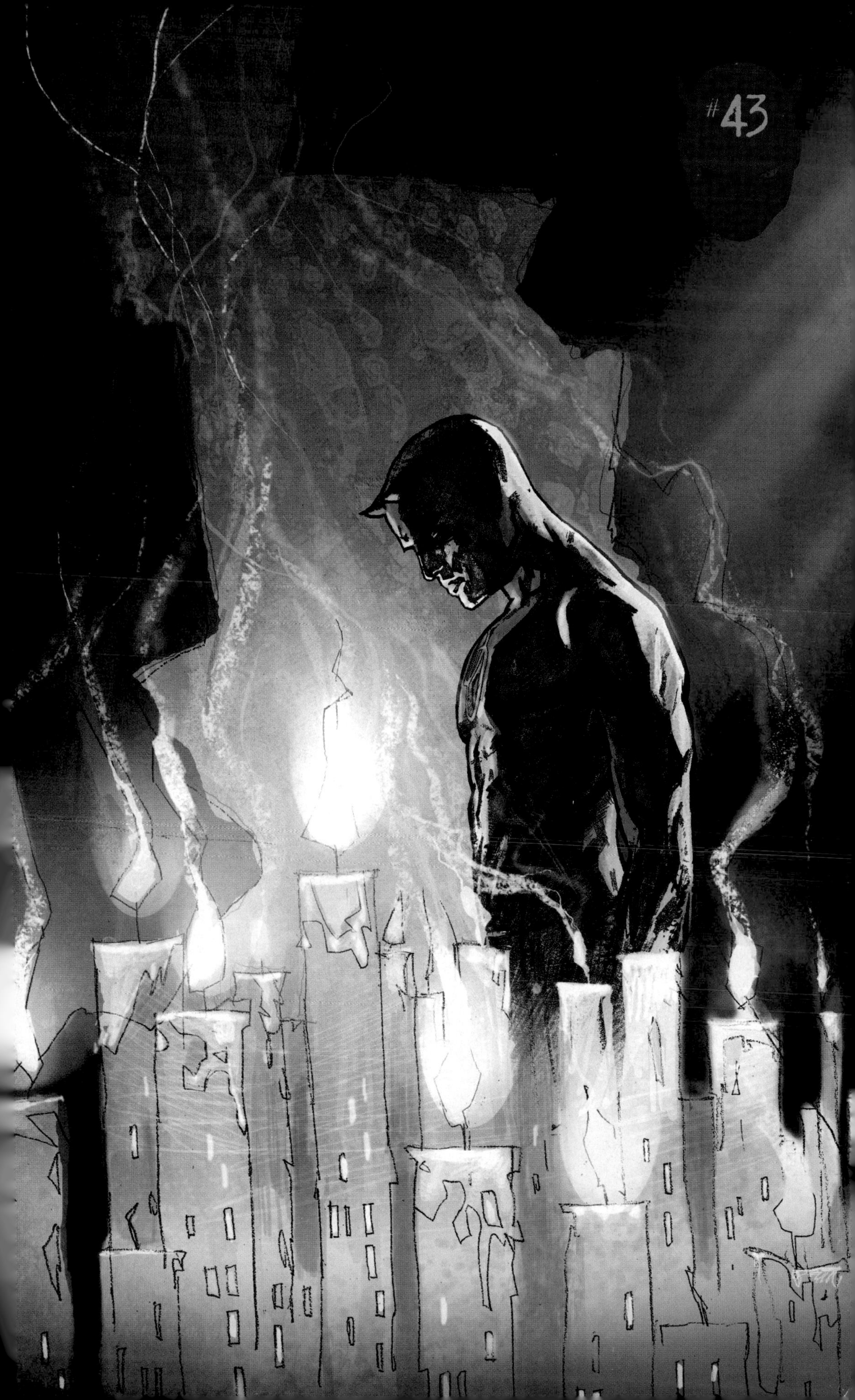
#43

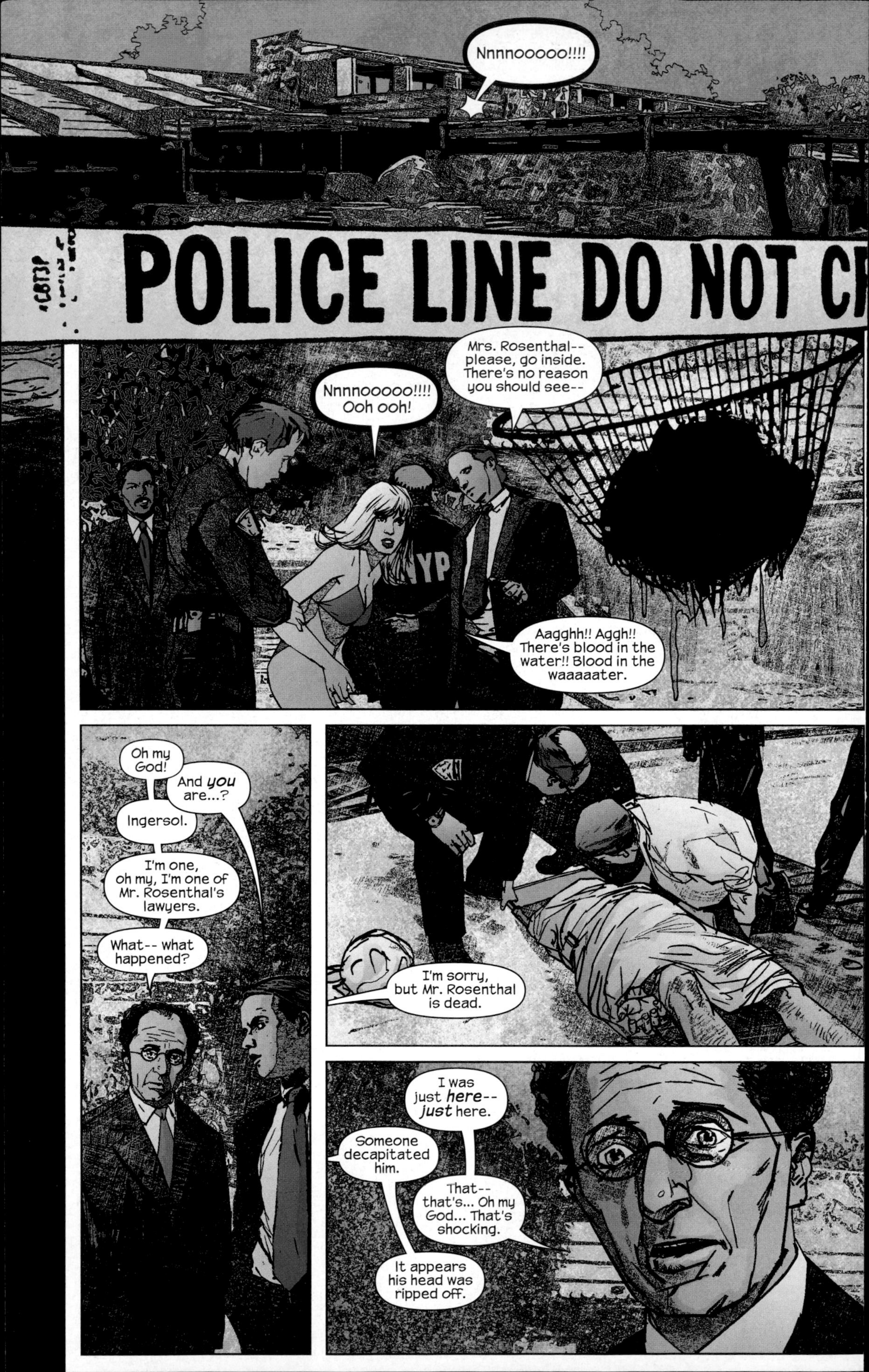
Nnnnooooo!!!!
POLICE LINE DO NOT
Nnnnooooo!!!! Ooh ooh!
Mrs. Rosenthal-- please, go inside. There's no reason you should see--
Aagghh!! Agghh!! There's blood in the water!! Blood in the waaaaater.
Oh my God!
And *you* are...?
Ingersol.
I'm one, oh my, I'm one of Mr. Rosenthal's lawyers.
What-- what happened?
I'm sorry, but Mr. Rosenthal is dead.
I was just **here**-- **just** here.
Someone decapitated him.
That-- that's... Oh my God... That's shocking.
It appears his head was ripped off.

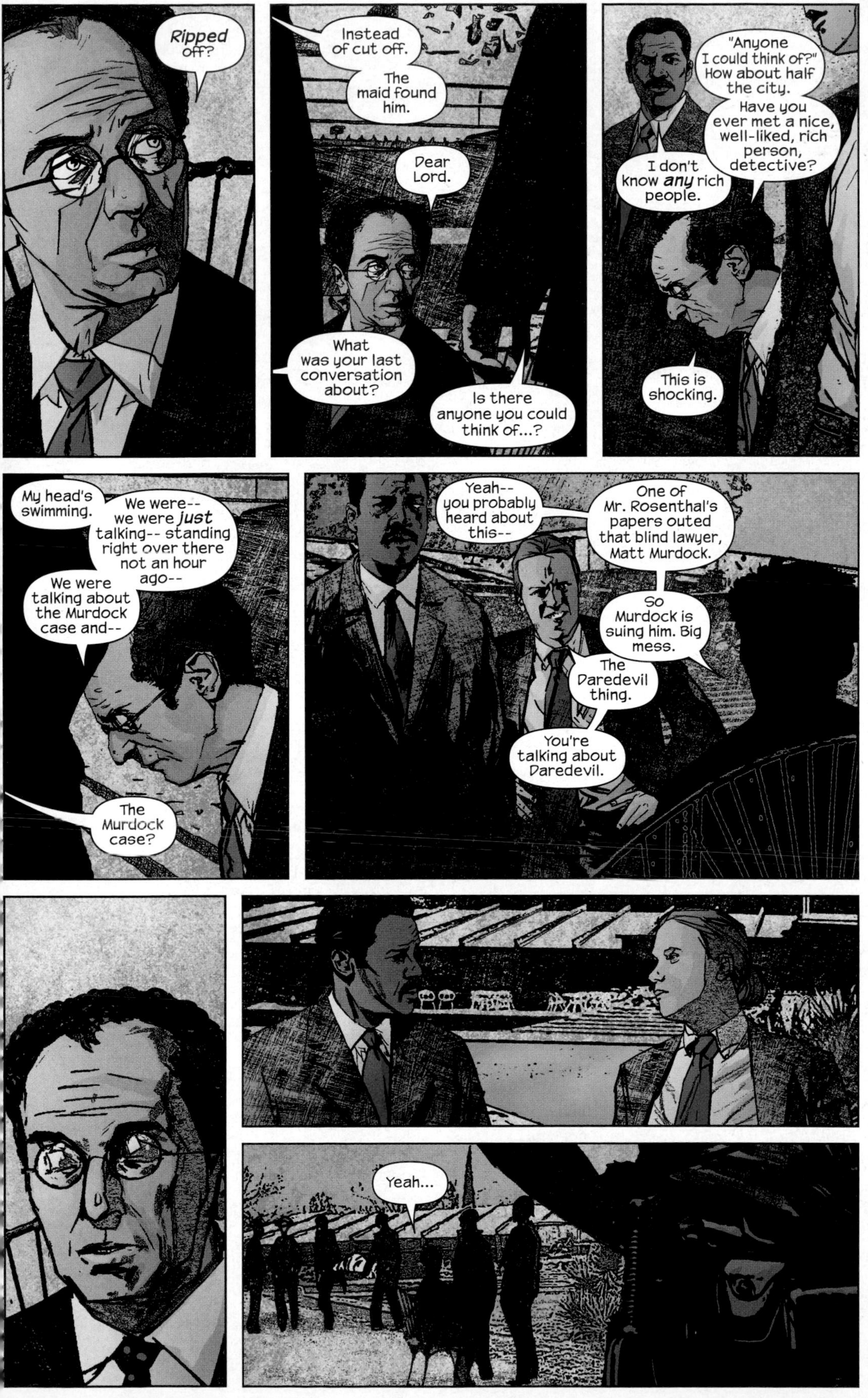
Ripped off?
Instead of cut off.
The maid found him.
Dear Lord.
What was your last conversation about?
Is there anyone you could think of...?
I don't know any rich people.
"Anyone I could think of?" How about half the city.
Have you ever met a nice, well-liked, rich person, detective?
This is shocking.
My head's swimming.
We were-- we were just talking-- standing right over there not an hour ago--
We were talking about the Murdock case and--
The Murdock case?
Yeah-- you probably heard about this--
One of Mr. Rosenthal's papers outed that blind lawyer, Matt Murdock.
So Murdock is suing him. Big mess.
The Daredevil thing.
You're talking about Daredevil.
Yeah...

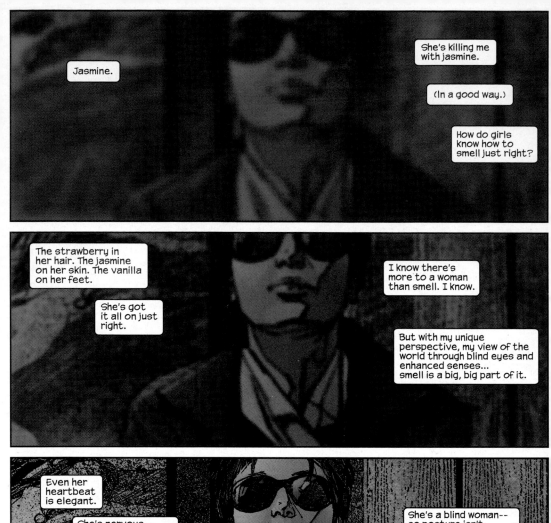

Jasmine.

She's killing me with jasmine.

(In a good way.)

How do girls know how to smell just right?

The strawberry in her hair. The jasmine on her skin. The vanilla on her feet.

She's got it all on just right.

I know there's more to a woman than smell. I know.

But with my unique perspective, my view of the world through blind eyes and enhanced senses... smell is a big, big part of it.

Even her heartbeat is elegant.

She's nervous-- embarrassed but her posture doesn't give her away.

She's a blind woman-- so posture isn't something practiced-- it's something inherent.

I let my radar fill in the blanks.

So I can 'see' what my other senses can't give me.

I feel her form.

Her silky, shiny hair.

Her precious, pale skin.

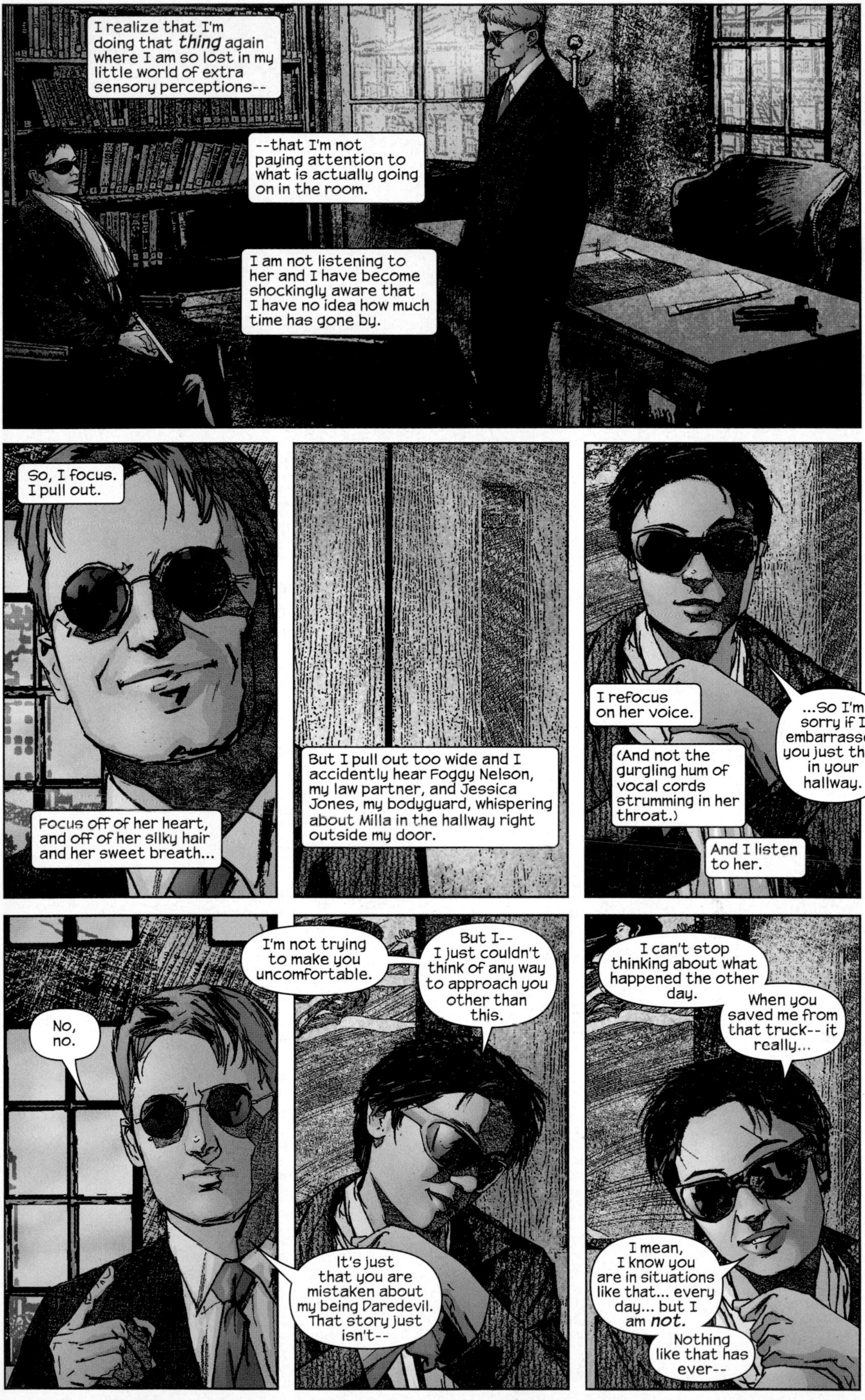

I realize that I'm doing that *thing* again where I am so lost in my little world of extra sensory perceptions--
--that I'm not paying attention to what is actually going on in the room.
I am not listening to her and I have become shockingly aware that I have no idea how much time has gone by.
So, I focus. I pull out.
Focus off of her heart, and off of her silky hair and her sweet breath...
But I pull out too wide and I accidently hear Foggy Nelson, my law partner, and Jessica Jones, my bodyguard, whispering about Milla in the hallway right outside my door.
I refocus on her voice.
(And not the gurgling hum of vocal cords strumming in her throat.)
...So I'm sorry if I embarrassed you just then in your hallway.
And I listen to her.
No, no.
It's just that you are mistaken about my being Daredevil. That story just isn't--
I'm not trying to make you uncomfortable.
But I-- I just couldn't think of any way to approach you other than this.
I can't stop thinking about what happened the other day.
When you saved me from that truck-- it really...
I mean, I know you are in situations like that... every day... but I am *not*.
Nothing like that has ever--

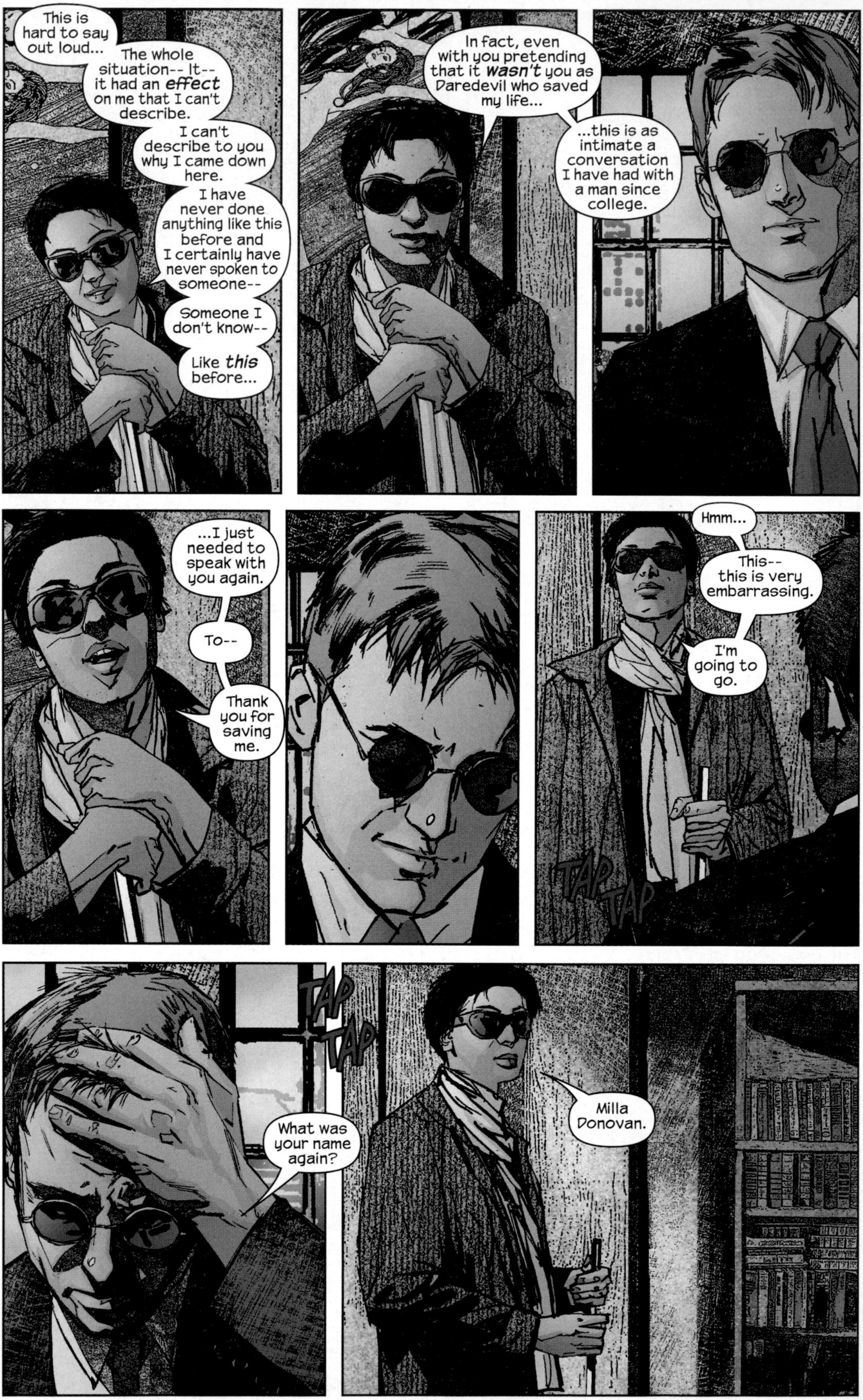
This is hard to say out loud...
The whole situation-- It-- it had an *effect* on me that I can't describe.
I can't describe to you why I came down here.
I have never done anything like this before and I certainly have never spoken to someone--
Someone I don't know--
Like *this* before...
In fact, even with you pretending that it *wasn't* you as Daredevil who saved my life...
...this is as intimate a conversation I have had with a man since college.
...I just needed to speak with you again.
To--
Thank you for saving me.
Hmm...
This-- this is very embarrassing.
I'm going to go.
TAP TAP
TAP TAP
What was your name again?
Milla Donovan.

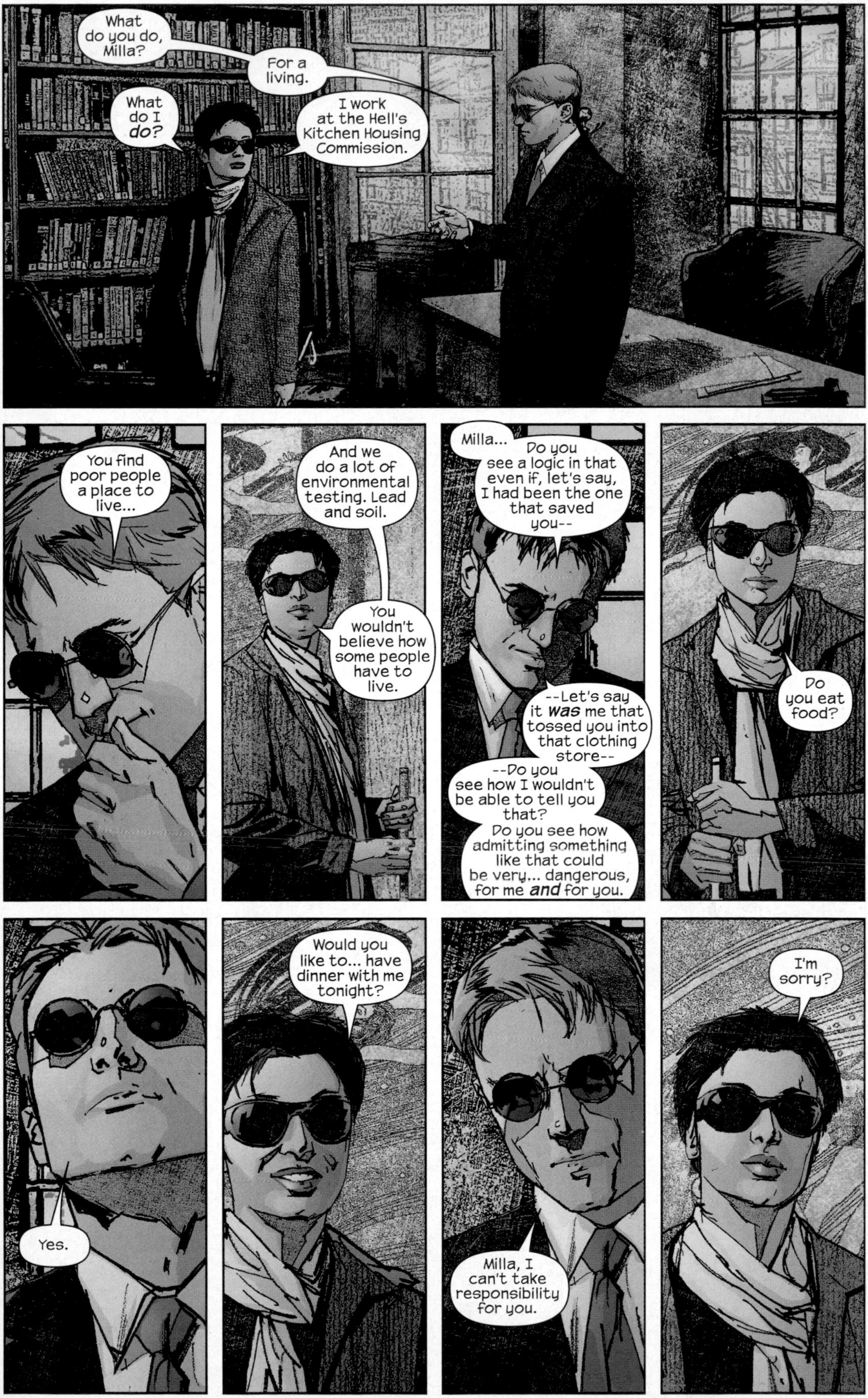

What do you do, Milla?
For a living.
What do I *do?*
I work at the Hell's Kitchen Housing Commission.
You find poor people a place to live...
And we do a lot of environmental testing. Lead and soil.
You wouldn't believe how some people have to live.
Milla...
Do you see a logic in that even if, let's say, I had been the one that saved you--
--Let's say it *was* me that tossed you into that clothing store--
--Do you see how I wouldn't be able to tell you that?
Do you see how admitting something like that could be very... dangerous, for me *and* for you.
Do you eat food?
Yes.
Would you like to... have dinner with me tonight?
Milla, I can't take responsibility for you.
I'm sorry?

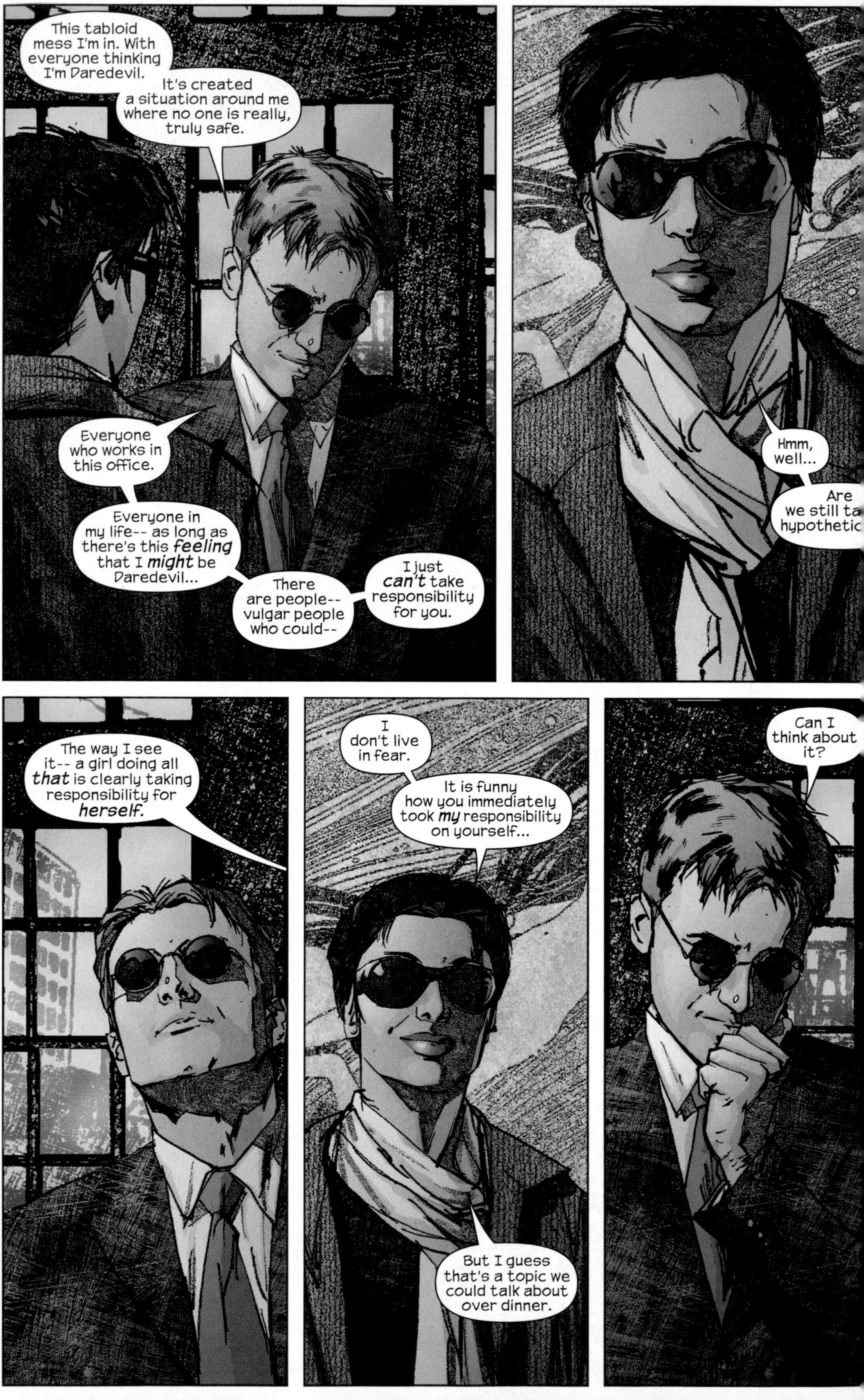

This tabloid mess I'm in. With everyone thinking I'm Daredevil.
It's created a situation around me where no one is really, truly safe.
Everyone who works in this office.
Everyone in my life-- as long as there's this *feeling* that I *might* be Daredevil...
There are people-- vulgar people who could--
I just *can't* take responsibility for you.
Hmm, well...
Are we still ta hypothetic
The way I see it-- a girl doing all *that* is clearly taking responsibility for *herself.*
I don't live in fear.
It is funny how you immediately took *my* responsibility on yourself...
But I guess that's a topic we could talk about over dinner.
Can I think about it?

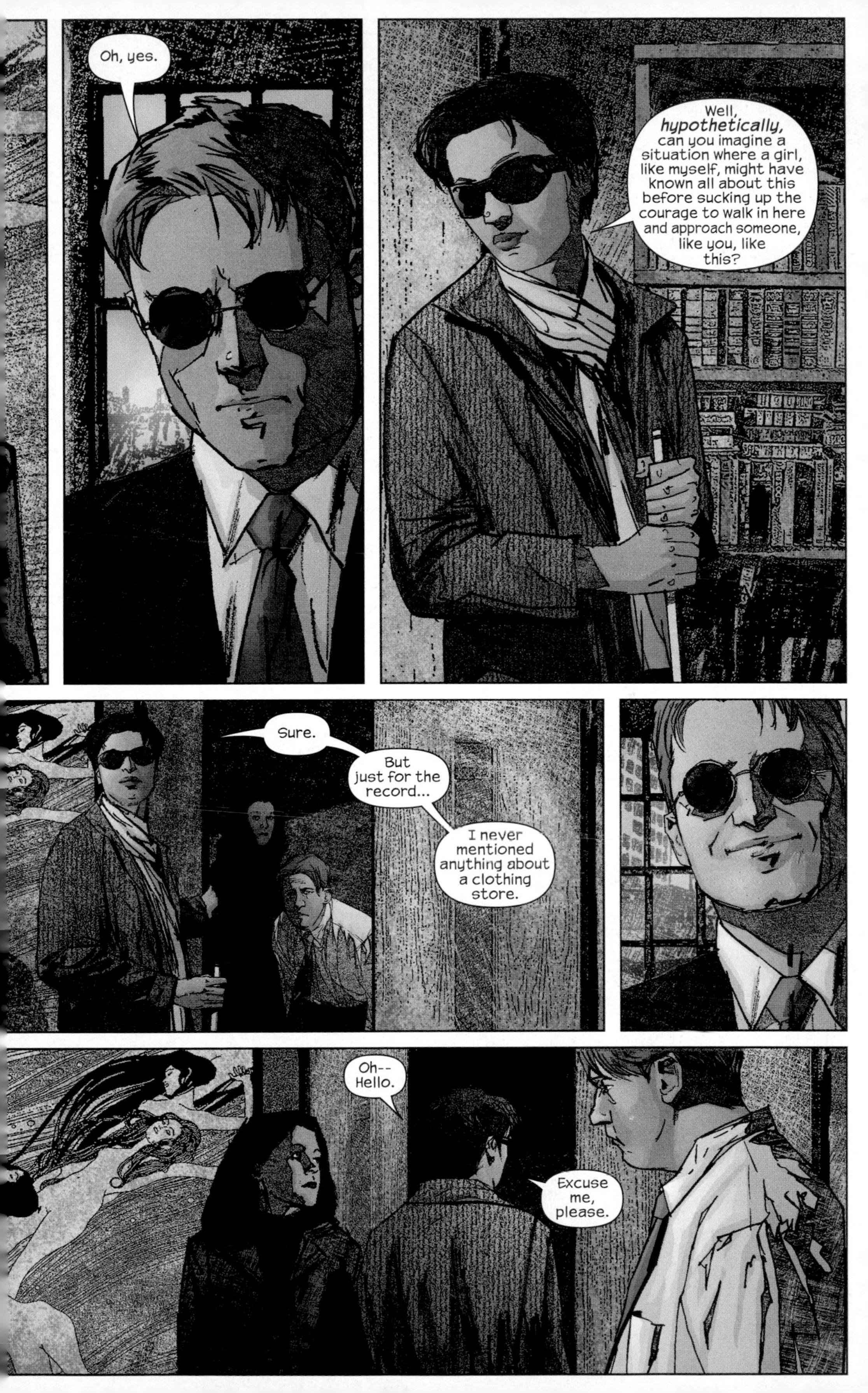

Oh, yes.
Well, *hypothetically,* can you imagine a situation where a girl, like myself, might have known all about this before sucking up the courage to walk in here and approach someone, like you, like this?
Sure.
But just for the record...
I never mentioned anything about a clothing store.
Oh-- Hello.
Excuse me, please.

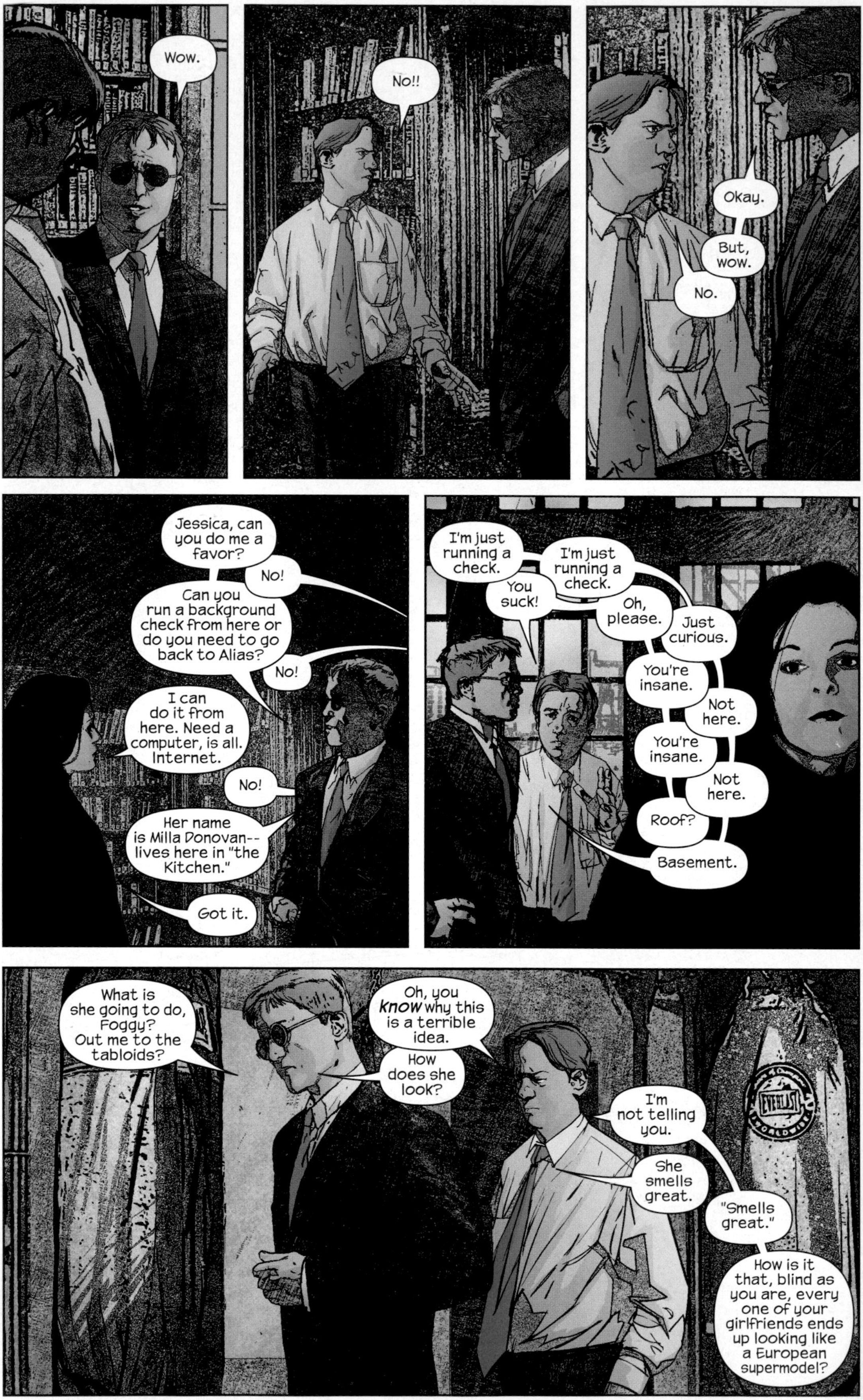
Wow.
No!!
Okay.
But, wow.
No.
Jessica, can you do me a favor?
No!
Can you run a background check from here or do you need to go back to Alias?
No!
I can do it from here. Need a computer, is all. Internet.
No!
Her name is Milla Donovan-- lives here in "the Kitchen."
Got it.
I'm just running a check.
I'm just running a check.
You suck!
Oh, please.
Just curious.
You're insane.
Not here.
You're insane.
Not here.
Roof?
Basement.
What is she going to do, Foggy? Out me to the tabloids?
Oh, you ***know*** why this is a terrible idea.
How does she look?
I'm not telling you.
She smells great.
"Smells great."
How is it that, blind as you are, every one of your girlfriends ends up looking like a European supermodel?
EVERLAST

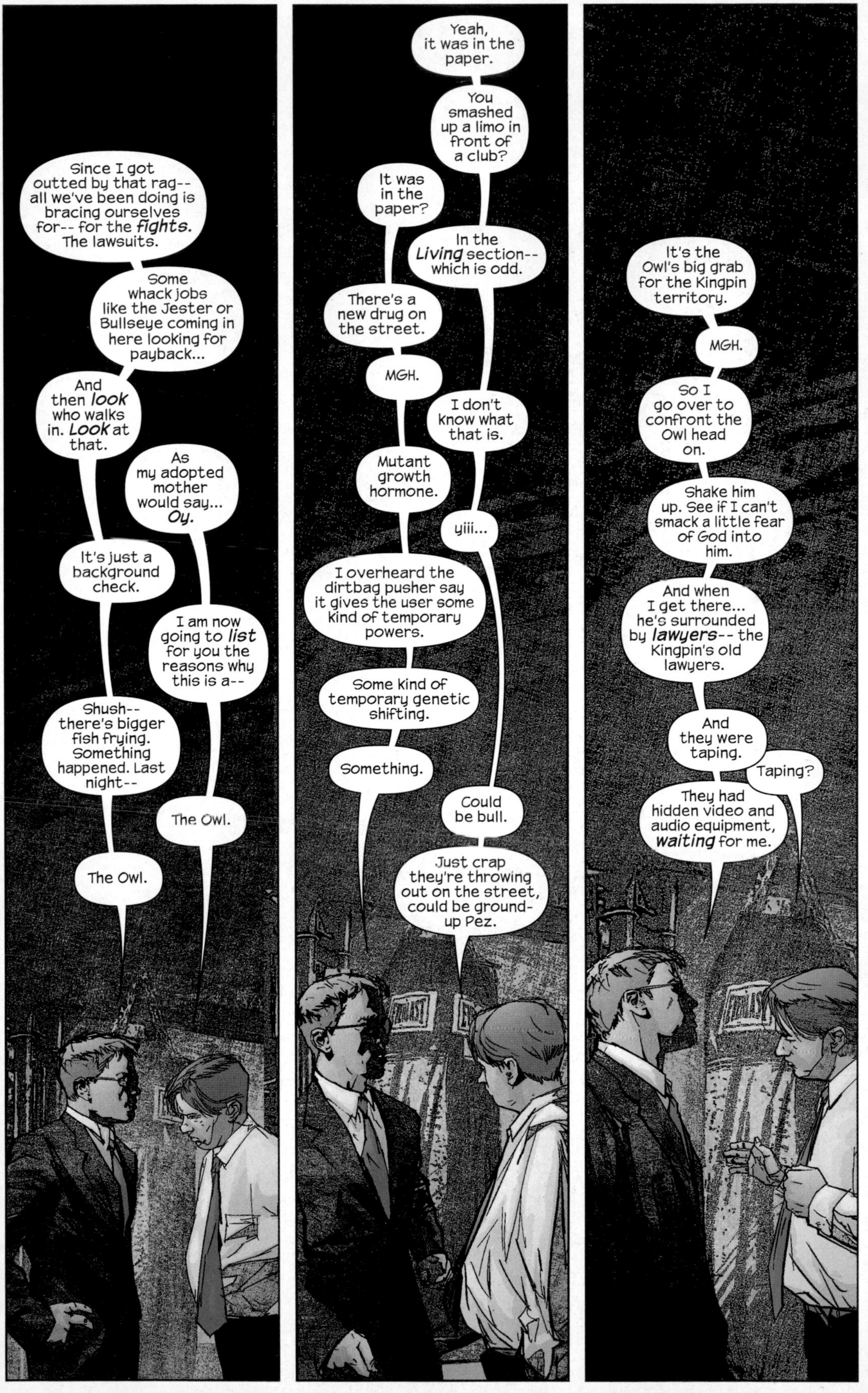
Since I got outted by that rag-- all we've been doing is bracing ourselves for-- for the fights. The lawsuits.
Some whack jobs like the Jester or Bullseye coming in here looking for payback...
And then look who walks in. Look at that.
As my adopted mother would say... Oy.
It's just a background check.
I am now going to list for you the reasons why this is a--
Shush-- there's bigger fish frying. Something happened. Last night--
The Owl.
The Owl.
Yeah, it was in the paper.
You smashed up a limo in front of a club?
It was in the paper?
In the Living section-- which is odd.
There's a new drug on the street.
MGH.
I don't know what that is.
Mutant growth hormone.
yiii...
I overheard the dirtbag pusher say it gives the user some kind of temporary powers.
Some kind of temporary genetic shifting.
Something.
Could be bull.
Just crap they're throwing out on the street, could be ground-up Pez.
It's the Owl's big grab for the Kingpin territory.
MGH.
So I go over to confront the Owl head on.
Shake him up. See if I can't smack a little fear of God into him.
And when I get there... he's surrounded by lawyers-- the Kingpin's old lawyers.
And they were taping.
Taping?
They had hidden video and audio equipment, waiting for me.

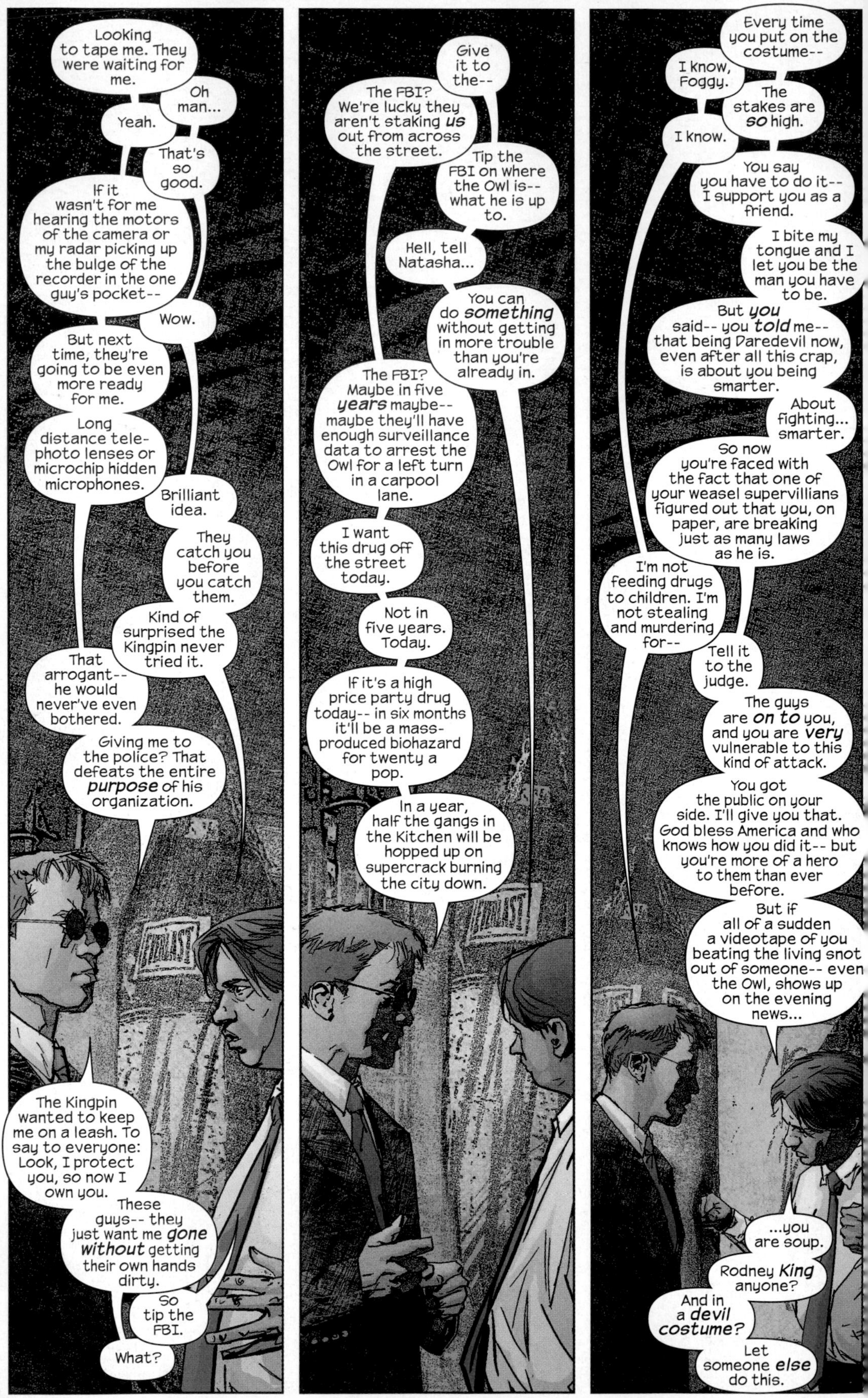

Looking to tape me. They were waiting for me.
Oh man...
Yeah.
That's so good.
If it wasn't for me hearing the motors of the camera or my radar picking up the bulge of the recorder in the one guy's pocket--
Wow.
But next time, they're going to be even more ready for me.
Long distance tele-photo lenses or microchip hidden microphones.
Brilliant idea.
They catch you before you catch them.
Kind of surprised the Kingpin never tried it.
That arrogant-- he would never've even bothered.
Giving me to the police? That defeats the entire purpose of his organization.
The Kingpin wanted to keep me on a leash. To say to everyone: Look, I protect you, so now I own you.
These guys-- they just want me gone without getting their own hands dirty.
So tip the FBI.
What?
Give it to the--
The FBI? We're lucky they aren't staking us out from across the street.
Tip the FBI on where the Owl is-- what he is up to.
Hell, tell Natasha...
You can do something without getting in more trouble than you're already in.
The FBI? Maybe in five years maybe-- maybe they'll have enough surveillance data to arrest the Owl for a left turn in a carpool lane.
I want this drug off the street today.
Not in five years. Today.
If it's a high price party drug today-- in six months it'll be a mass-produced biohazard for twenty a pop.
In a year, half the gangs in the Kitchen will be hopped up on supercrack burning the city down.
Every time you put on the costume--
I know, Foggy.
The stakes are so high.
I know.
You say you have to do it-- I support you as a friend.
I bite my tongue and I let you be the man you have to be.
But you said-- you told me-- that being Daredevil now, even after all this crap, is about you being smarter.
About fighting... smarter.
So now you're faced with the fact that one of your weasel supervillians figured out that you, on paper, are breaking just as many laws as he is.
I'm not feeding drugs to children. I'm not stealing and murdering for--
Tell it to the judge.
The guys are on to you, and you are very vulnerable to this kind of attack.
You got the public on your side. I'll give you that. God bless America and who knows how you did it-- but you're more of a hero to them than ever before.
But if all of a sudden a videotape of you beating the living snot out of someone-- even the Owl, shows up on the evening news...
...you are soup.
Rodney King anyone?
And in a devil costume?
Let someone else do this.

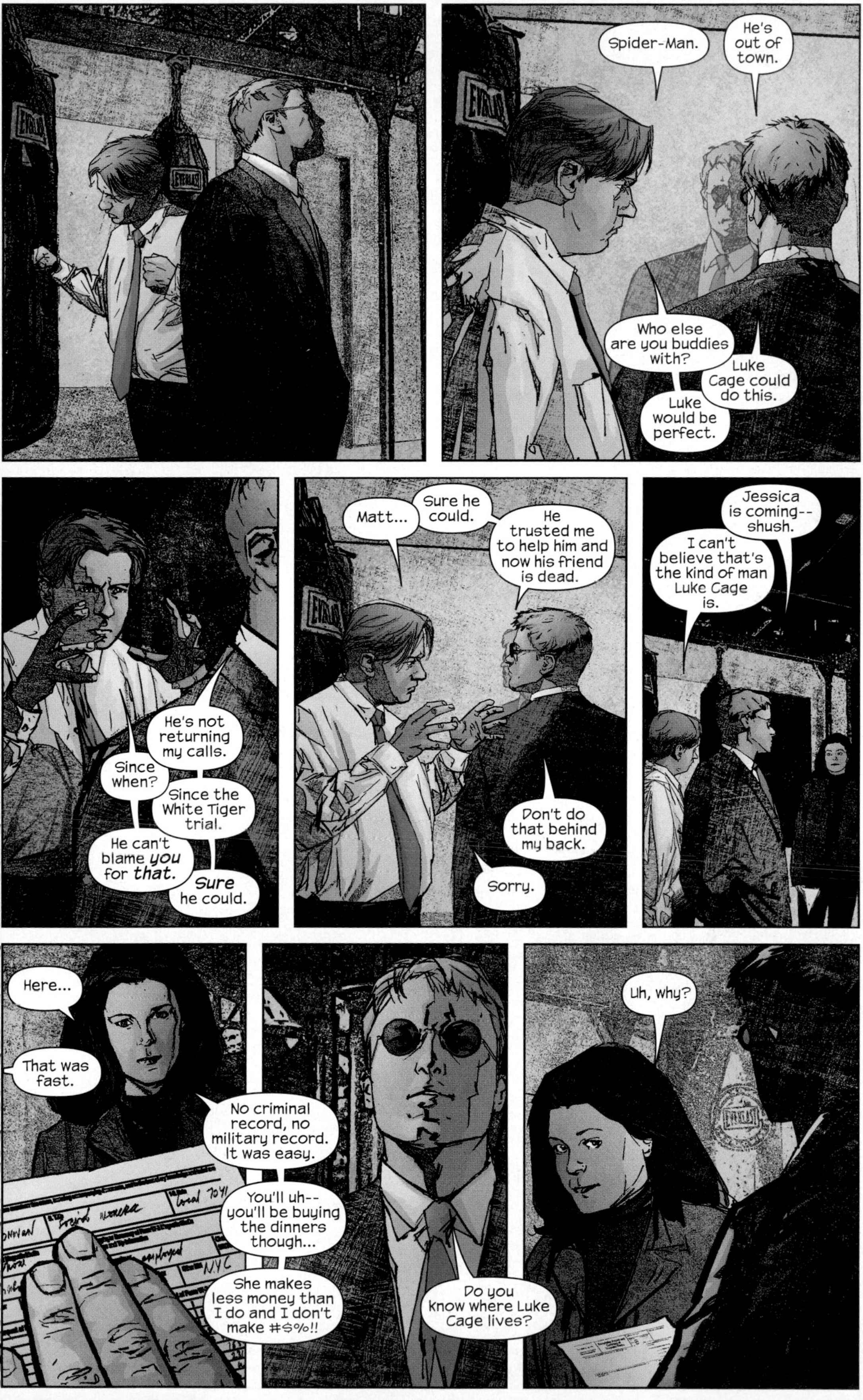
Spider-Man.
He's out of town.
Who else are you buddies with?
Luke Cage could do this.
Luke would be perfect.
He's not returning my calls.
Since when?
Since the White Tiger trial.
He can't blame *you* for *that*.
Sure he could.
Matt...
Sure he could.
He trusted me to help him and now his friend is dead.
Don't do that behind my back.
Sorry.
Jessica is coming--shush.
I can't believe that's the kind of man Luke Cage is.
Here...
That was fast.
No criminal record, no military record. It was easy.
You'll uh--you'll be buying the dinners though...
She makes less money than I do and I don't make #$%!!
Do you know where Luke Cage lives?
Uh, why?

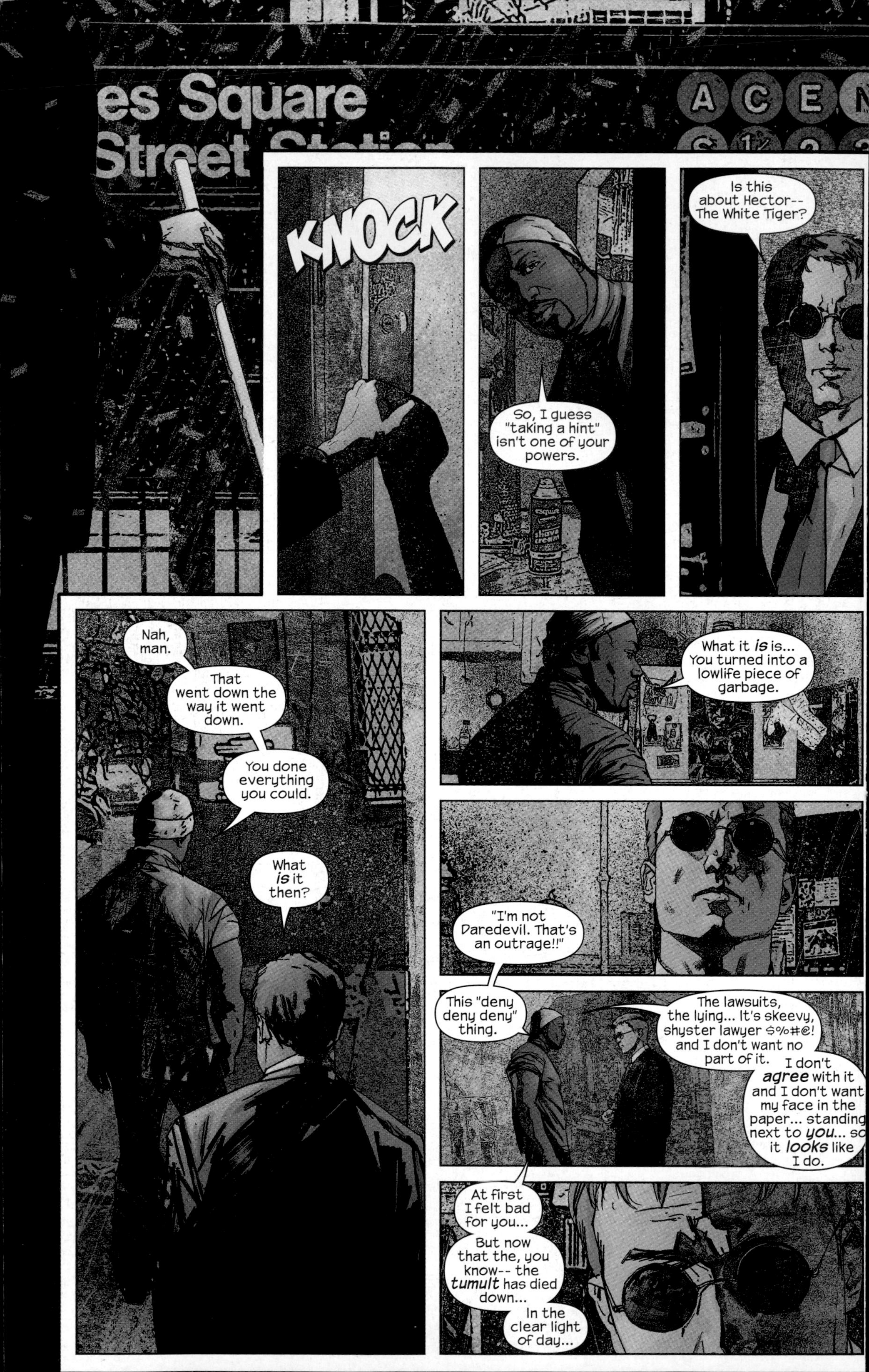

es Square
Street Station
A C E N
KNOCK
So, I guess "taking a hint" isn't one of your powers.
Is this about Hector-- The White Tiger?
Nah, man.
That went down the way it went down.
You done everything you could.
What *is* it then?
What it *is* is... You turned into a lowlife piece of garbage.
"I'm not Daredevil. That's an outrage!!"
This "deny deny deny" thing.
The lawsuits, the lying... It's skeevy, shyster lawyer $%#@! and I don't want no part of it.
I don't *agree* with it and I don't want my face in the paper... standing next to *you*... so it *looks* like I do.
At first I felt bad for you...
But now that the, you know-- the *tumult* has died down...
In the clear light of day...

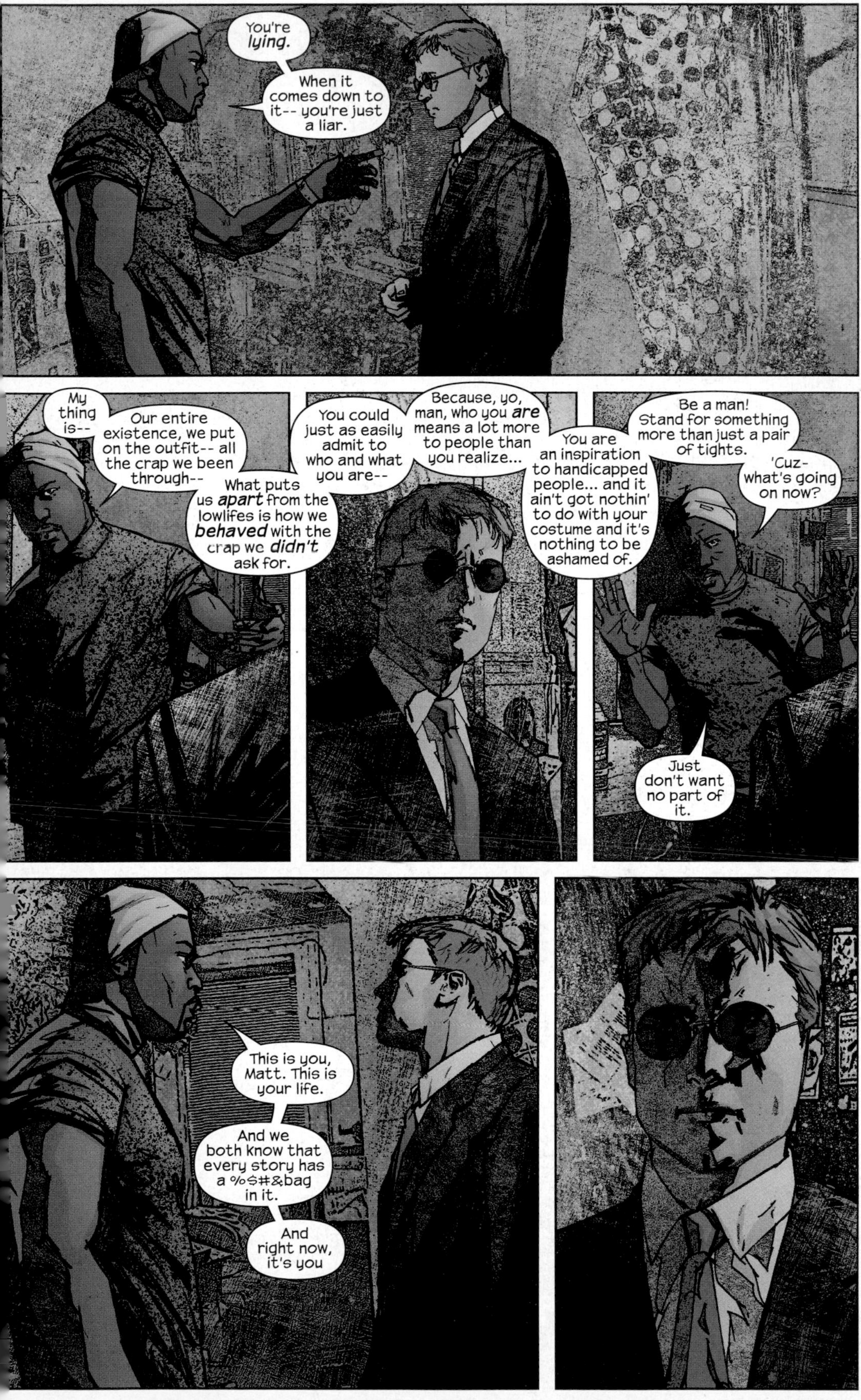
You're lying.
When it comes down to it-- you're just a liar.
My thing is--
Our entire existence, we put on the outfit-- all the crap we been through--
What puts us apart from the lowlifes is how we behaved with the crap we didn't ask for.
You could just as easily admit to who and what you are--
Because, yo, man, who you are means a lot more to people than you realize...
You are an inspiration to handicapped people... and it ain't got nothin' to do with your costume and it's nothing to be ashamed of.
Be a man! Stand for something more than just a pair of tights.
'Cuz- what's going on now?
Just don't want no part of it.
This is you, Matt. This is your life.
And we both know that every story has a %$#&bag in it.
And right now, it's you

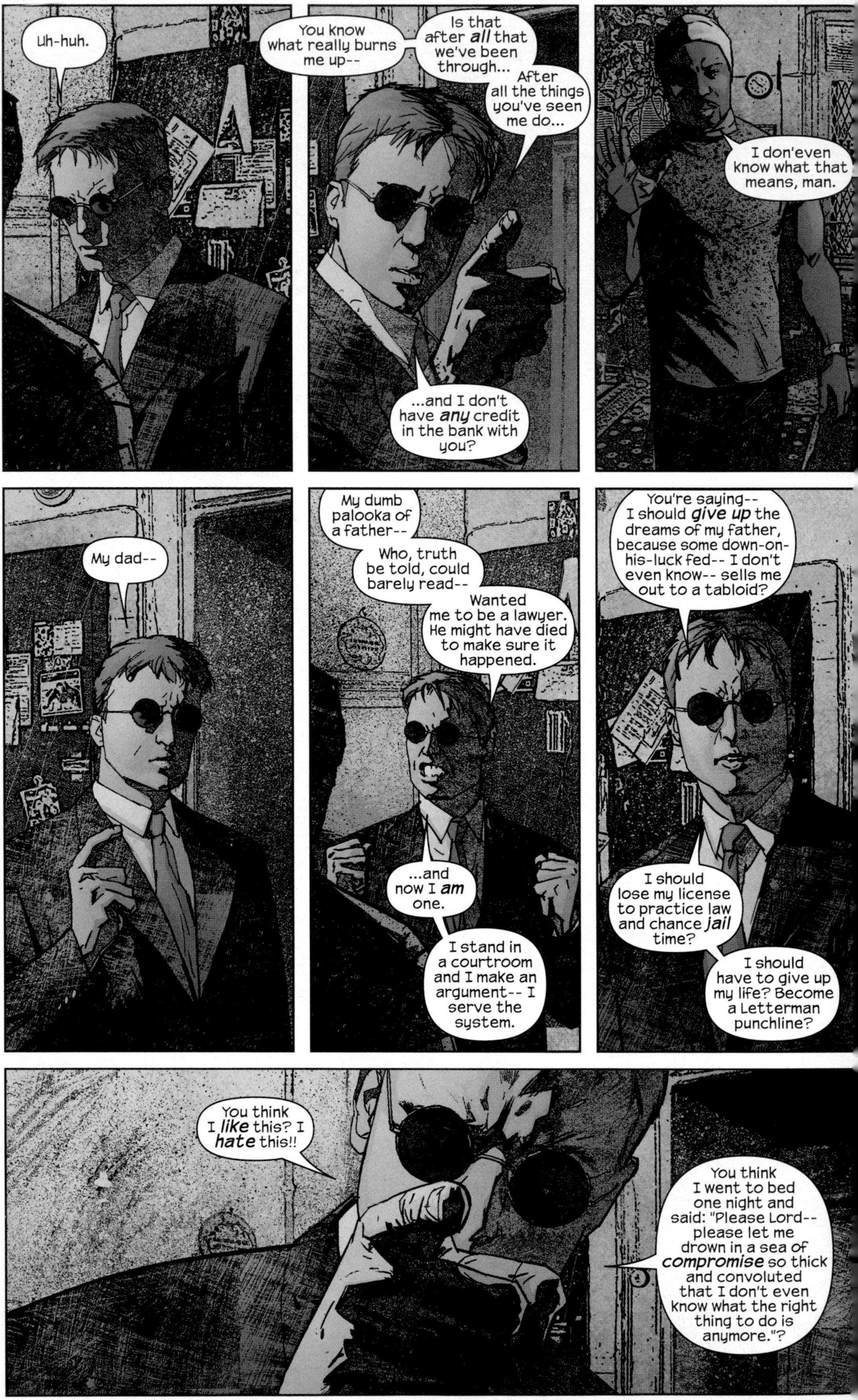
Uh-huh.
You know what really burns me up--
Is that after all that we've been through...
After all the things you've seen me do...
...and I don't have any credit in the bank with you?
I don'even know what that means, man.
My dad--
My dumb palooka of a father--
Who, truth be told, could barely read--
Wanted me to be a lawyer. He might have died to make sure it happened.
...and now I am one.
I stand in a courtroom and I make an argument-- I serve the system.
You're saying-- I should give up the dreams of my father, because some down-on-his-luck fed-- I don't even know-- sells me out to a tabloid?
I should lose my license to practice law and chance jail time?
I should have to give up my life? Become a Letterman punchline?
You think I like this? I hate this!!
You think I went to bed one night and said: "Please Lord-- please let me drown in a sea of compromise so thick and convoluted that I don't even know what the right thing to do is anymore."?

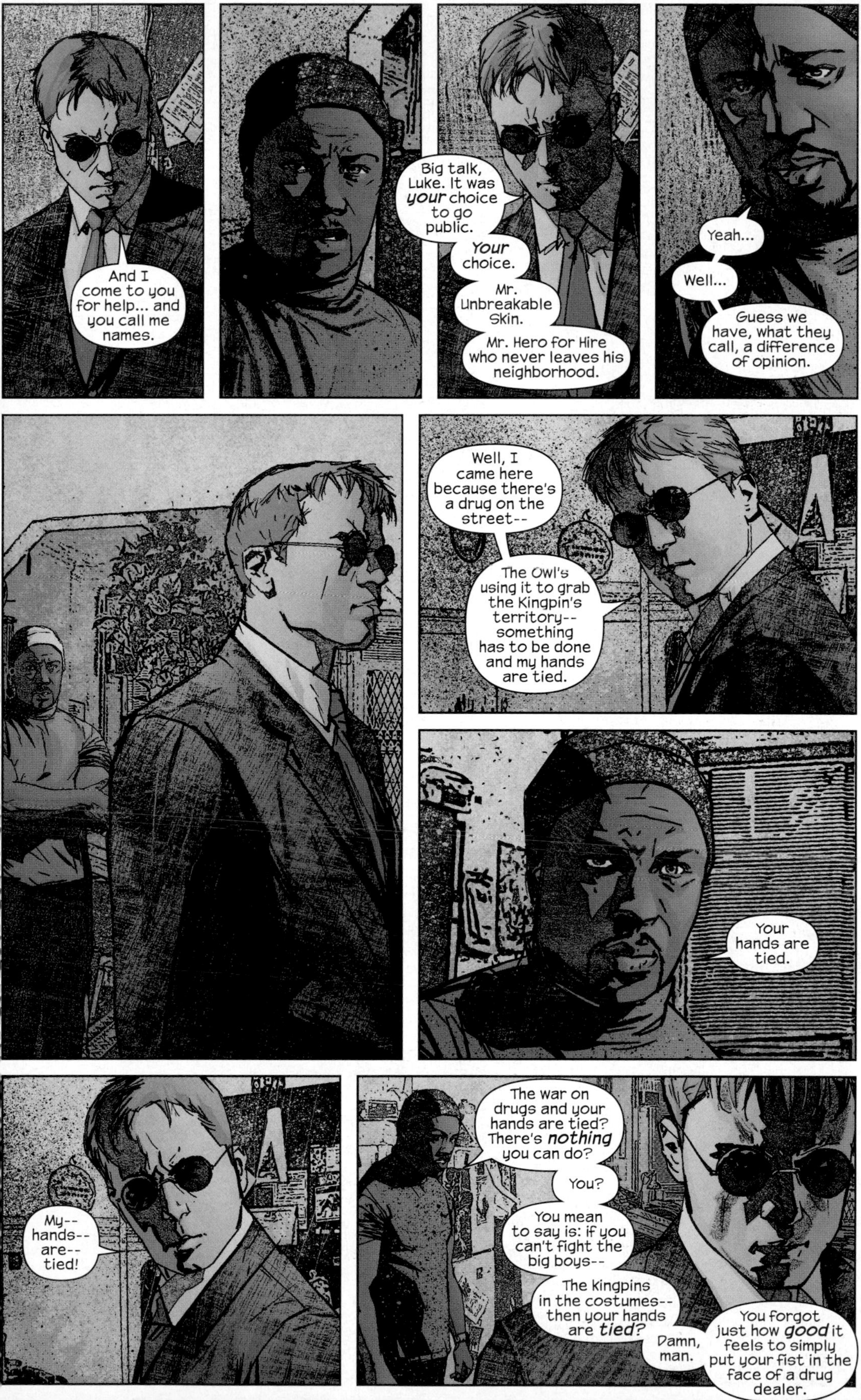
And I come to you for help... and you call me names.
Big talk, Luke. It was *your* choice to go public.
Your choice.
Mr. Unbreakable Skin.
Mr. Hero for Hire who never leaves his neighborhood.
Yeah...
Well...
Guess we have, what they call, a difference of opinion.
Well, I came here because there's a drug on the street--
The Owl's using it to grab the Kingpin's territory-- something has to be done and my hands are tied.
Your hands are tied.
My-- hands-- are-- tied!
The war on drugs and your hands are tied? There's *nothing* you can do?
You?
You mean to say is: if you can't fight the big boys--
The kingpins in the costumes-- then your hands are *tied?*
Damn, man.
You forgot just how *good* it feels to simply put your fist in the face of a drug dealer.

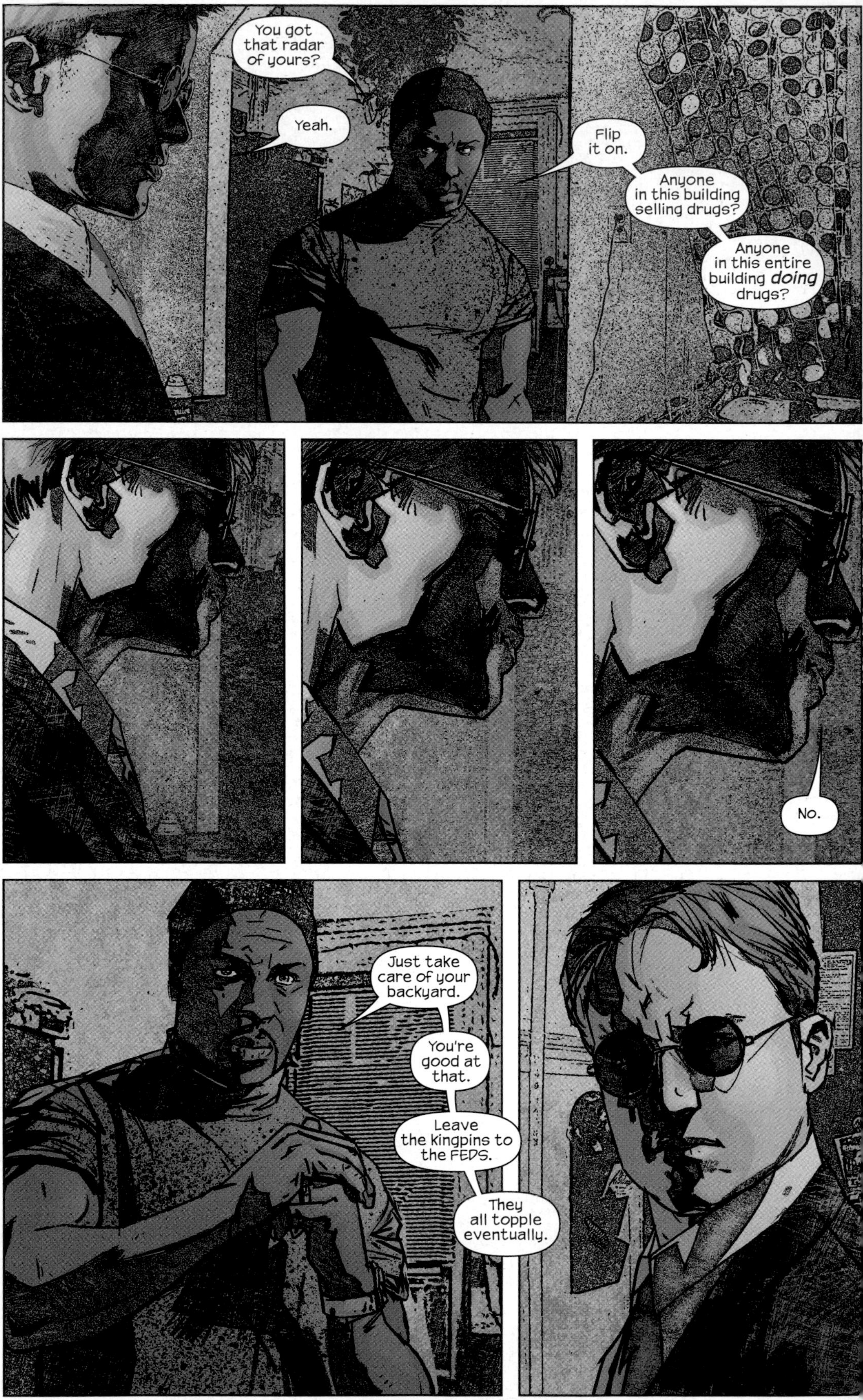
You got that radar of yours?
Yeah.
Flip it on.
Anyone in this building selling drugs?
Anyone in this entire building *doing* drugs?
No.
Just take care of your backyard.
You're good at that.
Leave the kingpins to the FEDS.
They all topple eventually.

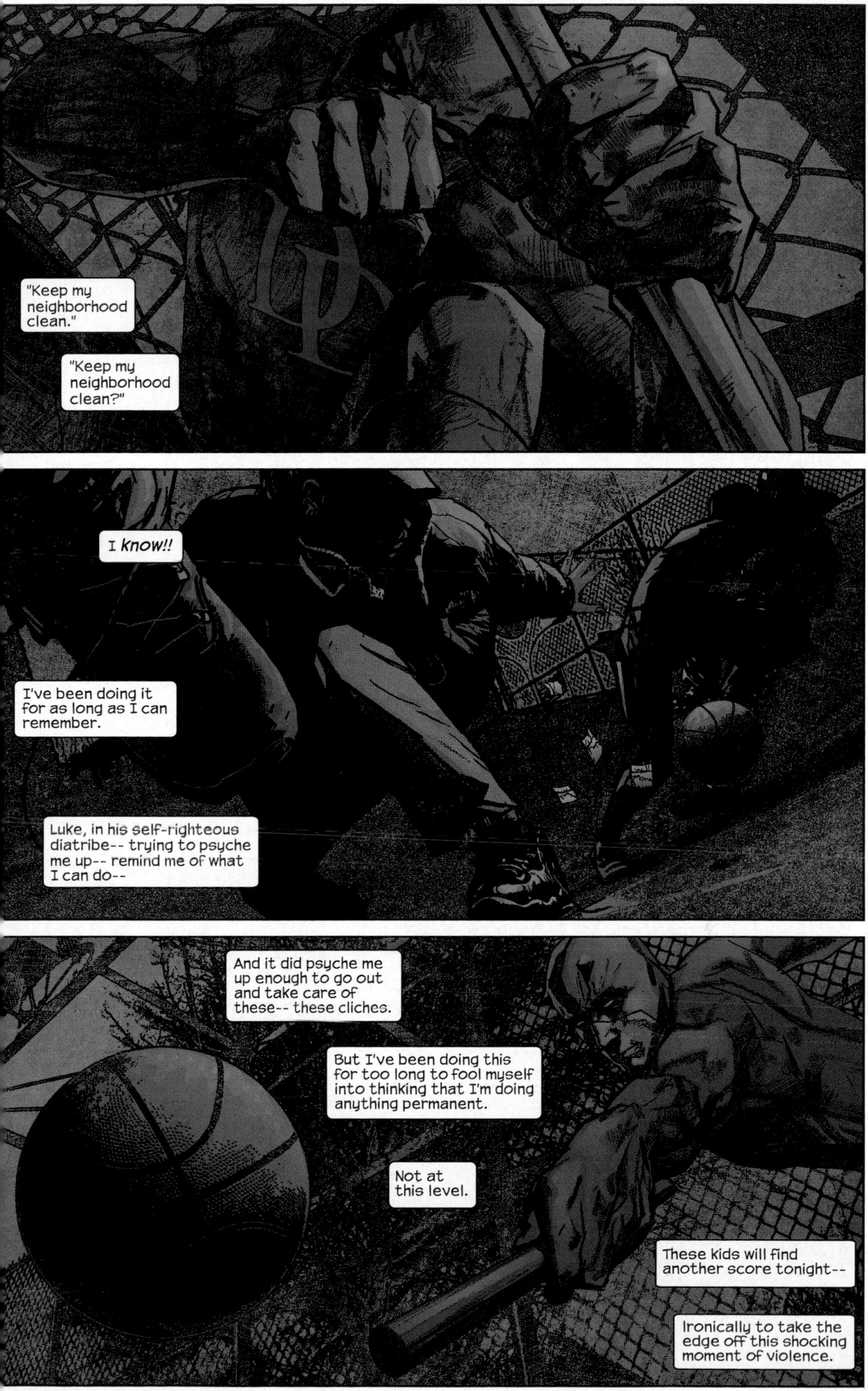
"Keep my neighborhood clean."
"Keep my neighborhood clean?"
I *know!!*
I've been doing it for as long as I can remember.
Luke, in his self-righteous diatribe-- trying to psyche me up-- remind me of what I can do--
And it did psyche me up enough to go out and take care of these-- these cliches.
But I've been doing this for too long to fool myself into thinking that I'm doing anything permanent.
Not at this level.
These kids will find another score tonight--
Ironically to take the edge off this shocking moment of violence.

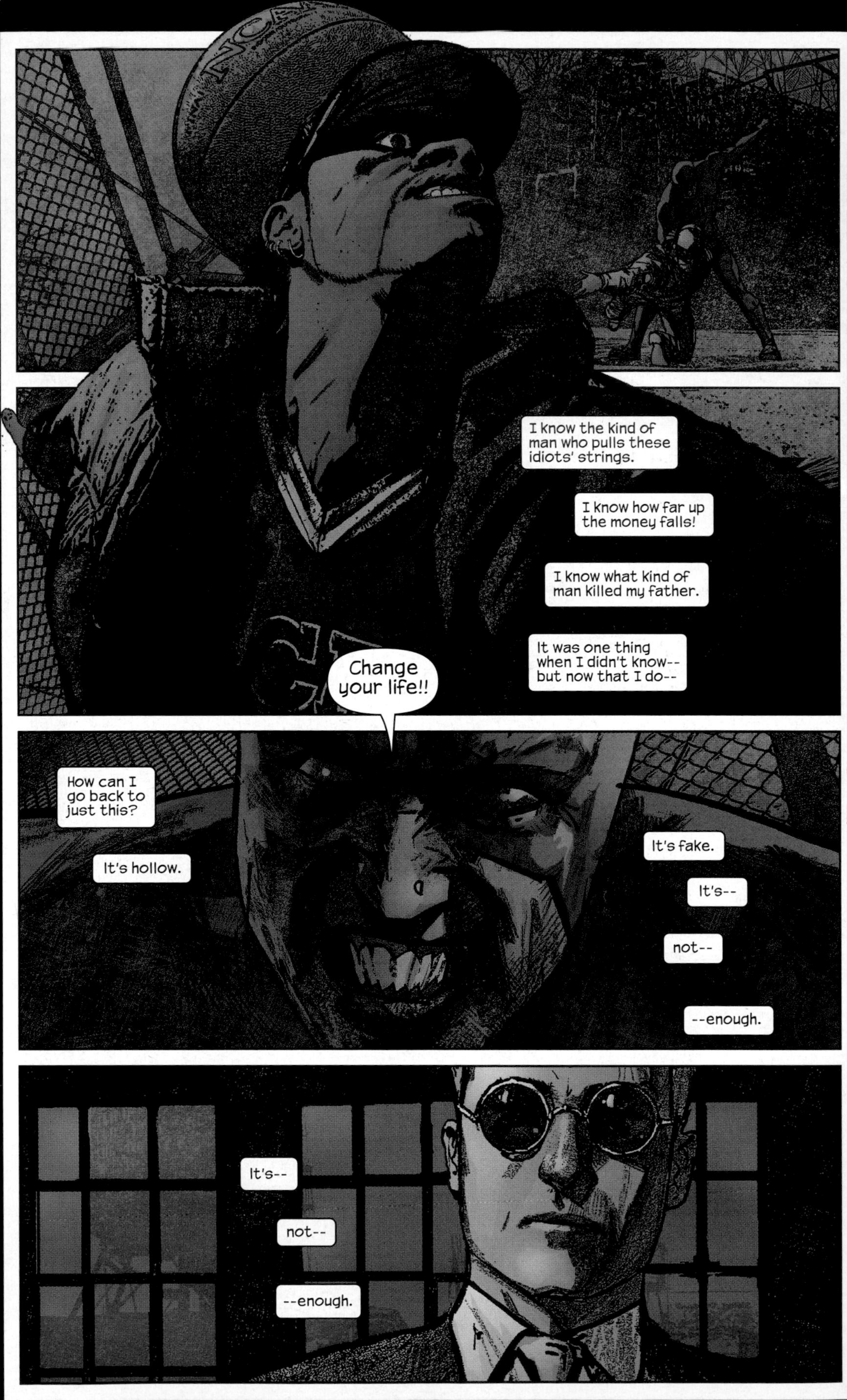

I know the kind of man who pulls these idiots' strings.
I know how far up the money falls!
I know what kind of man killed my father.
It was one thing when I didn't know-- but now that I do--
Change your life!!
How can I go back to just this?
It's hollow.
It's fake.
It's--
not--
--enough.
It's--
not--
--enough.

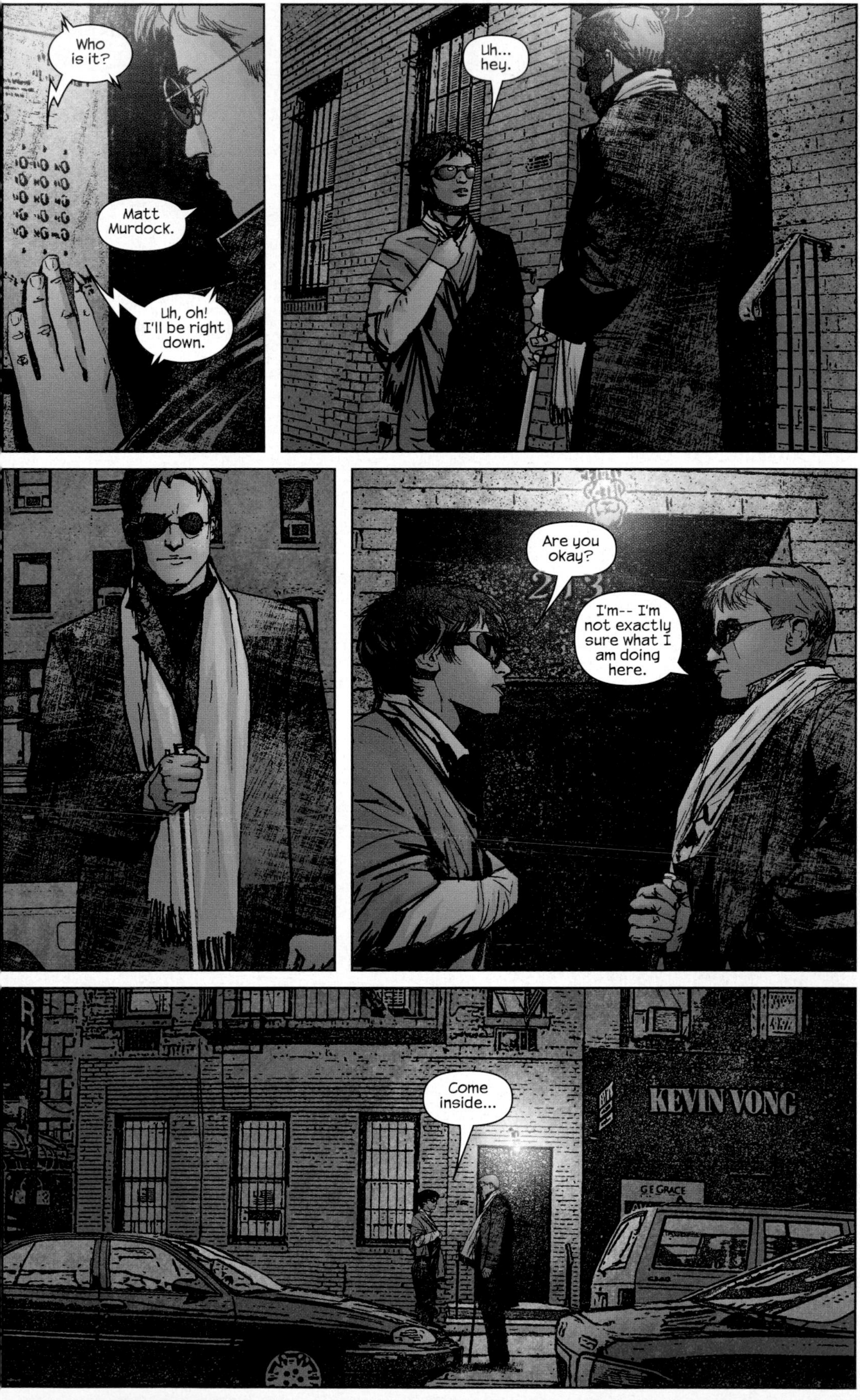
Who is it?
Matt Murdock.
Uh, oh! I'll be right down.
Uh... hey.
Are you okay?
I'm-- I'm not exactly sure what I am doing here.
Come inside...
KEVIN VONG
G E GRACE

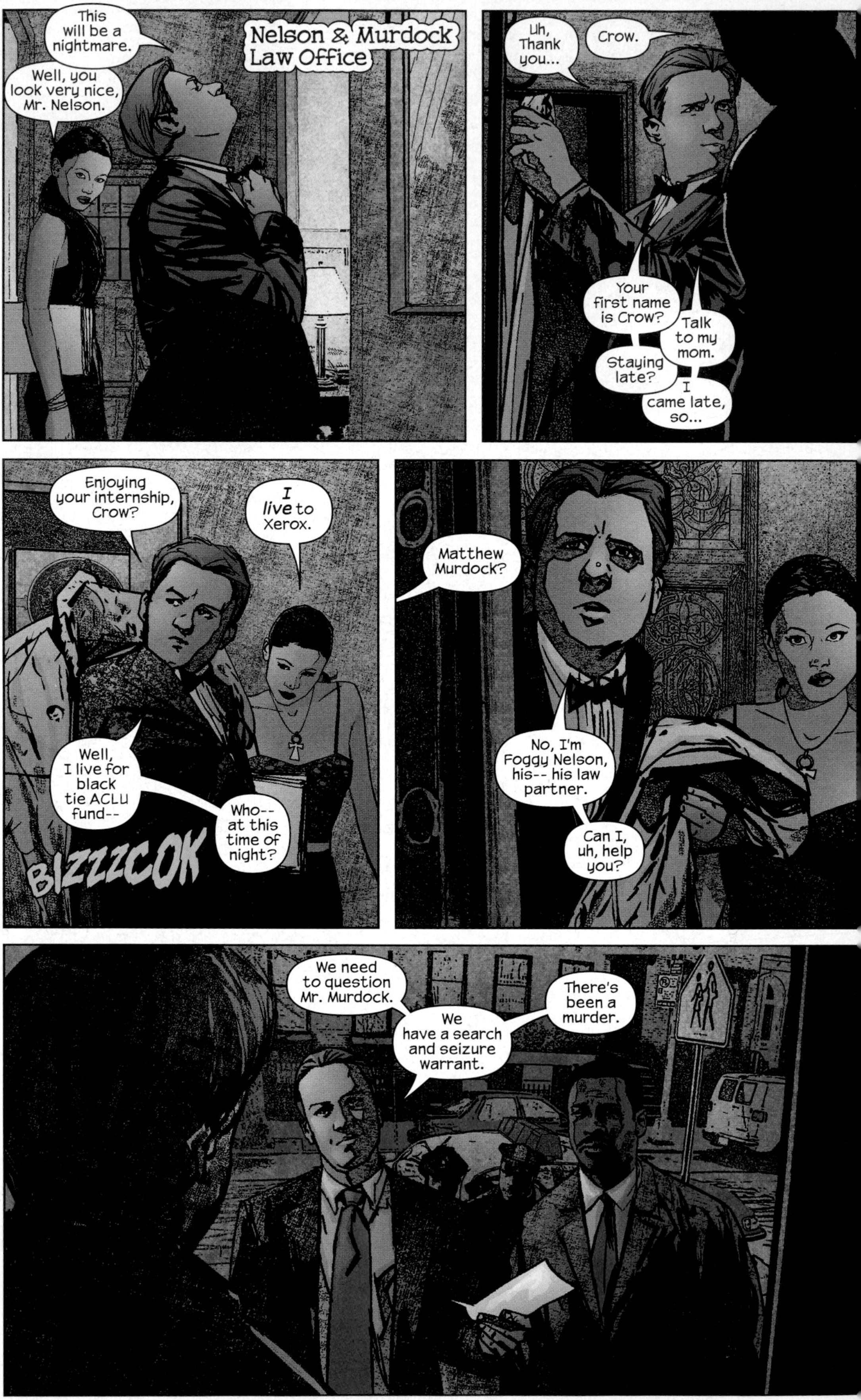
Nelson & Murdock Law Office
This will be a nightmare.
Well, you look very nice, Mr. Nelson.
Uh, Thank you...
Crow.
Your first name is Crow?
Talk to my mom.
Staying late?
I came late, so...
Enjoying your internship, Crow?
I live to Xerox.
Well, I live for black tie ACLU fund--
Who-- at this time of night?
BIZZZCOK
Matthew Murdock?
No, I'm Foggy Nelson, his-- his law partner.
Can I, uh, help you?
We need to question Mr. Murdock.
We have a search and seizure warrant.
There's been a murder.

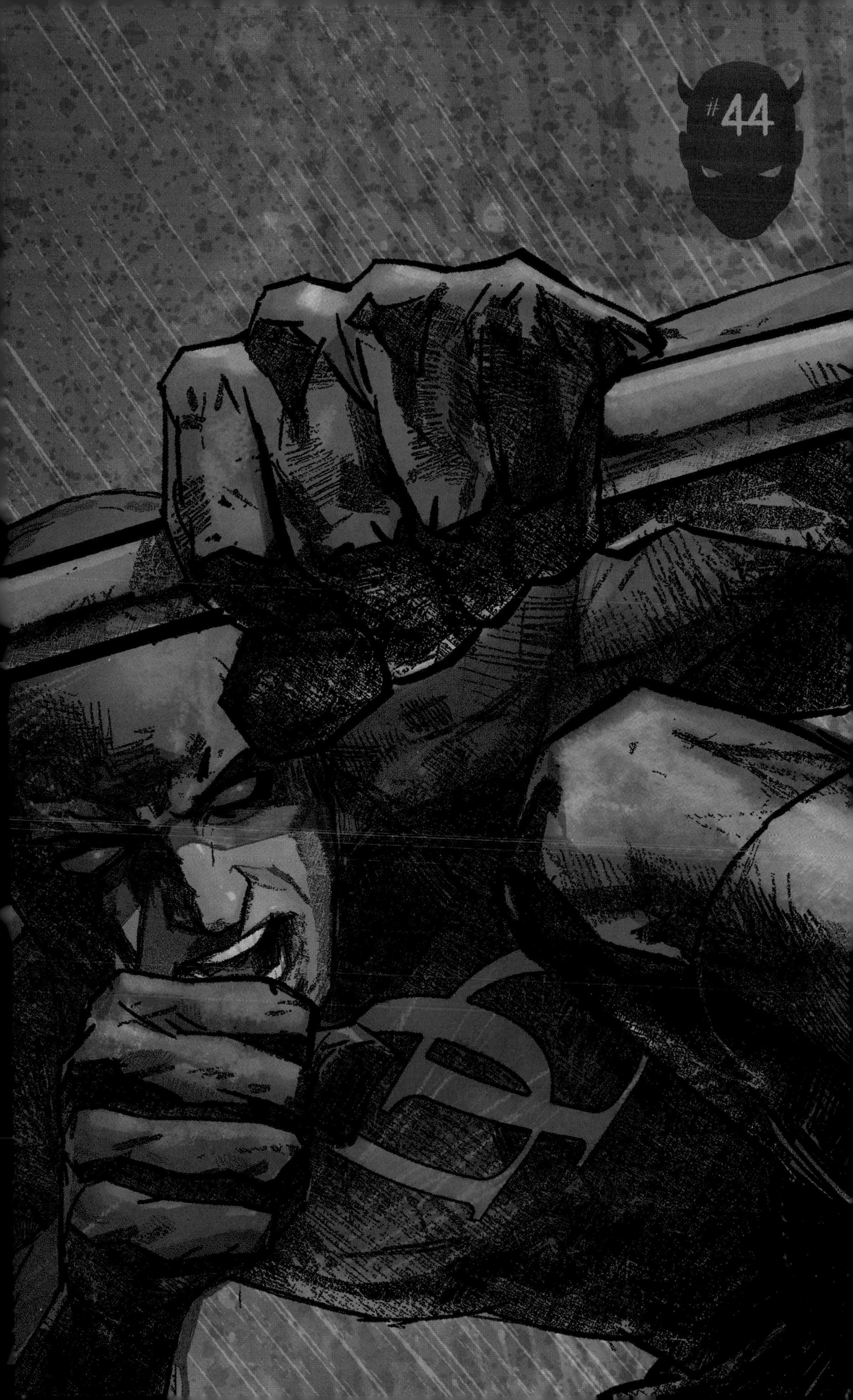
#44

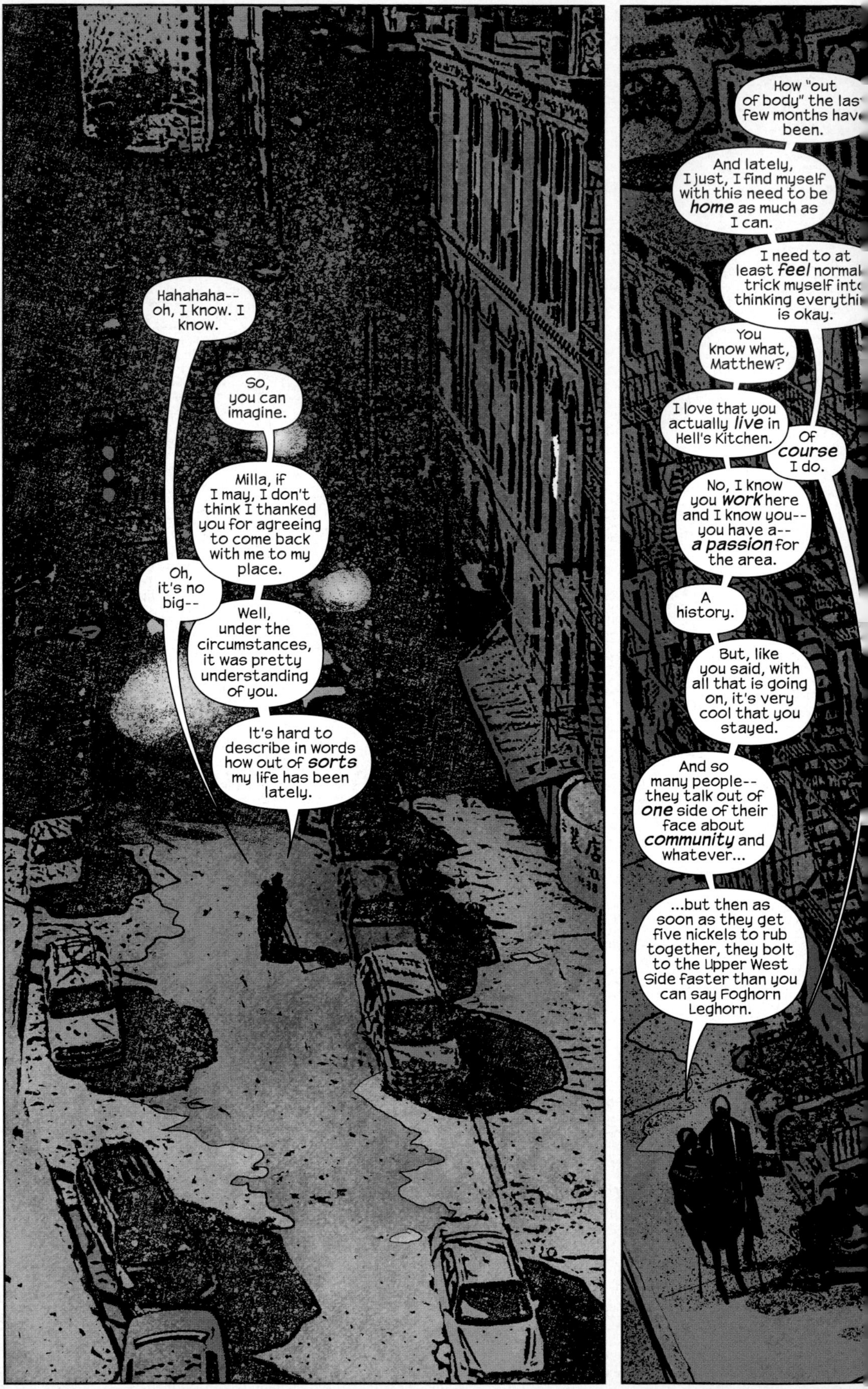
Hahahaha--oh, I know. I know.
So, you can imagine.
Milla, if I may, I don't think I thanked you for agreeing to come back with me to my place.
Oh, it's no big--
Well, under the circumstances, it was pretty understanding of you.
It's hard to describe in words how out of *sorts* my life has been lately.
How "out of body" the las few months hav been.
And lately, I just, I find myself with this need to be *home* as much as I can.
I need to at least *feel* normal trick myself int thinking everythi is okay.
You know what, Matthew?
I love that you actually *live* in Hell's Kitchen.
Of *course* I do.
No, I know you *work* here and I know you--you have a--*a passion* for the area.
A history.
But, like you said, with all that is going on, it's very cool that you stayed.
And so many people--they talk out of *one* side of their face about *community* and whatever...
...but then as soon as they get five nickels to rub together, they bolt to the Upper West Side faster than you can say Foghorn Leghorn.

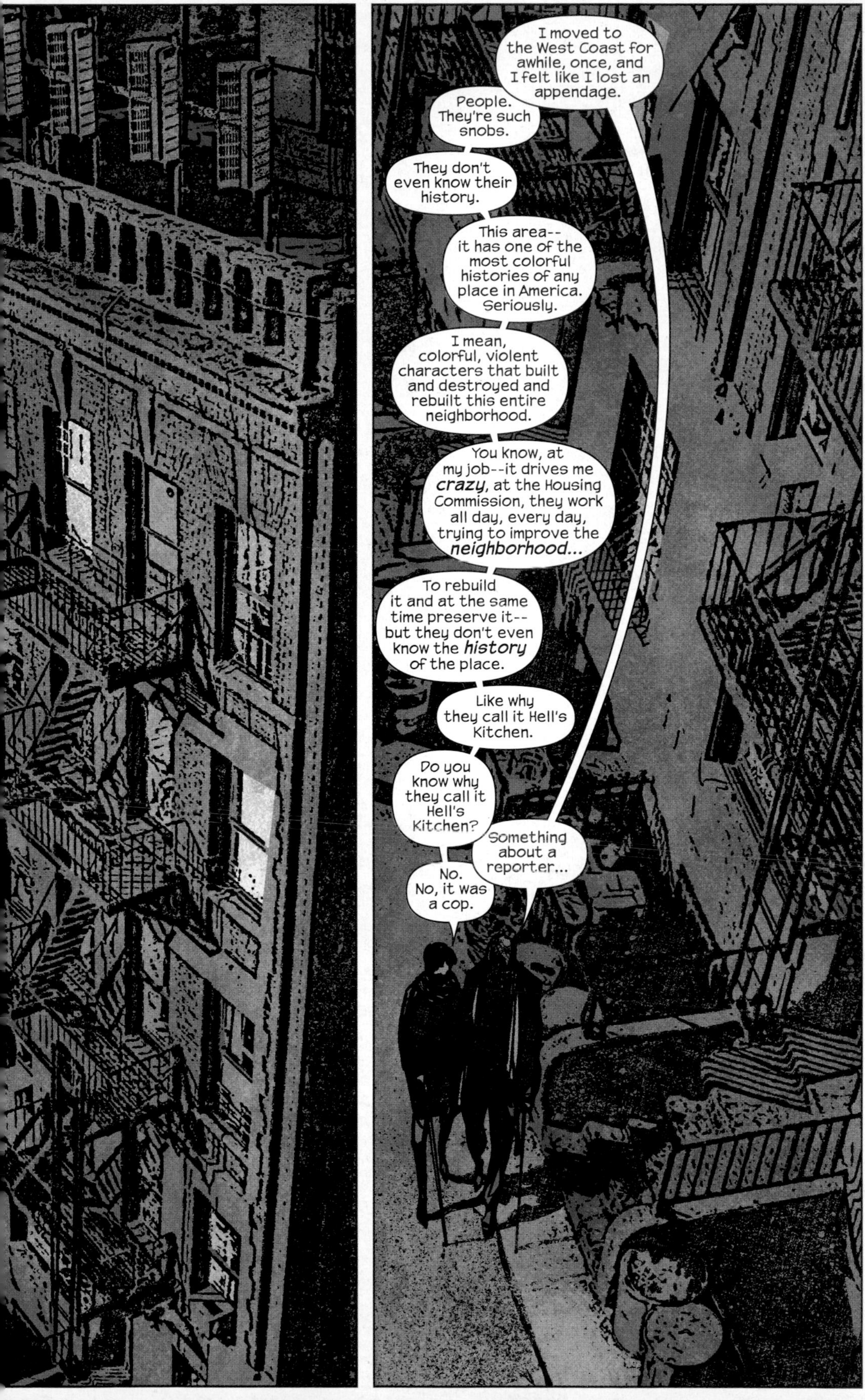
I moved to the West Coast for awhile, once, and I felt like I lost an appendage.
People. They're such snobs.
They don't even know their history.
This area--it has one of the most colorful histories of any place in America. Seriously.
I mean, colorful, violent characters that built and destroyed and rebuilt this entire neighborhood.
You know, at my job--it drives me *crazy*, at the Housing Commission, they work all day, every day, trying to improve the *neighborhood...*
To rebuild it and at the same time preserve it--but they don't even know the *history* of the place.
Like why they call it Hell's Kitchen.
Do you know why they call it Hell's Kitchen?
Something about a reporter...
No. No, it was a cop.

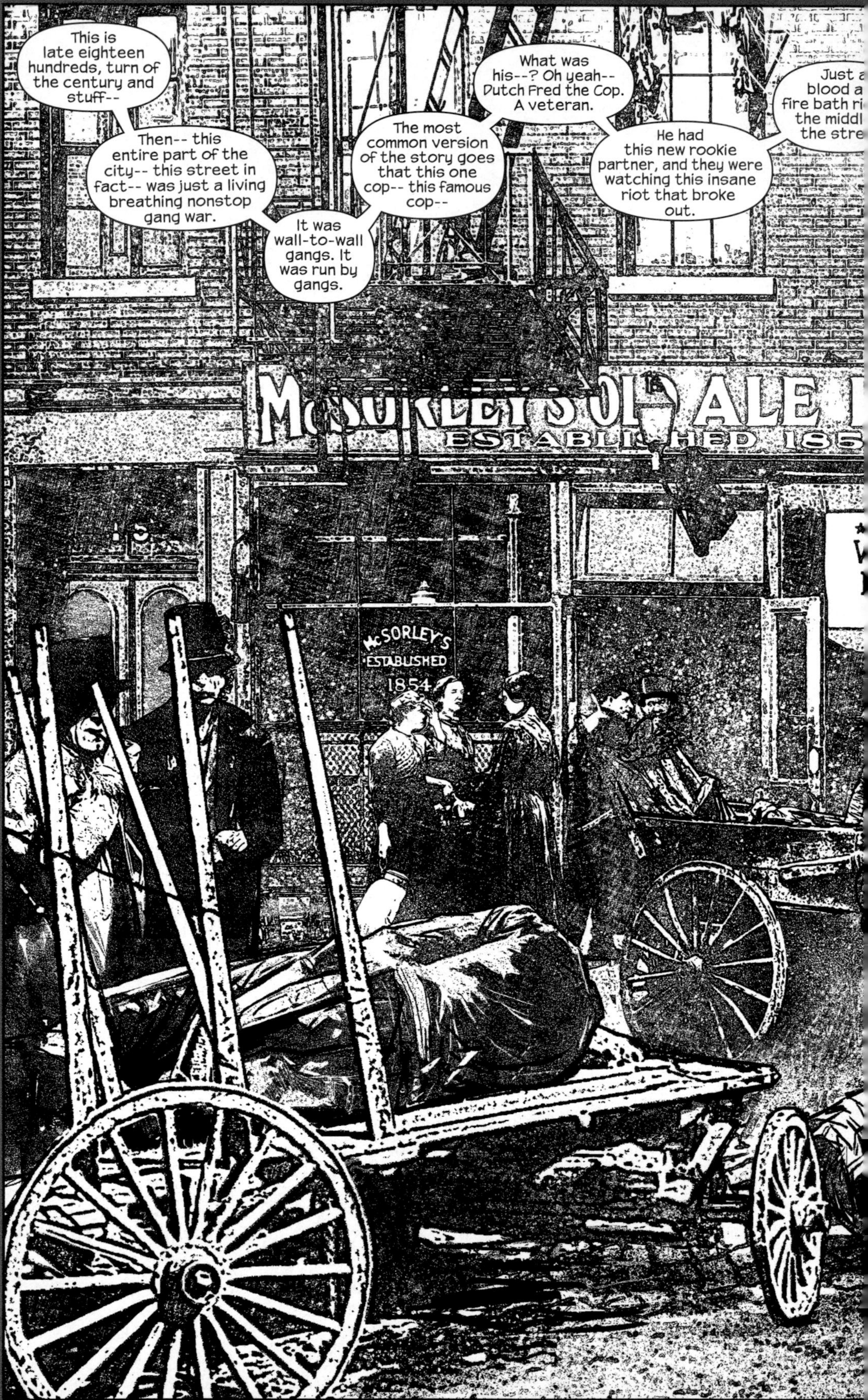

This is late eighteen hundreds, turn of the century and stuff--
Then-- this entire part of the city-- this street in fact-- was just a living breathing nonstop gang war.
It was wall-to-wall gangs. It was run by gangs.
The most common version of the story goes that this one cop-- this famous cop--
What was his--? Oh yeah-- Dutch Fred the Cop. A veteran.
He had this new rookie partner, and they were watching this insane riot that broke out.
Just a blood a fire bath ri the middl the stre
ESTABLISHED 185
McSORLEY'S ESTABLISHED 1854

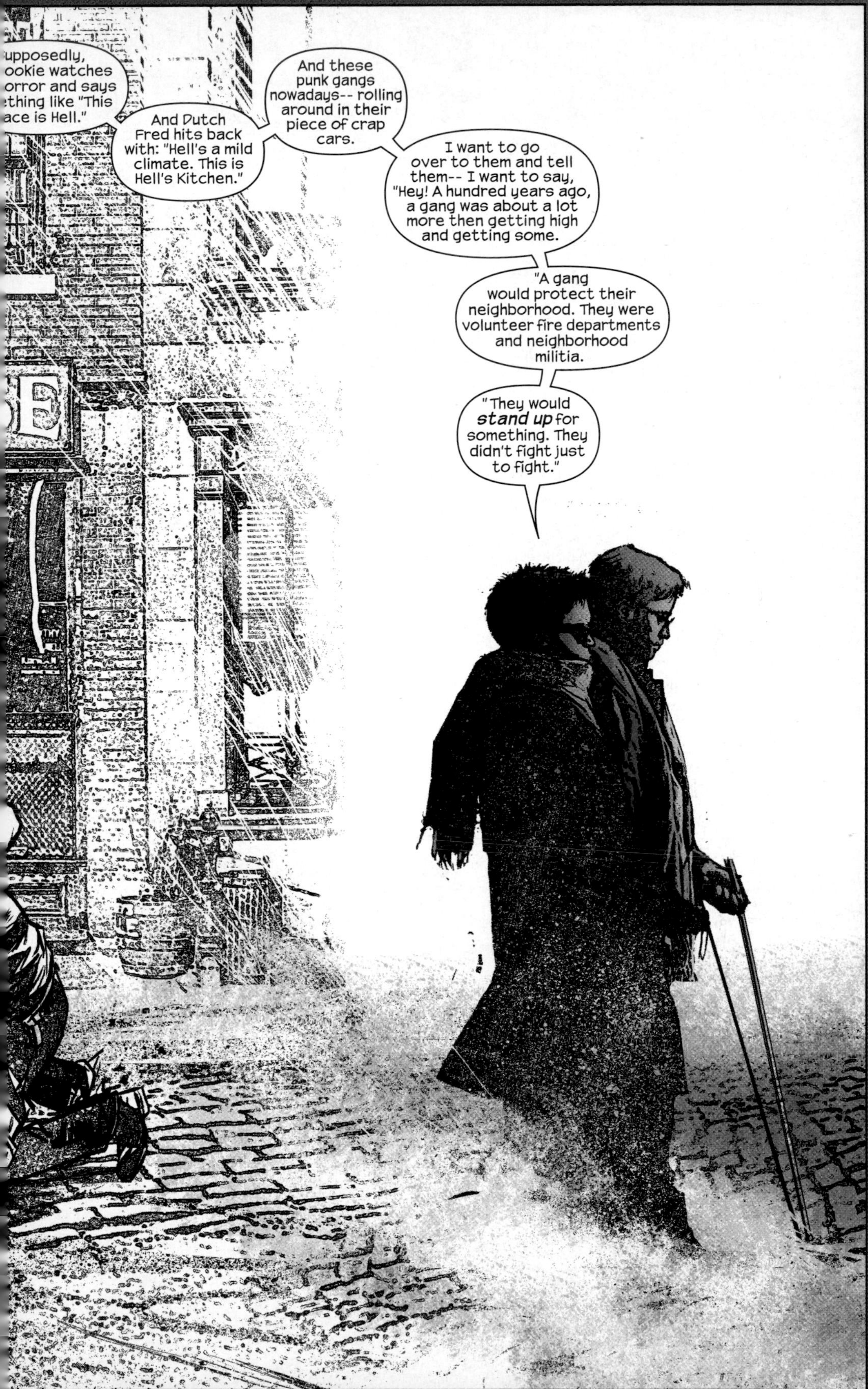

upposedly, ookie watches orror and says ething like "This ace is Hell."
And Dutch Fred hits back with: "Hell's a mild climate. This is Hell's Kitchen."
And these punk gangs nowadays-- rolling around in their piece of crap cars.
I want to go over to them and tell them-- I want to say, "Hey! A hundred years ago, a gang was about a lot more then getting high and getting some.
"A gang would protect their neighborhood. They were volunteer fire departments and neighborhood militia.
"They would **stand up** for something. They didn't fight just to fight."

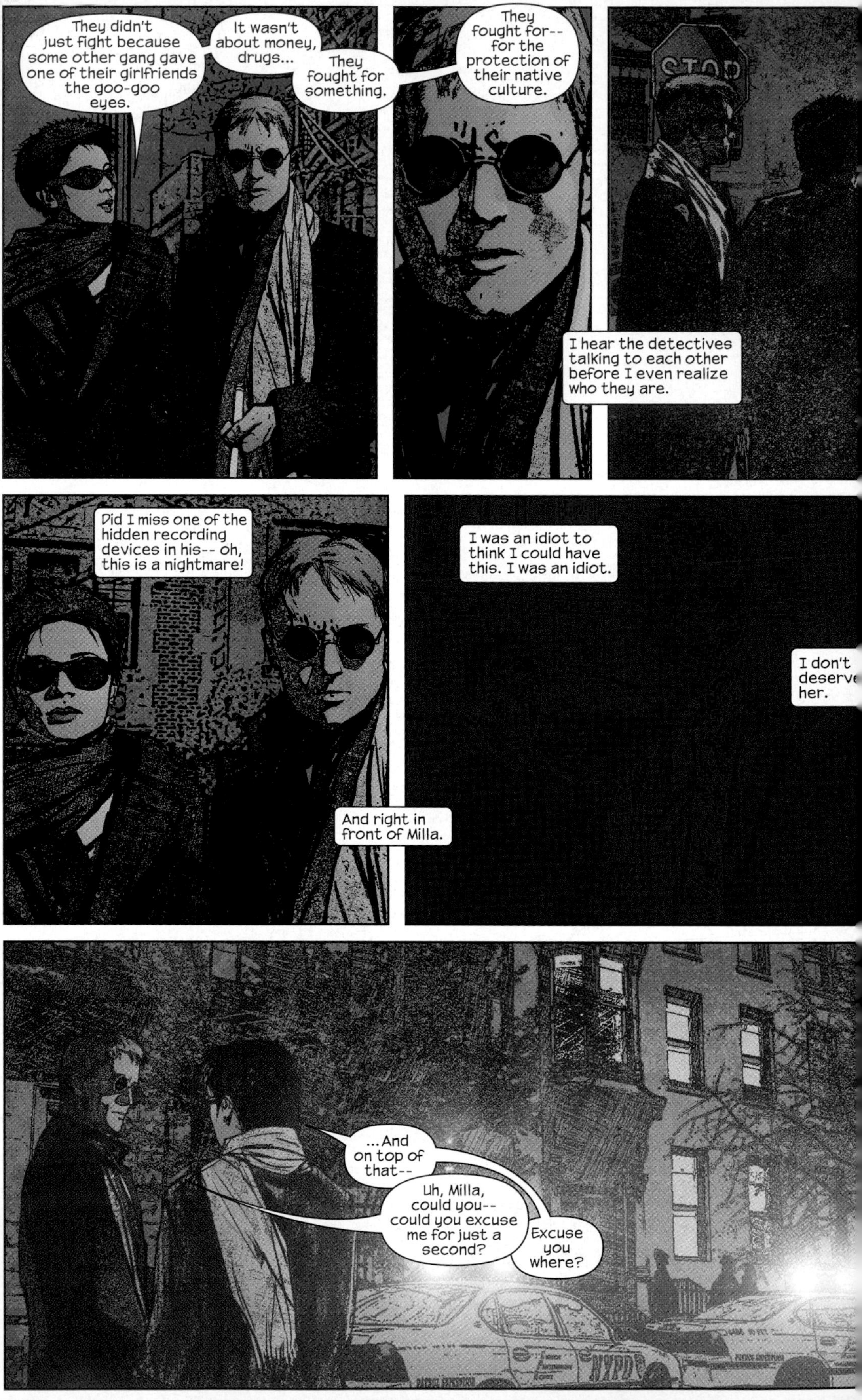
They didn't just fight because some other gang gave one of their girlfriends the goo-goo eyes.
It wasn't about money, drugs...
They fought for something.
They fought for-- for the protection of their native culture.
STOP
I hear the detectives talking to each other before I even realize who they are.
Did I miss one of the hidden recording devices in his-- oh, this is a nightmare!
And right in front of Milla.
I was an idiot to think I could have this. I was an idiot.
I don't deserv
her.
...And on top of that--
Uh, Milla, could you-- could you excuse me for just a second?
Excuse you where?
NYPD

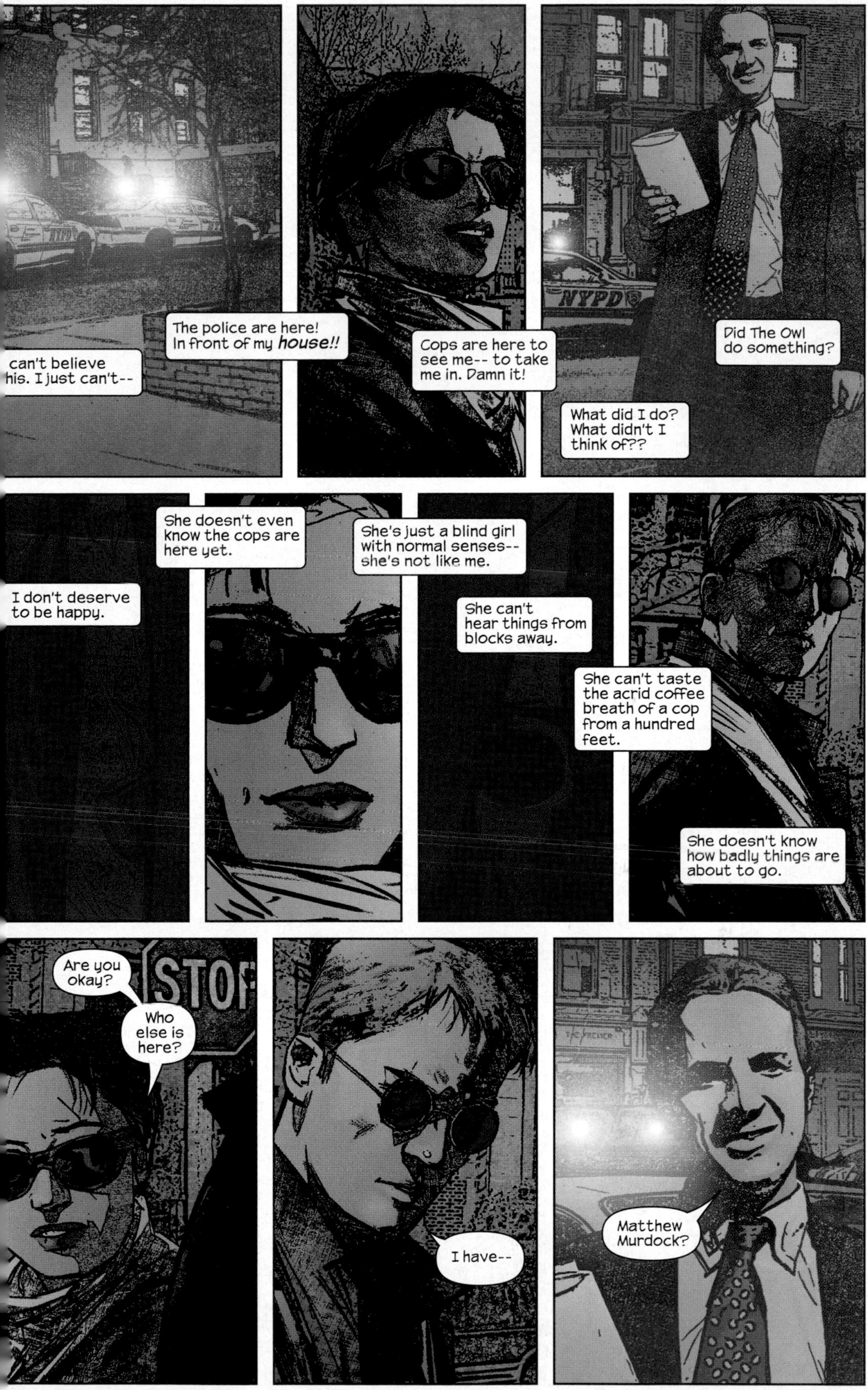
can't believe
his. I just can't--
The police are here! In front of my *house!!*
Cops are here to see me-- to take me in. Damn it!
Did The Owl do something?
What did I do? What didn't I think of??
I don't deserve to be happy.
She doesn't even know the cops are here yet.
She's just a blind girl with normal senses-- she's not like me.
She can't hear things from blocks away.
She can't taste the acrid coffee breath of a cop from a hundred feet.
She doesn't know how badly things are about to go.
Are you okay?
Who else is here?
STOP
I have--
Matthew Murdock?

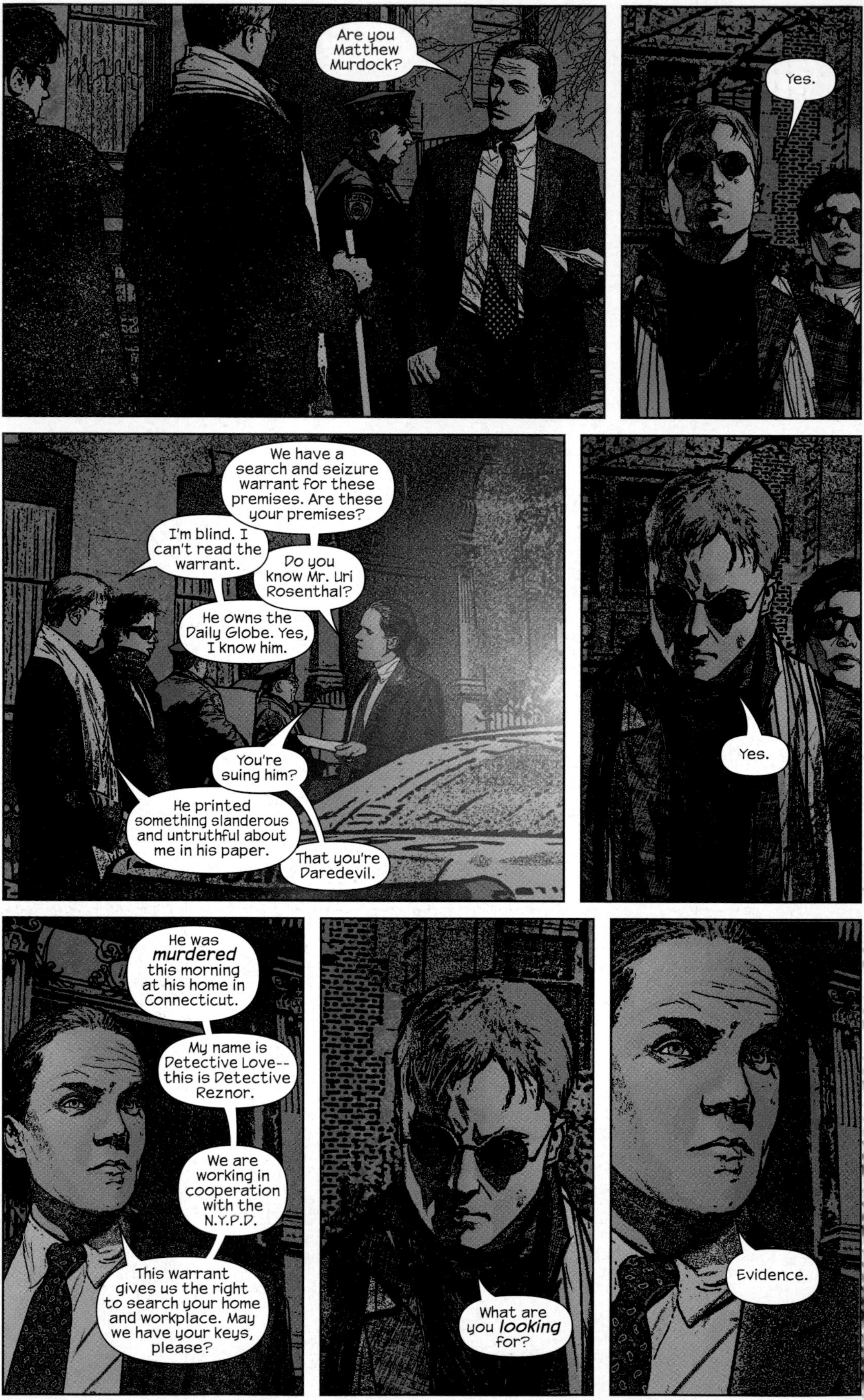
Are you Matthew Murdock?
Yes.
We have a search and seizure warrant for these premises. Are these your premises?
I'm blind. I can't read the warrant.
Do you know Mr. Uri Rosenthal?
He owns the Daily Globe. Yes, I know him.
You're suing him?
He printed something slanderous and untruthful about me in his paper.
That you're Daredevil.
Yes.
He was *murdered* this morning at his home in Connecticut.
My name is Detective Love-- this is Detective Reznor.
We are working in cooperation with the N.Y.P.D.
This warrant gives us the right to search your home and workplace. May we have your keys, please?
What are you *looking* for?
Evidence.

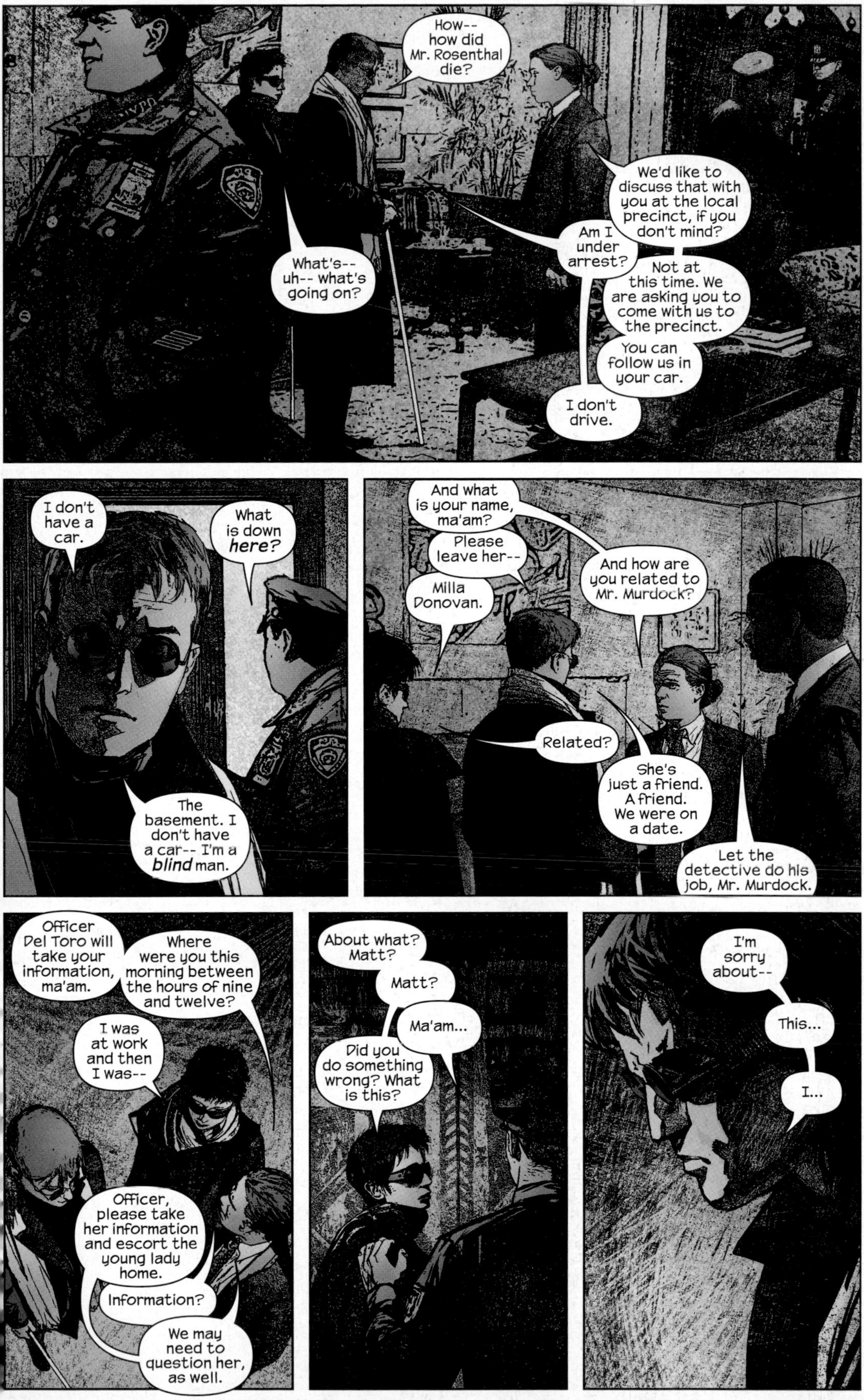
How-- how did Mr. Rosenthal die?
We'd like to discuss that with you at the local precinct, if you don't mind?
What's-- uh-- what's going on?
Am I under arrest?
Not at this time. We are asking you to come with us to the precinct.
You can follow us in your car.
I don't drive.
I don't have a car.
What is down *here?*
The basement. I don't have a car-- I'm a *blind* man.
And what is your name, ma'am?
Please leave her--
Milla Donovan.
And how are you related to Mr. Murdock?
Related?
She's just a friend. A friend. We were on a date.
Let the detective do his job, Mr. Murdock.
Officer Del Toro will take your information, ma'am.
Where were you this morning between the hours of nine and twelve?
I was at work and then I was--
Officer, please take her information and escort the young lady home.
Information?
We may need to question her, as well.
About what? Matt?
Matt?
Ma'am...
Did you do something wrong? What is this?
I'm sorry about--
This...
I...

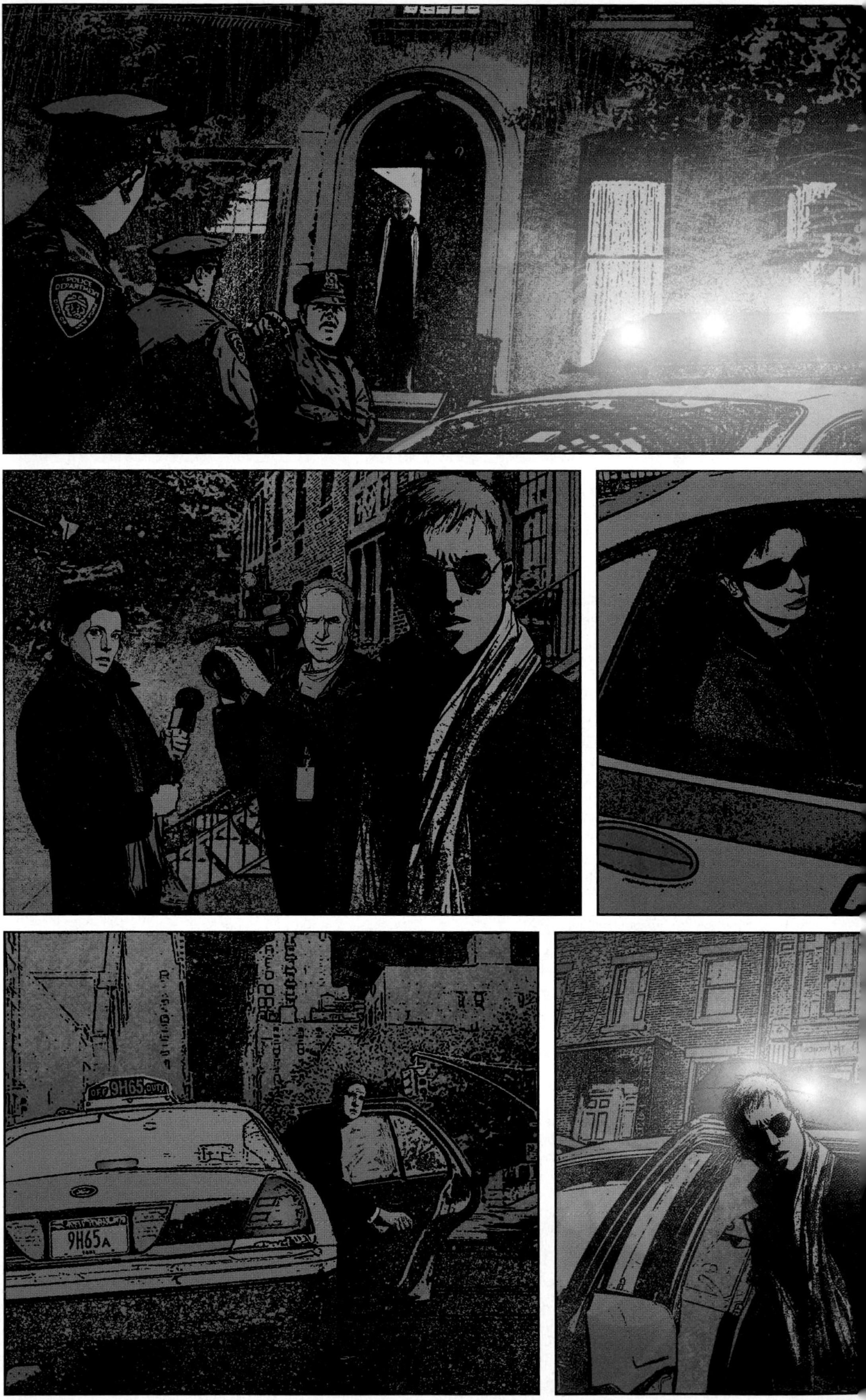
POLICE DEPARTMENT
9H65
9H65A

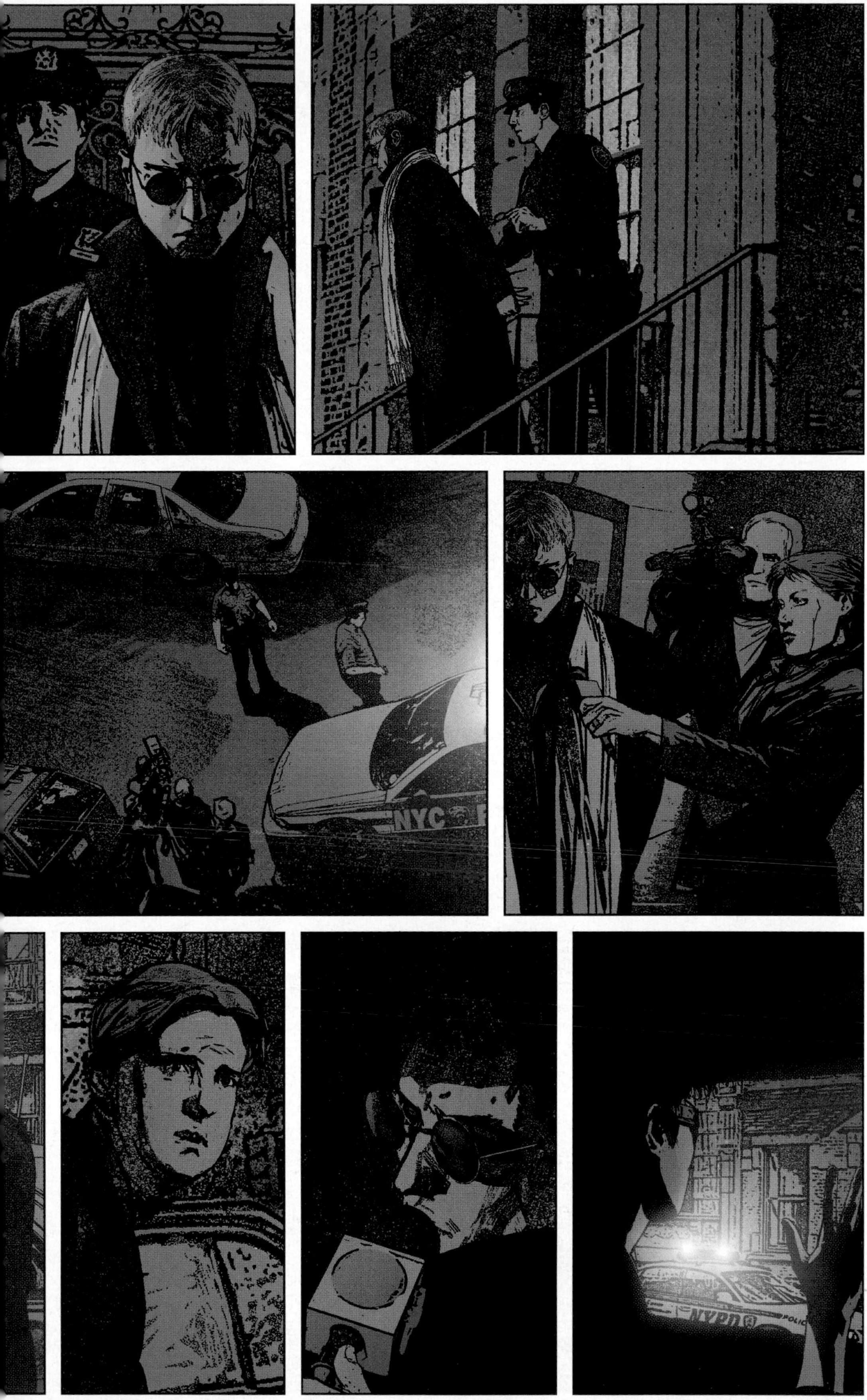
NYC
NYPD

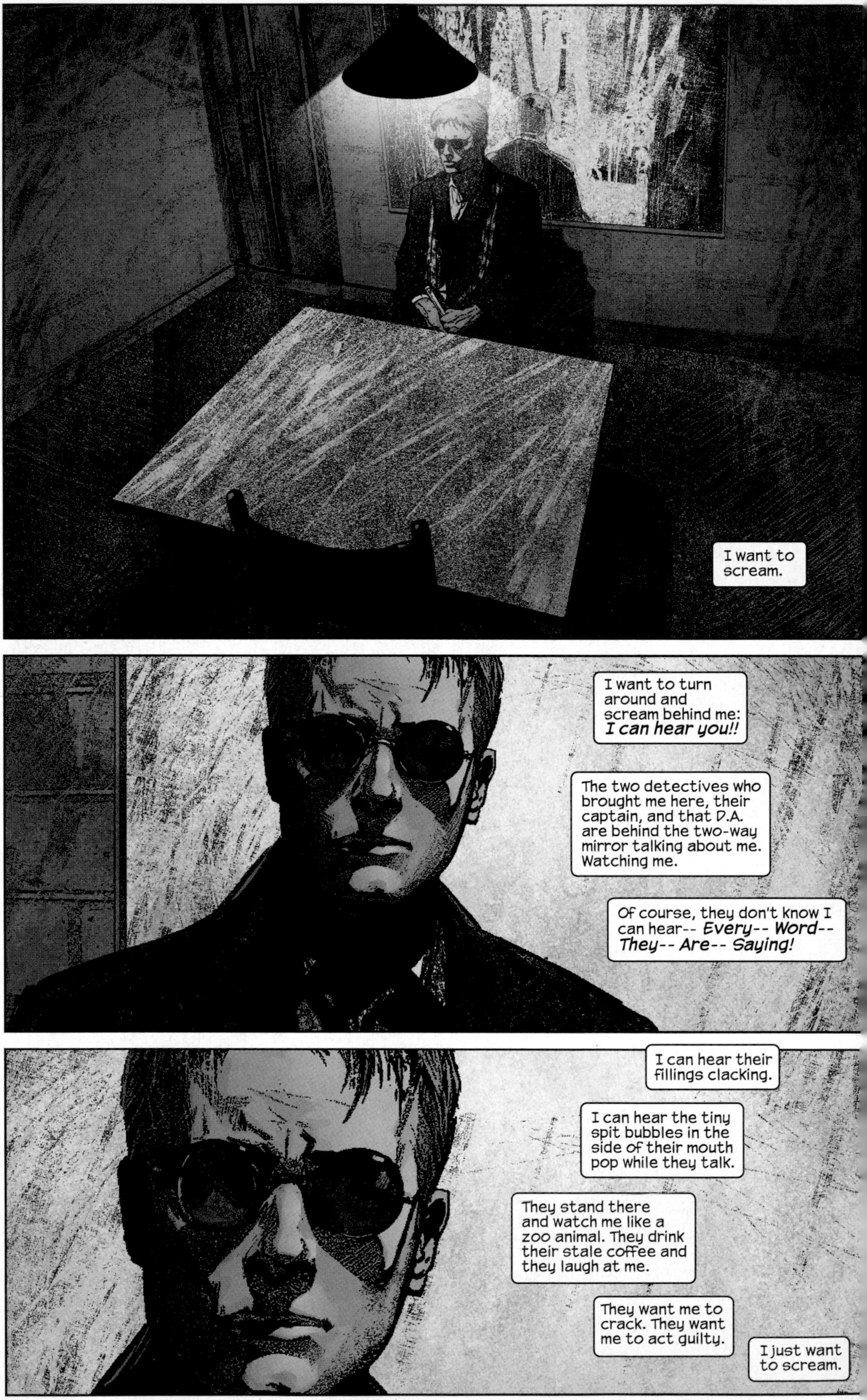
I want to scream.
I want to turn around and scream behind me: *I can hear you!!*
The two detectives who brought me here, their captain, and that D.A. are behind the two-way mirror talking about me. Watching me.
Of course, they don't know I can hear-- *Every-- Word-- They-- Are-- Saying!*
I can hear their fillings clacking.
I can hear the tiny spit bubbles in the side of their mouth pop while they talk.
They stand there and watch me like a zoo animal. They drink their stale coffee and they laugh at me.
They want me to crack. They want me to act guilty.
I just want to scream.

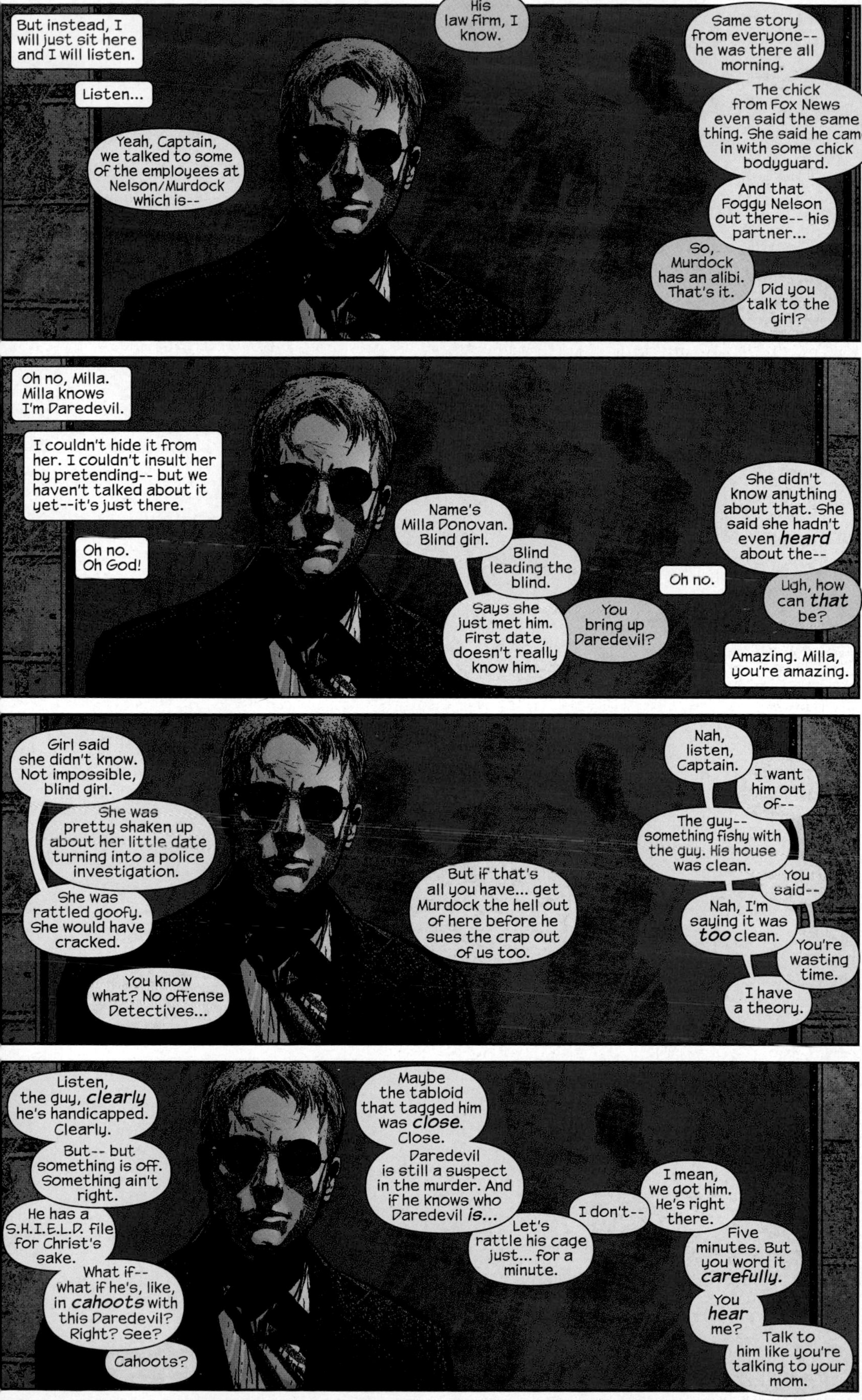

But instead, I will just sit here and I will listen.
Listen...
Yeah, Captain, we talked to some of the employees at Nelson/Murdock which is--
His law firm, I know.
Same story from everyone-- he was there all morning.
The chick from Fox News even said the same thing. She said he came in with some chick bodyguard.
And that Foggy Nelson out there-- his partner...
So, Murdock has an alibi. That's it.
Did you talk to the girl?
Oh no, Milla. Milla knows I'm Daredevil.
I couldn't hide it from her. I couldn't insult her by pretending-- but we haven't talked about it yet--it's just there.
Oh no. Oh God!
Name's Milla Donovan. Blind girl.
Blind leading the blind.
Says she just met him. First date, doesn't really know him.
You bring up Daredevil?
She didn't know anything about that. She said she hadn't even heard about the--
Oh no.
Ugh, how can that be?
Amazing. Milla, you're amazing.
Girl said she didn't know. Not impossible, blind girl.
She was pretty shaken up about her little date turning into a police investigation.
She was rattled goofy. She would have cracked.
You know what? No offense Detectives...
But if that's all you have... get Murdock the hell out of here before he sues the crap out of us too.
Nah, listen, Captain.
I want him out of--
The guy-- something fishy with the guy. His house was clean.
You said--
Nah, I'm saying it was too clean.
You're wasting time.
I have a theory.
Listen, the guy, clearly he's handicapped. Clearly.
But-- but something is off. Something ain't right.
He has a S.H.I.E.L.D. file for Christ's sake.
What if-- what if he's, like, in cahoots with this Daredevil? Right? See?
Cahoots?
Maybe the tabloid that tagged him was close. Close.
Daredevil is still a suspect in the murder. And if he knows who Daredevil is...
Let's rattle his cage just... for a minute.
I don't--
I mean, we got him. He's right there.
Five minutes. But you word it carefully.
You hear me?
Talk to him like you're talking to your mom.

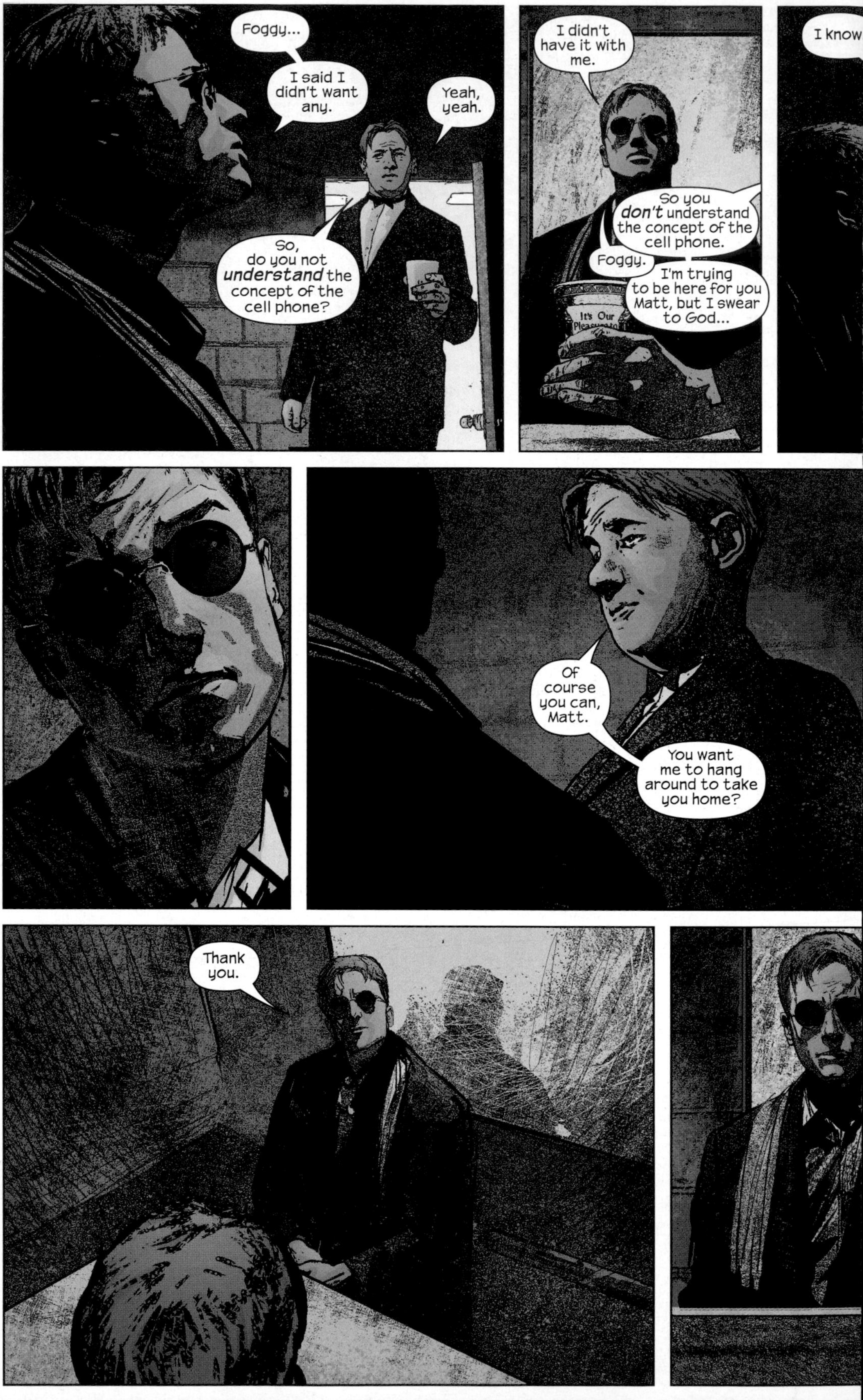
Foggy...
I said I didn't want any.
Yeah, yeah.
So, do you not *understand* the concept of the cell phone?
I didn't have it with me.
So you *don't* understand the concept of the cell phone.
Foggy.
I'm trying to be here for you Matt, but I swear to God...
It's Our Pleasure to
I know
Of course you can, Matt.
You want me to hang around to take you home?
Thank you.

I'll handle the detectives when they...

I'm sorry?

...an...le...

...can...ndle...t.

Wow.

That's pretty stubborn on many levels.

I have nothing to hide, Foggy.

I can represent myself in this simple misunderstanding.

You understand...

Would you?

Of course, pal.

Foggy?

It's Our Pleasure to Serve You

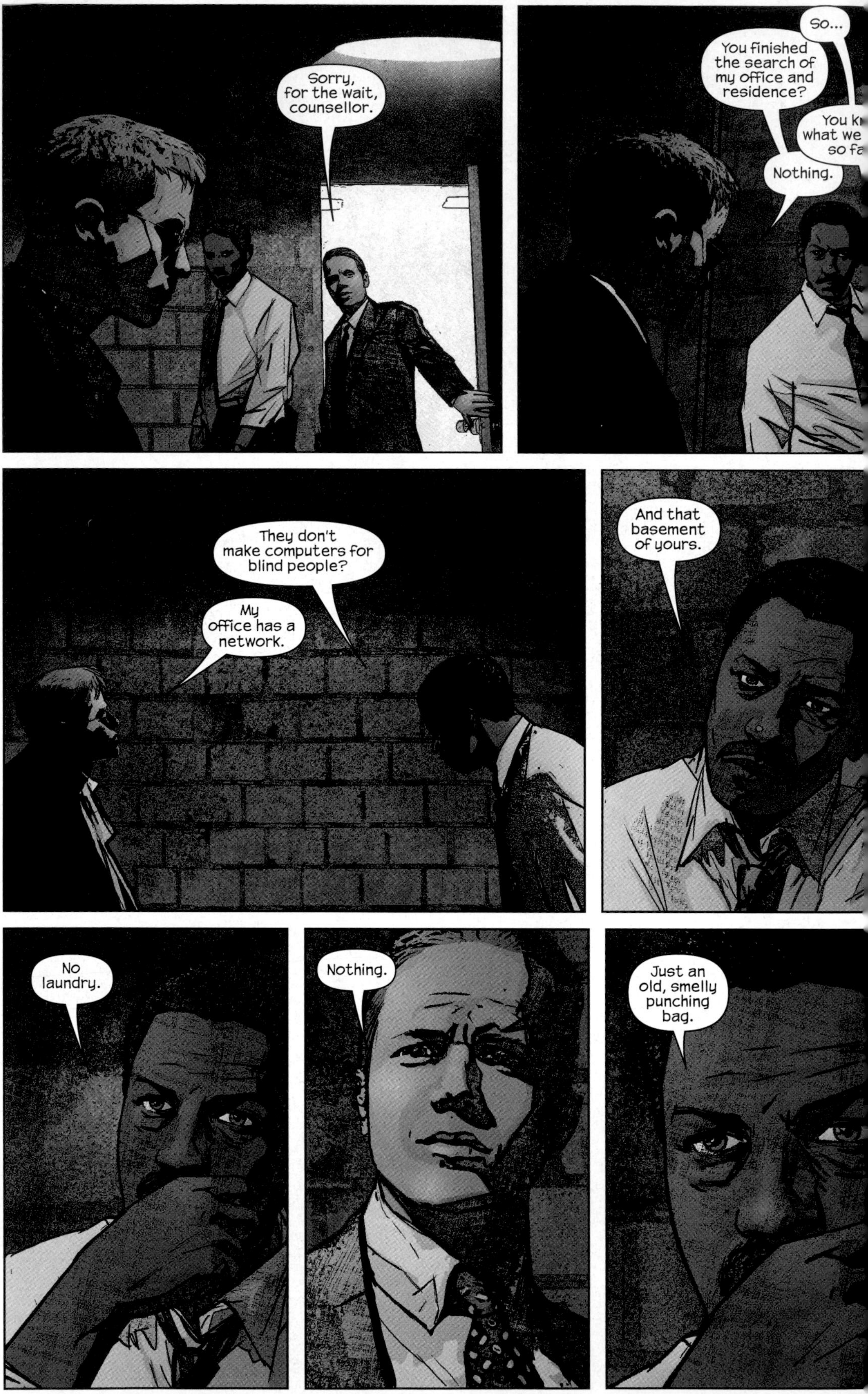
Sorry, for the wait, counsellor.
So...
You finished the search of my office and residence?
You k what we so fa
Nothing.
They don't make computers for blind people?
My office has a network.
And that basement of yours.
No laundry.
Nothing.
Just an old, smelly punching bag.

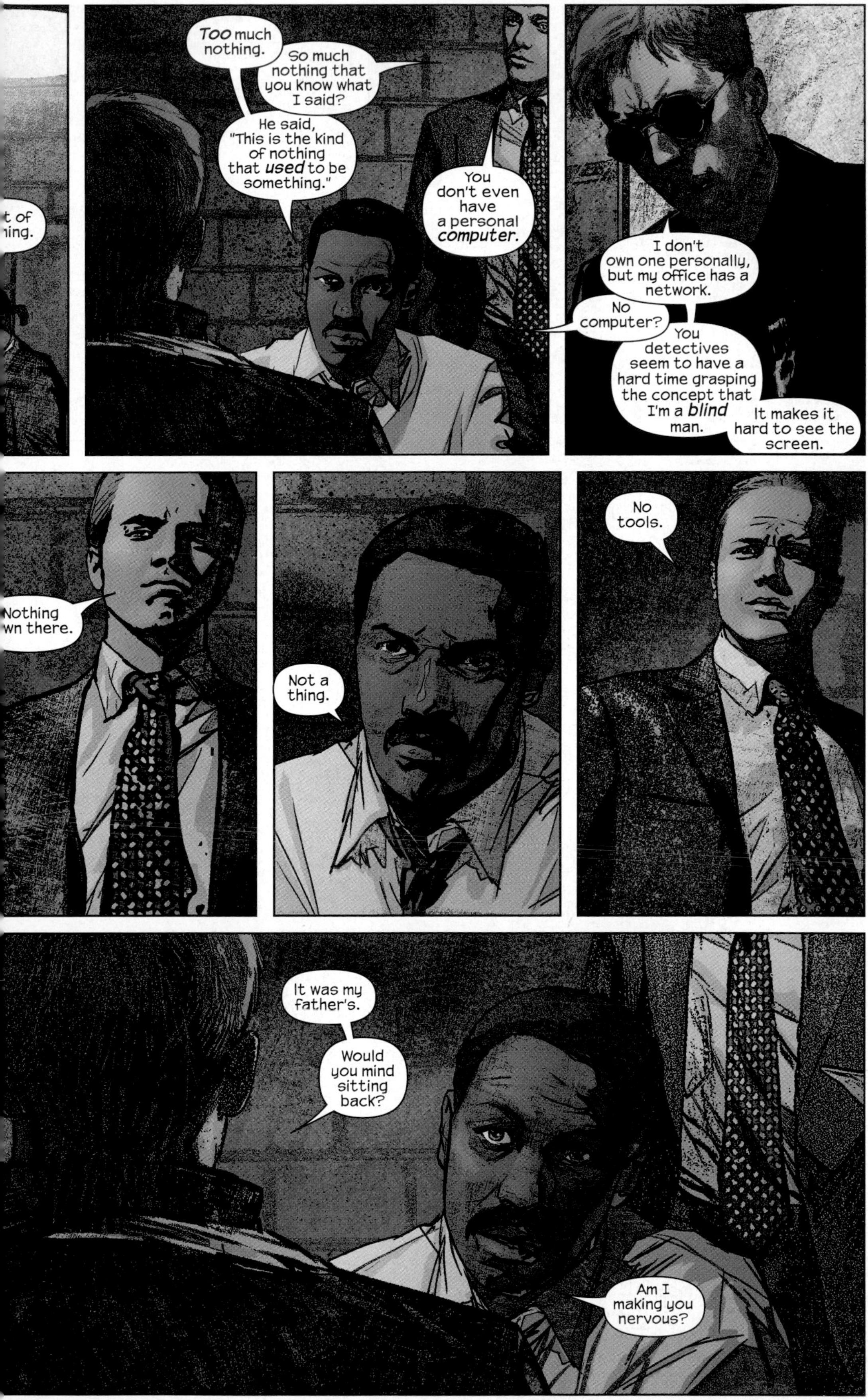
t of
ning.
Too much nothing.
So much nothing that you know what I said?
He said, "This is the kind of nothing that *used* to be something."
You don't even have a personal *computer*.
I don't own one personally, but my office has a network.
No computer?
You detectives seem to have a hard time grasping the concept that I'm a *blind* man.
It makes it hard to see the screen.
Nothing
wn there.
Not a thing.
No tools.
It was my father's.
Would you mind sitting back?
Am I making you nervous?

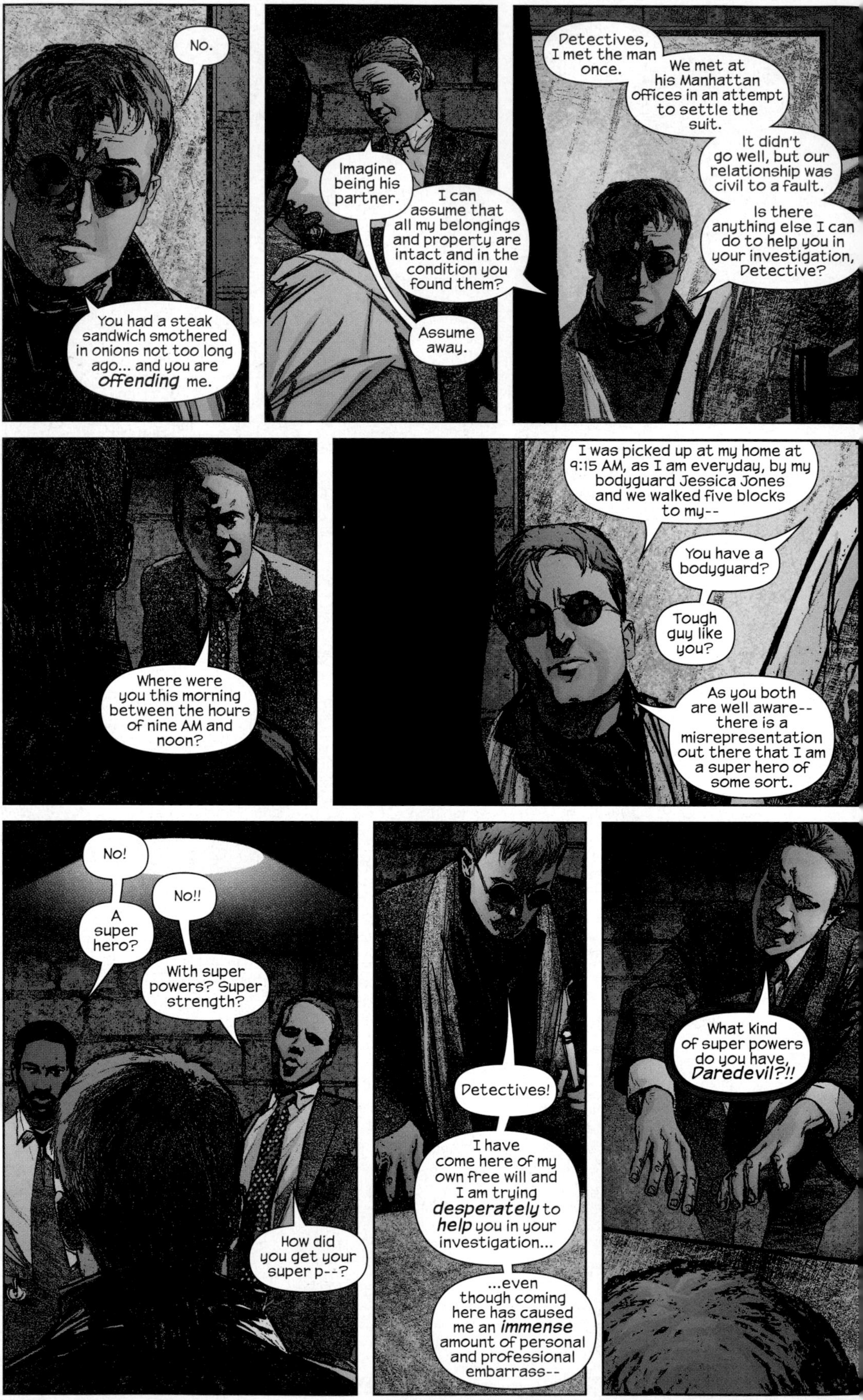
No.
You had a steak sandwich smothered in onions not too long ago... and you are *offending* me.
Imagine being his partner.
I can assume that all my belongings and property are intact and in the condition you found them?
Assume away.
Detectives, I met the man once.
We met at his Manhattan offices in an attempt to settle the suit.
It didn't go well, but our relationship was civil to a fault.
Is there anything else I can do to help you in your investigation, Detective?
Where were you this morning between the hours of nine AM and noon?
I was picked up at my home at 9:15 AM, as I am everyday, by my bodyguard Jessica Jones and we walked five blocks to my--
You have a bodyguard?
Tough guy like you?
As you both are well aware-- there is a misrepresentation out there that I am a super hero of some sort.
No!
A super hero?
No!!
With super powers? Super strength?
How did you get your super p--?
Detectives!
I have come here of my own free will and I am trying *desperately* to *help* you in your investigation...
...even though coming here has caused me an *immense* amount of personal and professional embarrass--
What kind of super powers do you have, *Daredevil*?!!

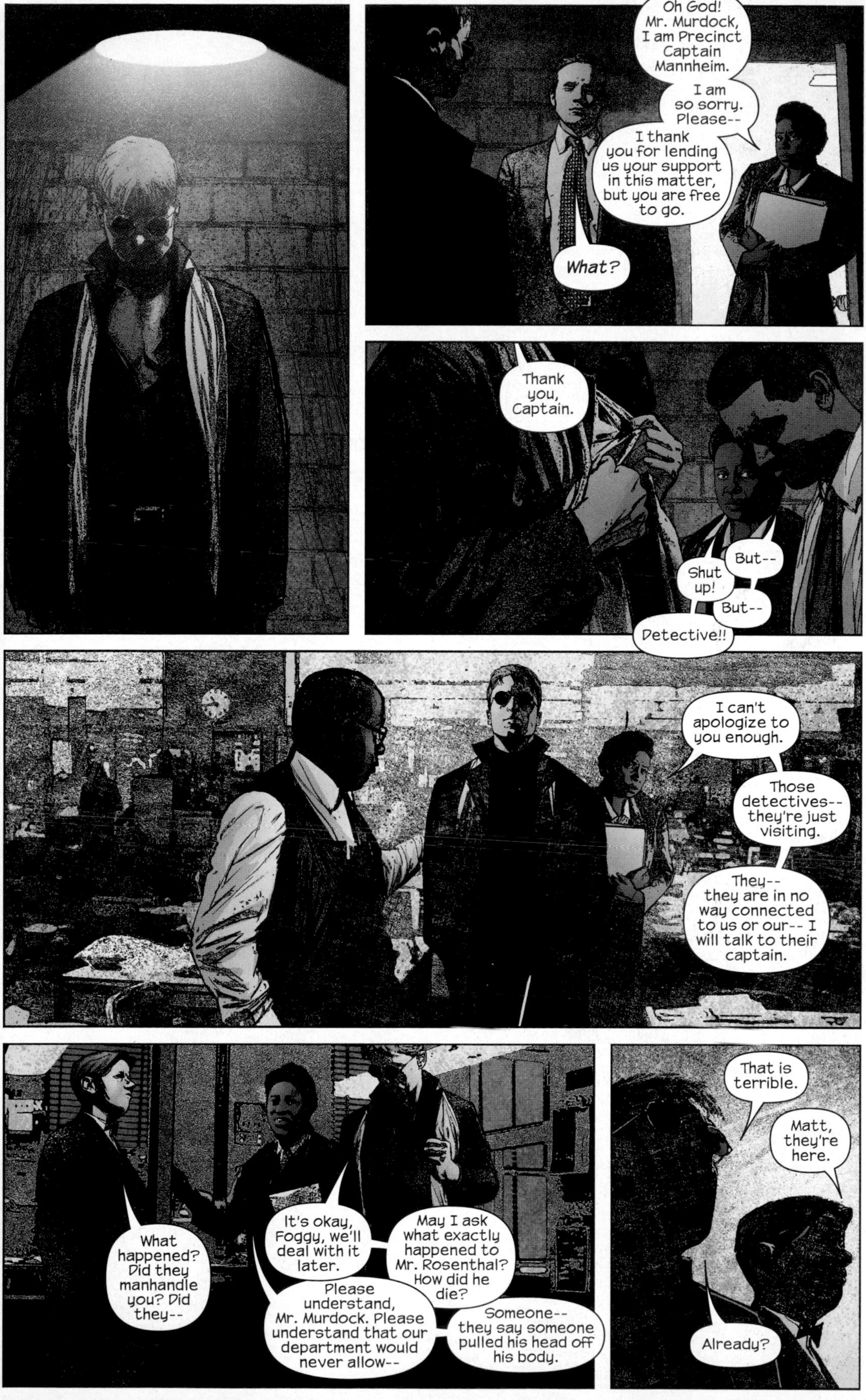

Oh God! Mr. Murdock, I am Precinct Captain Mannheim.
I am so sorry. Please--
I thank you for lending us your support in this matter, but you are free to go.
What?
Thank you, Captain.
But--
Shut up!
But--
Detective!!
I can't apologize to you enough.
Those detectives-- they're just visiting.
They-- they are in no way connected to us or our-- I will talk to their captain.
What happened? Did they manhandle you? Did they--
It's okay, Foggy, we'll deal with it later.
Please understand, Mr. Murdock. Please understand that our department would never allow--
May I ask what exactly happened to Mr. Rosenthal? How did he die?
Someone-- they say someone pulled his head off his body.
That is terrible.
Matt, they're here.
Already?

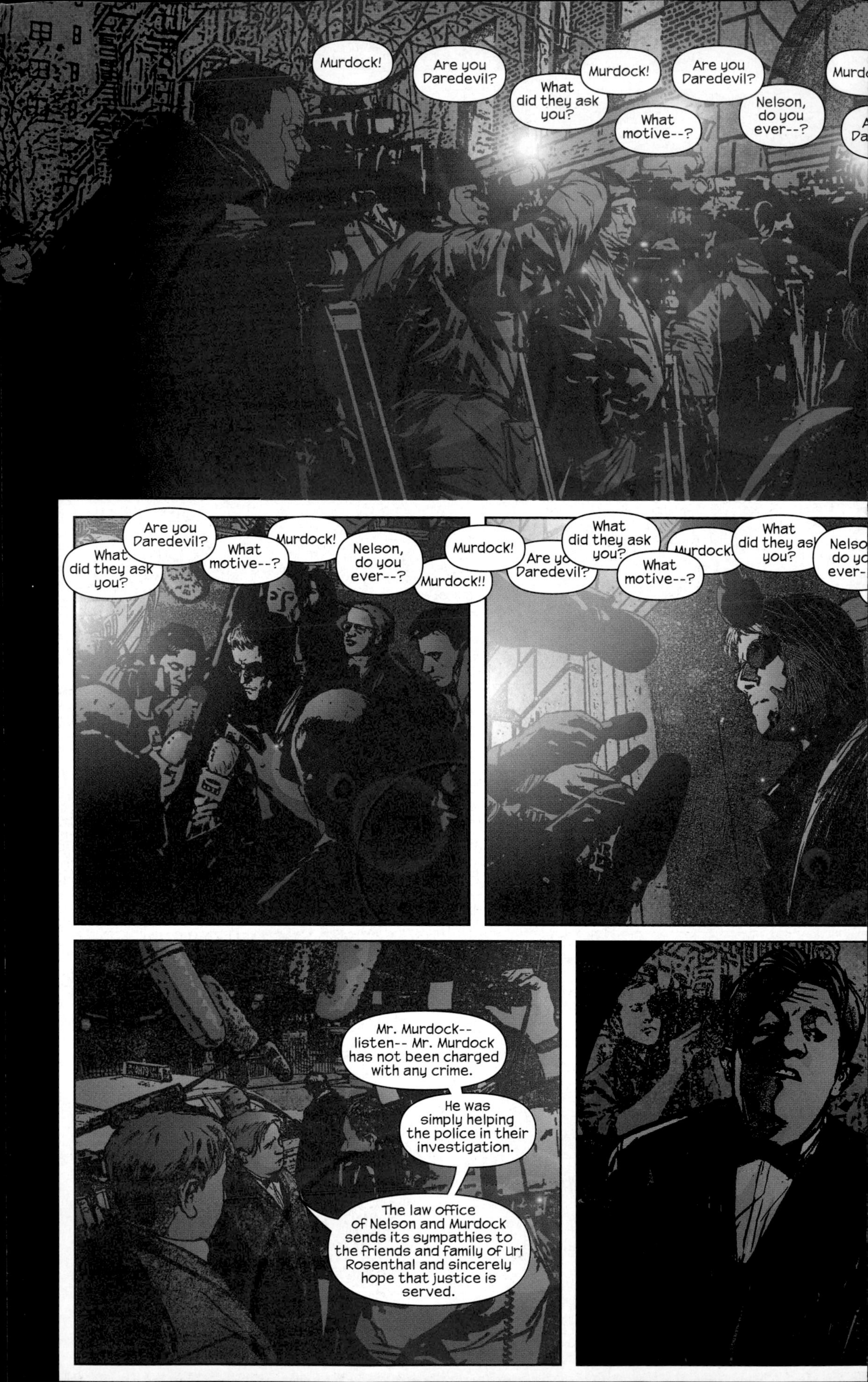
Murdock!
Are you Daredevil?
What did they ask you?
Murdock!
What motive--?
Are you Daredevil?
Nelson, do you ever--?
What did they ask you?
Are you Daredevil?
What motive--?
Murdock!
Nelson, do you ever--?
Murdock!
Murdock!!
What did they ask you?
What motive--?
What did they ask you?
Mr. Murdock-- listen-- Mr. Murdock has not been charged with any crime.
He was simply helping the police in their investigation.
The law office of Nelson and Murdock sends its sympathies to the friends and family of Uri Rosenthal and sincerely hope that justice is served.

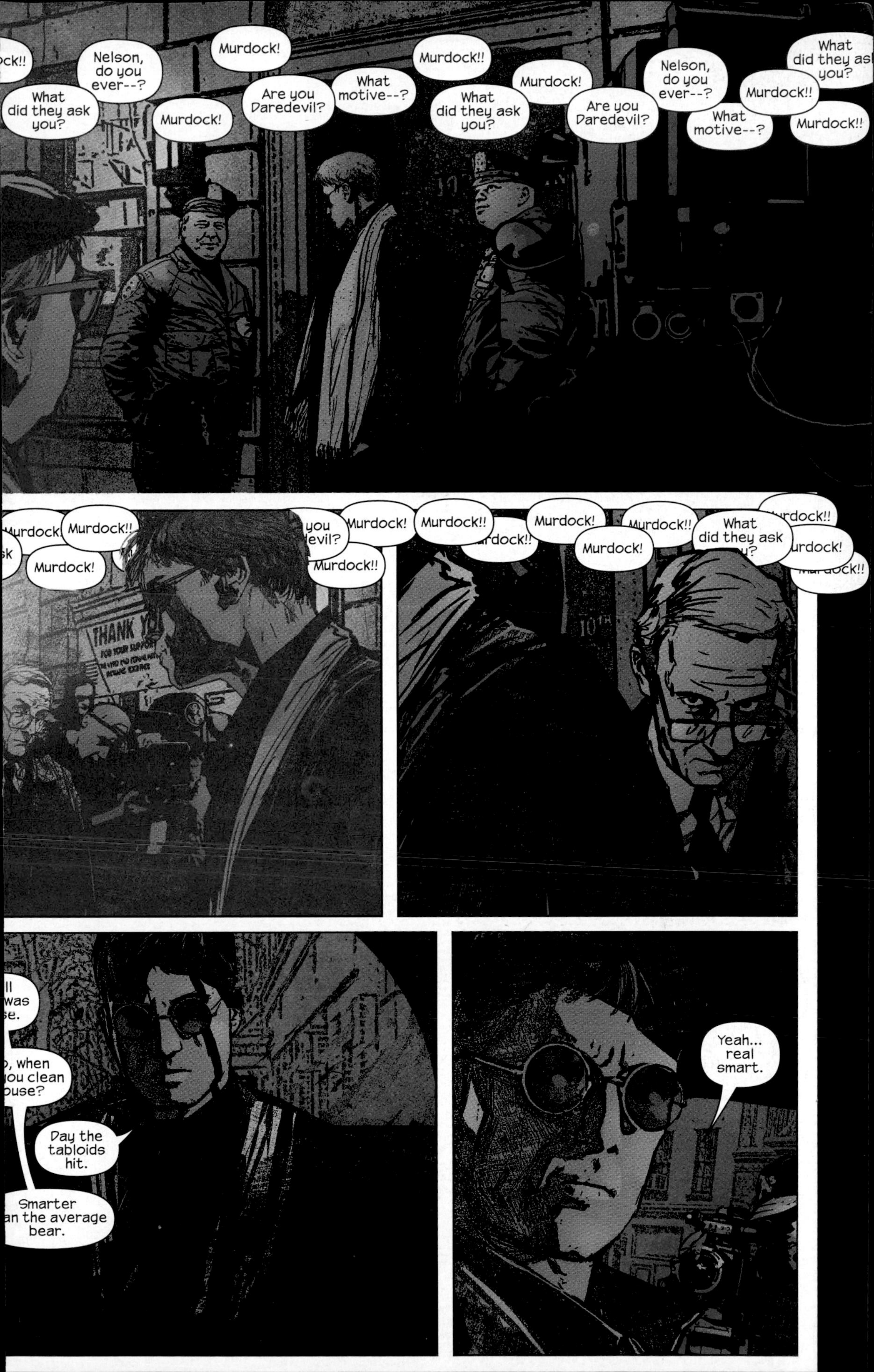
ck!!
Nelson, do you ever--?
What did they ask you?
Murdock!
Murdock!
Are you Daredevil?
What motive--?
Murdock!!
What did they ask you?
Murdock!
Are you Daredevil?
Nelson, do you ever--?
What motive--?
What did they ask you?
Murdock!!
Murdock!!
Murdock!!
Murdock!
Murdock!
Murdock!!
Murdock!!
Murdock!
Murdock!
What did they ask
Murdock!!
Day the tabloids hit.
Smarter an the average bear.
Yeah... real smart.

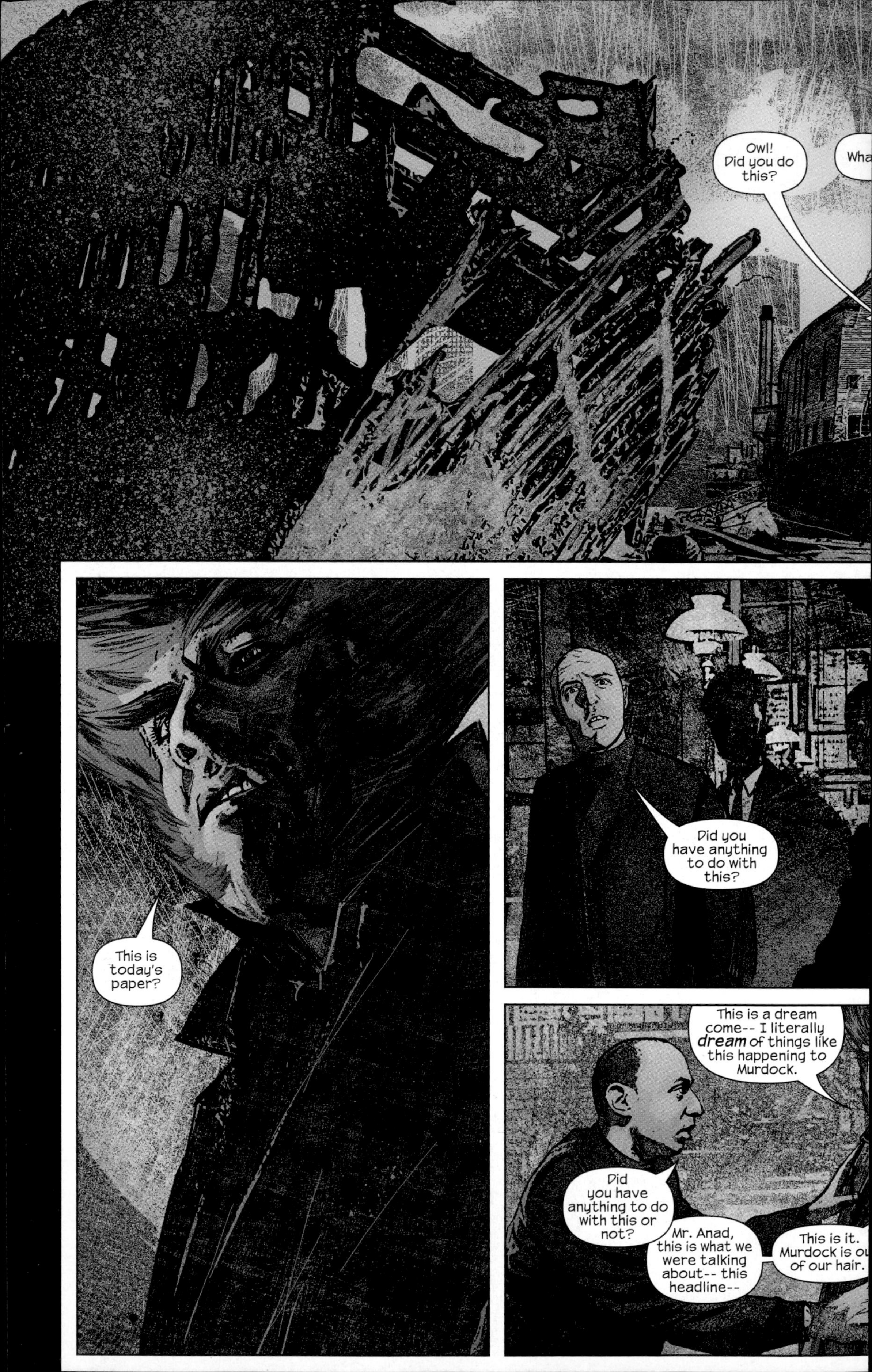

Owl! Did you do this?
Wha
This is today's paper?
Did you have anything to do with this?
This is a dream come-- I literally *dream* of things like this happening to Murdock.
Did you have anything to do with this or not?
Mr. Anad, this is what we were talking about-- this headline--
This is it. Murdock is ou of our hair.

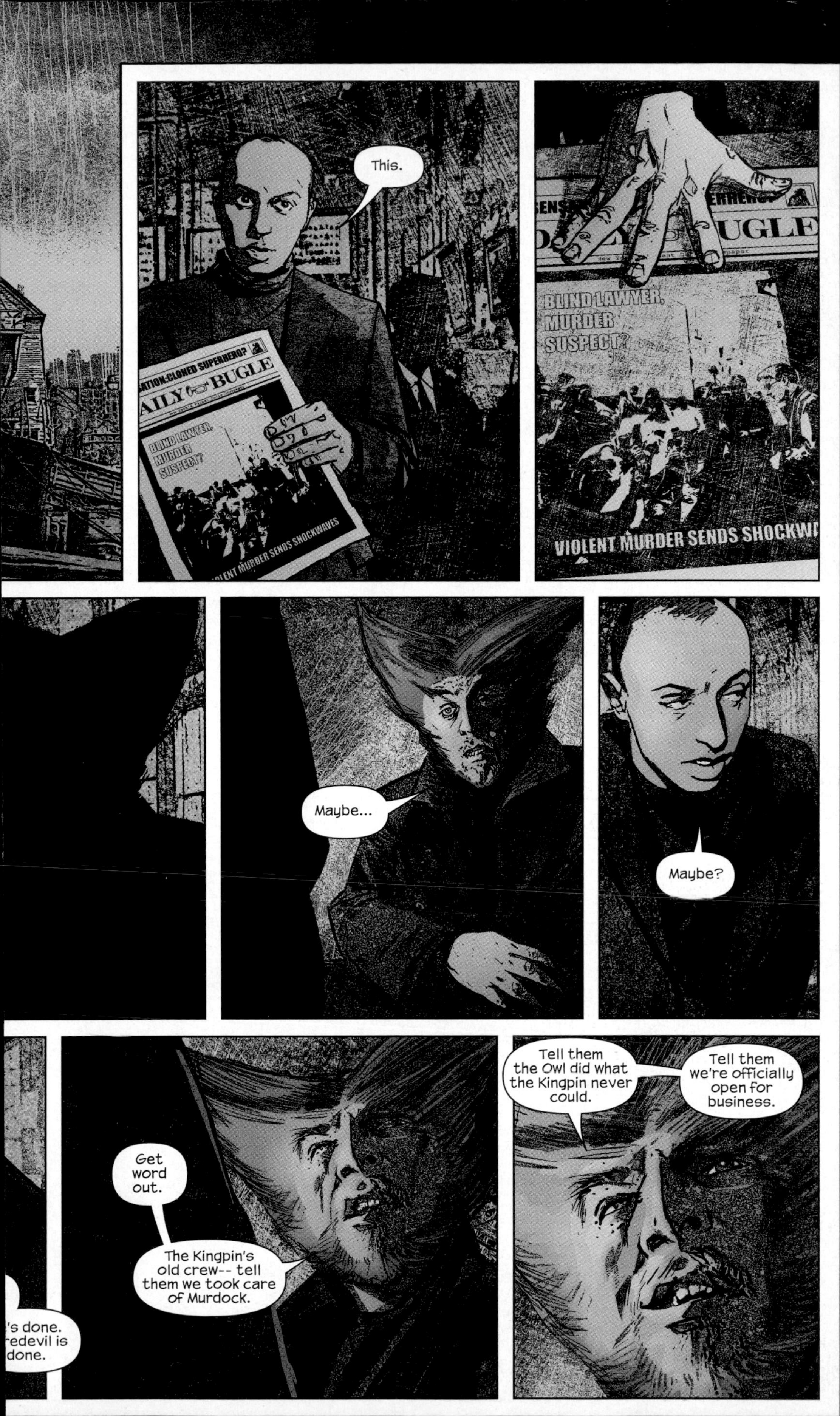
This.
BLIND LAWYER, MURDER SUSPECT?
VIOLENT MURDER SENDS SHOCKWAVES
BUGLE
BLIND LAWYER, MURDER SUSPECT?
VIOLENT MURDER SENDS SHOCKW
Maybe...
Maybe?
's done. redevil is done.
Get word out.
The Kingpin's old crew-- tell them we took care of Murdock.
Tell them the Owl did what the Kingpin never could.
Tell them we're officially open for business.

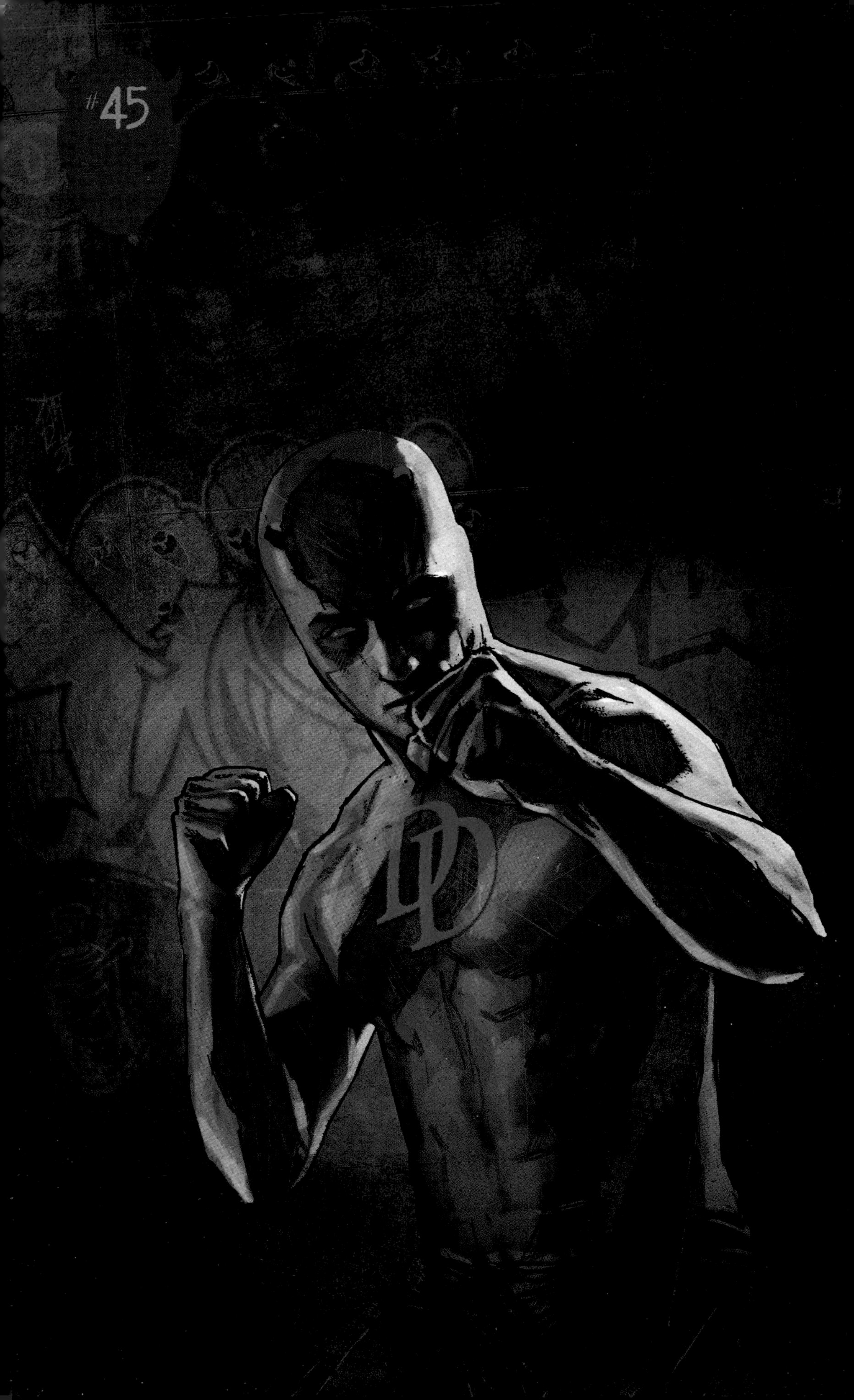

#45

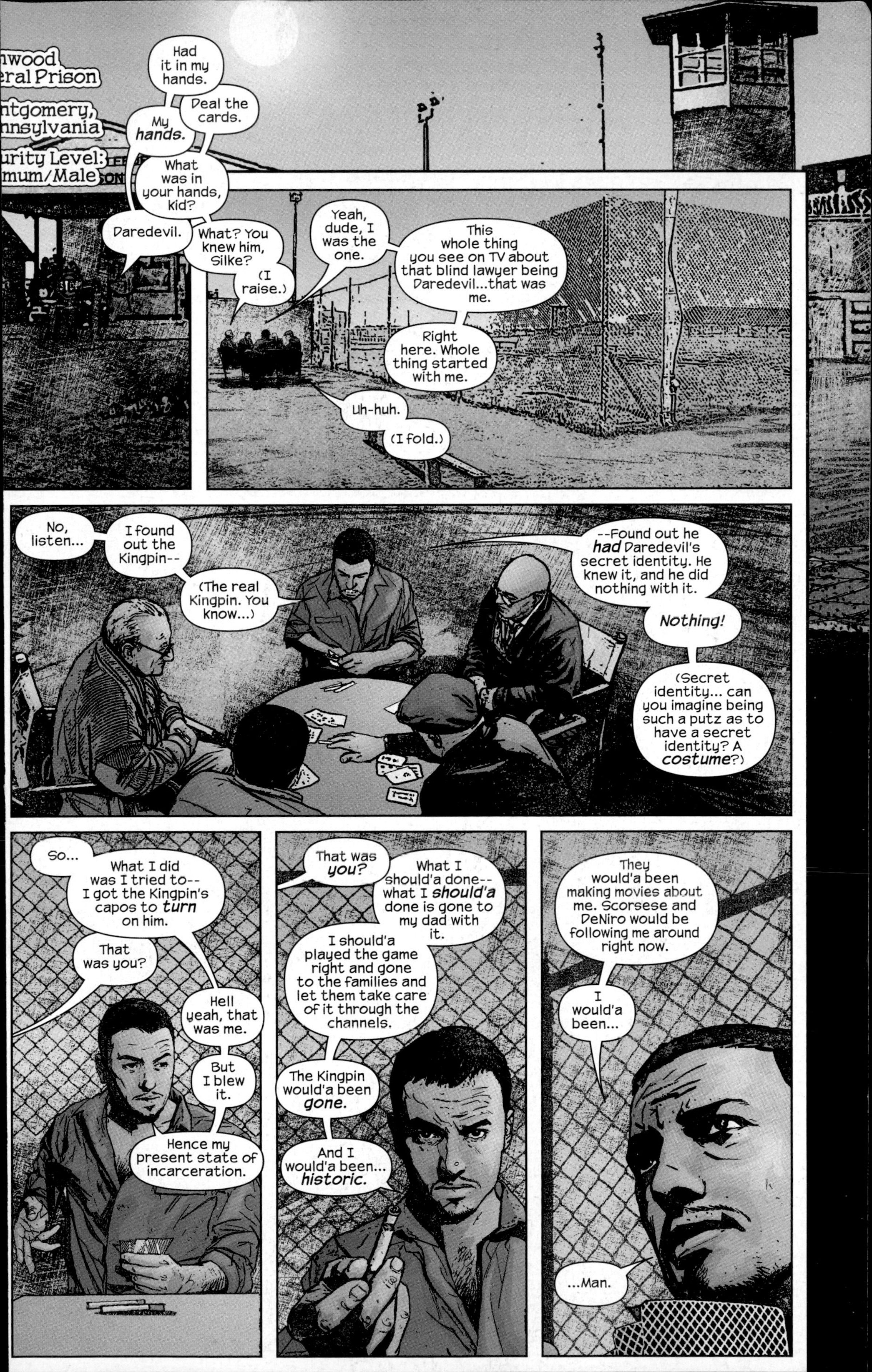

nwood
eral Prison
ntgomery,
nnsylvania
urity Level:
mum/Male
Had it in my hands.
Deal the cards.
My *hands.*
What was in your hands, kid?
Daredevil.
What? You knew him, Silke?
(I raise.)
Yeah, dude, I was the one.
This whole thing you see on TV about that blind lawyer being Daredevil...that was me.
Right here. Whole thing started with me.
Uh-huh.
(I fold.)
No, listen...
I found out the Kingpin--
(The real Kingpin. You know...)
--Found out he *had* Daredevil's secret identity. He knew it, and he did nothing with it.
Nothing!
(Secret identity... can you imagine being such a putz as to have a secret identity? A *costume*?)
So...
What I did was I tried to-- I got the Kingpin's capos to *turn* on him.
That was you?
Hell yeah, that was me.
But I blew it.
Hence my present state of incarceration.
That was *you?*
What I should'a done-- what I *should'a* done is gone to my dad with it.
I should'a played the game right and gone to the families and let them take care of it through the channels.
The Kingpin would'a been *gone.*
And I would'a been... *historic.*
They would'a been making movies about me. Scorsese and DeNiro would be following me around right now.
I would'a been...
...Man.

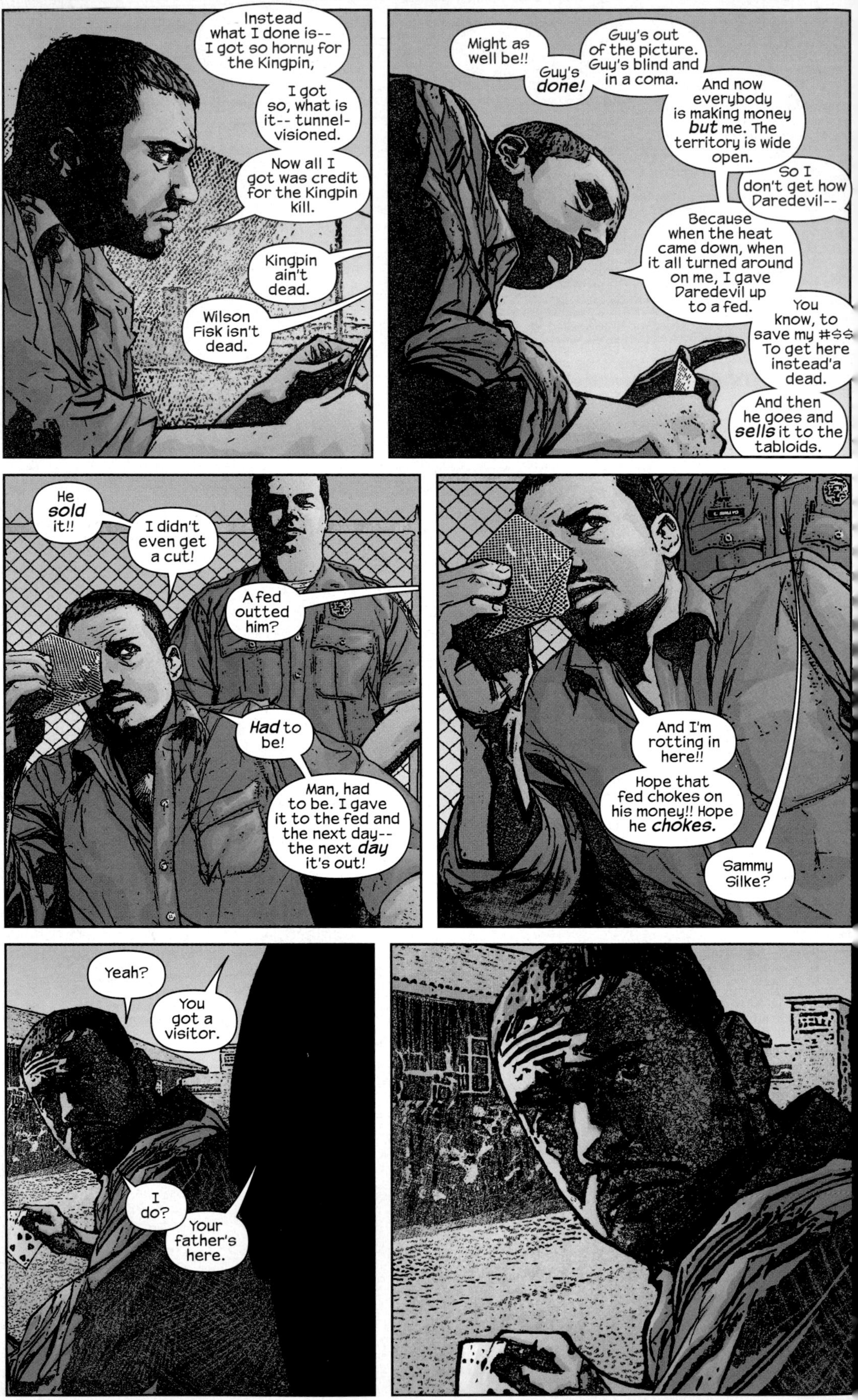
Instead what I done is-- I got so horny for the Kingpin,
I got so, what is it-- tunnel-visioned.
Now all I got was credit for the Kingpin kill.
Kingpin ain't dead.
Wilson Fisk isn't dead.
Might as well be!!
Guy's done!
Guy's out of the picture. Guy's blind and in a coma.
And now everybody is making money but me. The territory is wide open.
So I don't get how Daredevil--
Because when the heat came down, when it all turned around on me, I gave Daredevil up to a fed.
You know, to save my #$$ To get here instead'a dead.
And then he goes and sells it to the tabloids.
He sold it!!
I didn't even get a cut!
A fed outted him?
Had to be!
Man, had to be. I gave it to the fed and the next day-- the next day it's out!
And I'm rotting in here!!
Hope that fed chokes on his money!! Hope he chokes.
Sammy Silke?
Yeah?
You got a visitor.
I do?
Your father's here.

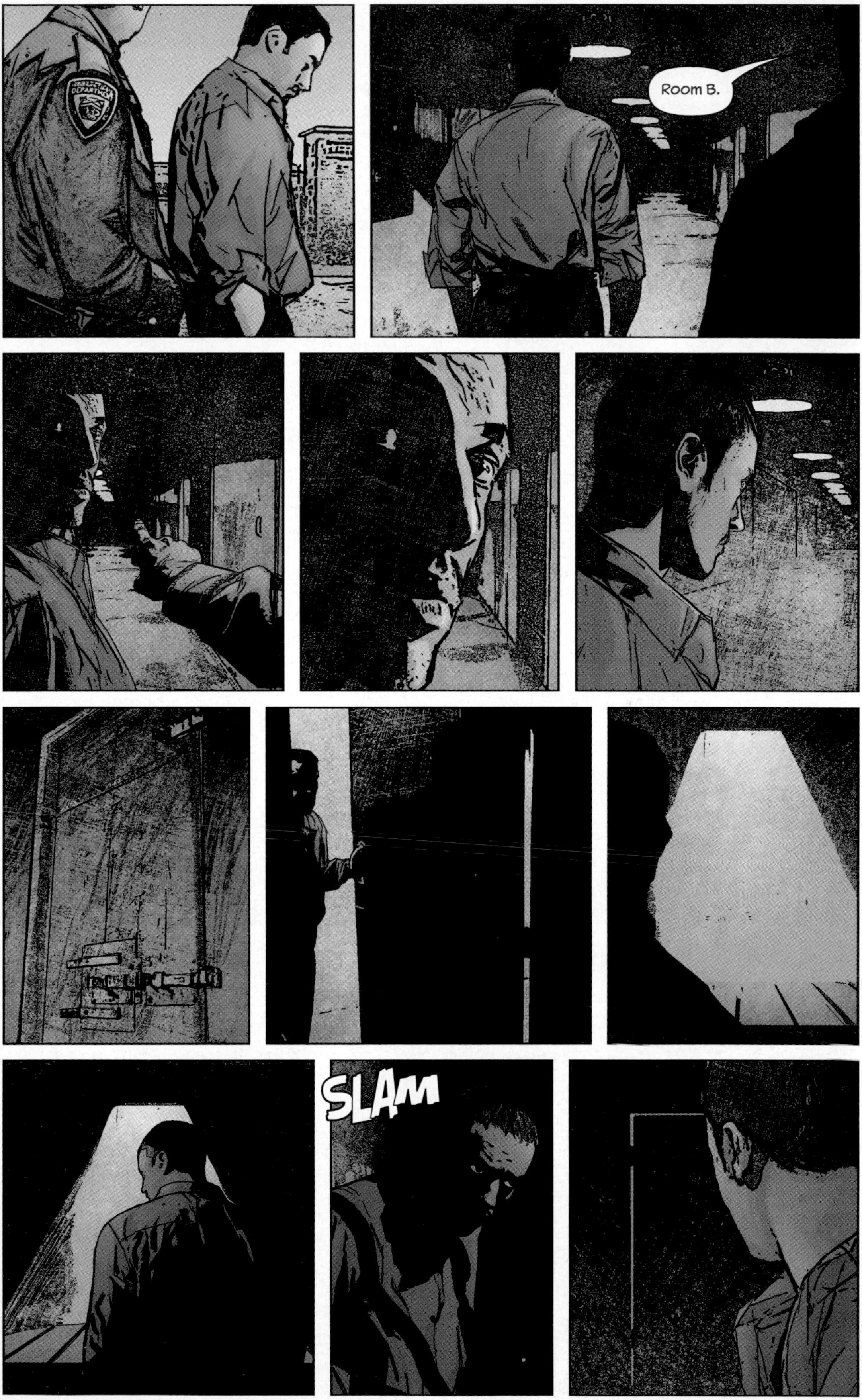
Room B.
SLAM

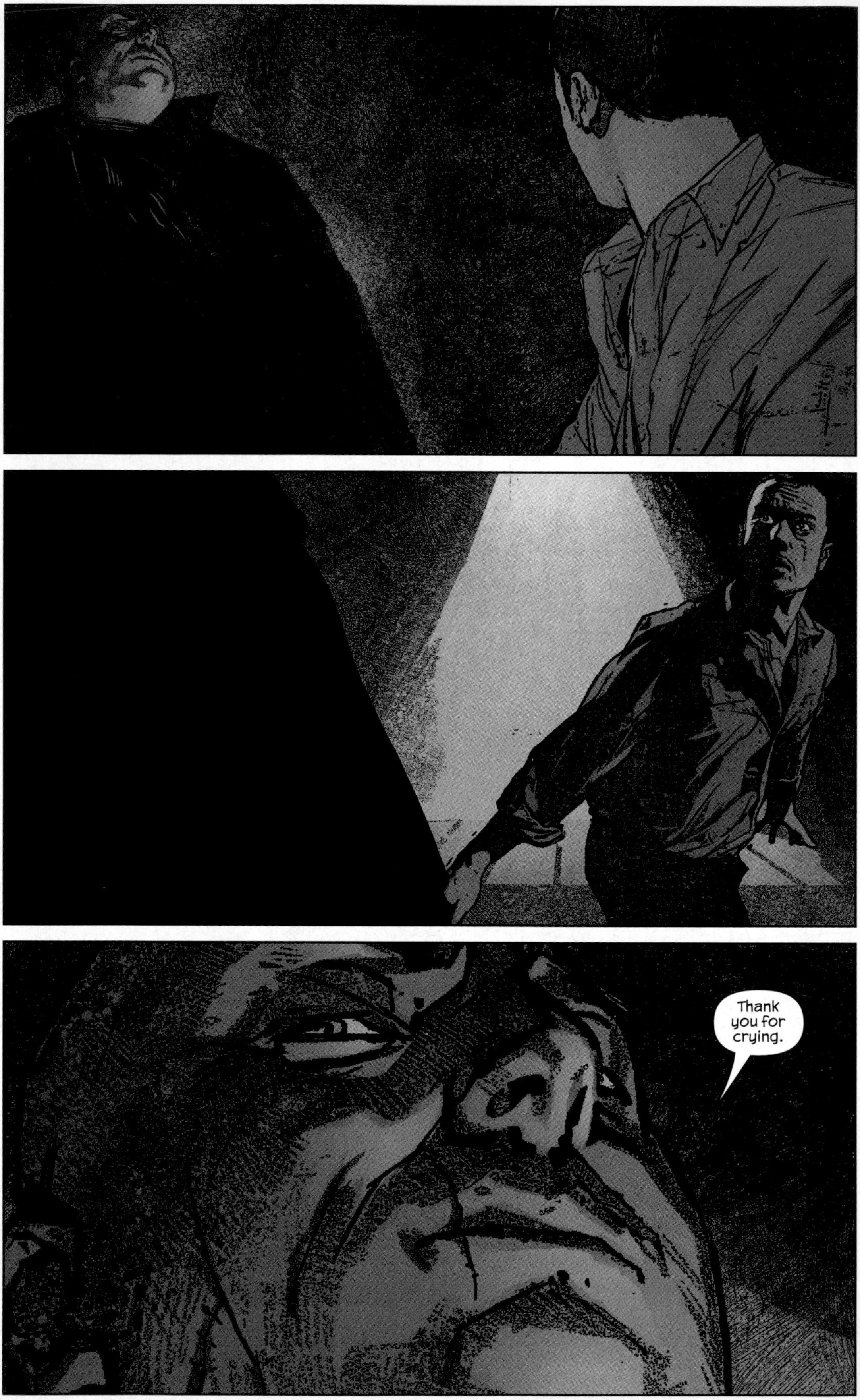
Thank you for crying.

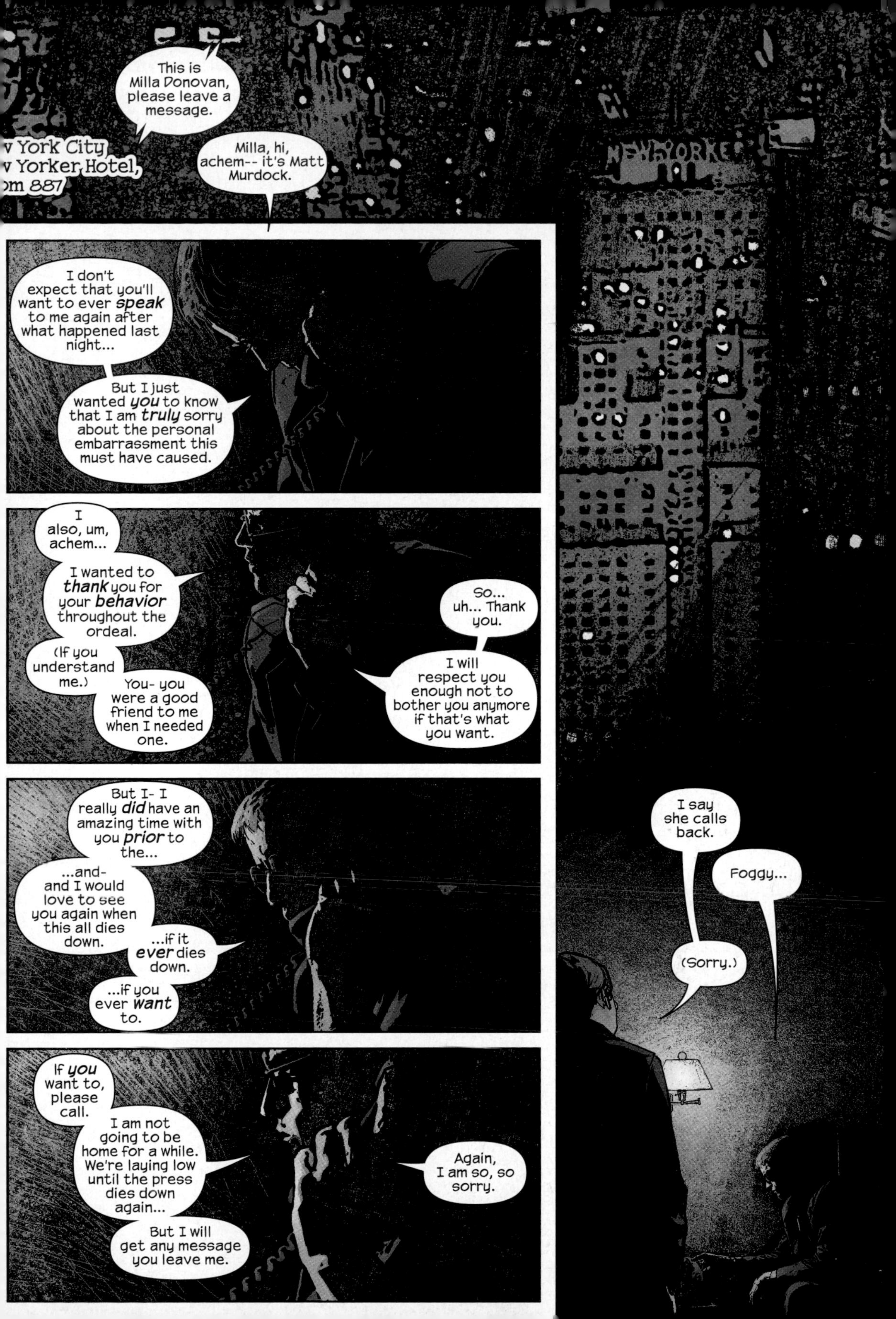

This is Milla Donovan, please leave a message.
v York City
v Yorker Hotel,
om 887
Milla, hi, achem-- it's Matt Murdock.
I don't expect that you'll want to ever *speak* to me again after what happened last night...
But I just wanted *you* to know that I am *truly* sorry about the personal embarrassment this must have caused.
I also, um, achem...
I wanted to *thank* you for your *behavior* throughout the ordeal.
(If you understand me.)
You- you were a good friend to me when I needed one.
So... uh... Thank you.
I will respect you enough not to bother you anymore if that's what you want.
But I- I really *did* have an amazing time with you *prior* to the...
...and- and I would love to see you again when this all dies down.
...if it *ever* dies down.
...if you ever *want* to.
If *you* want to, please call.
I am not going to be home for a while. We're laying low until the press dies down again...
But I will get any message you leave me.
Again, I am so, so sorry.
I say she calls back.
Foggy...
(Sorry.)

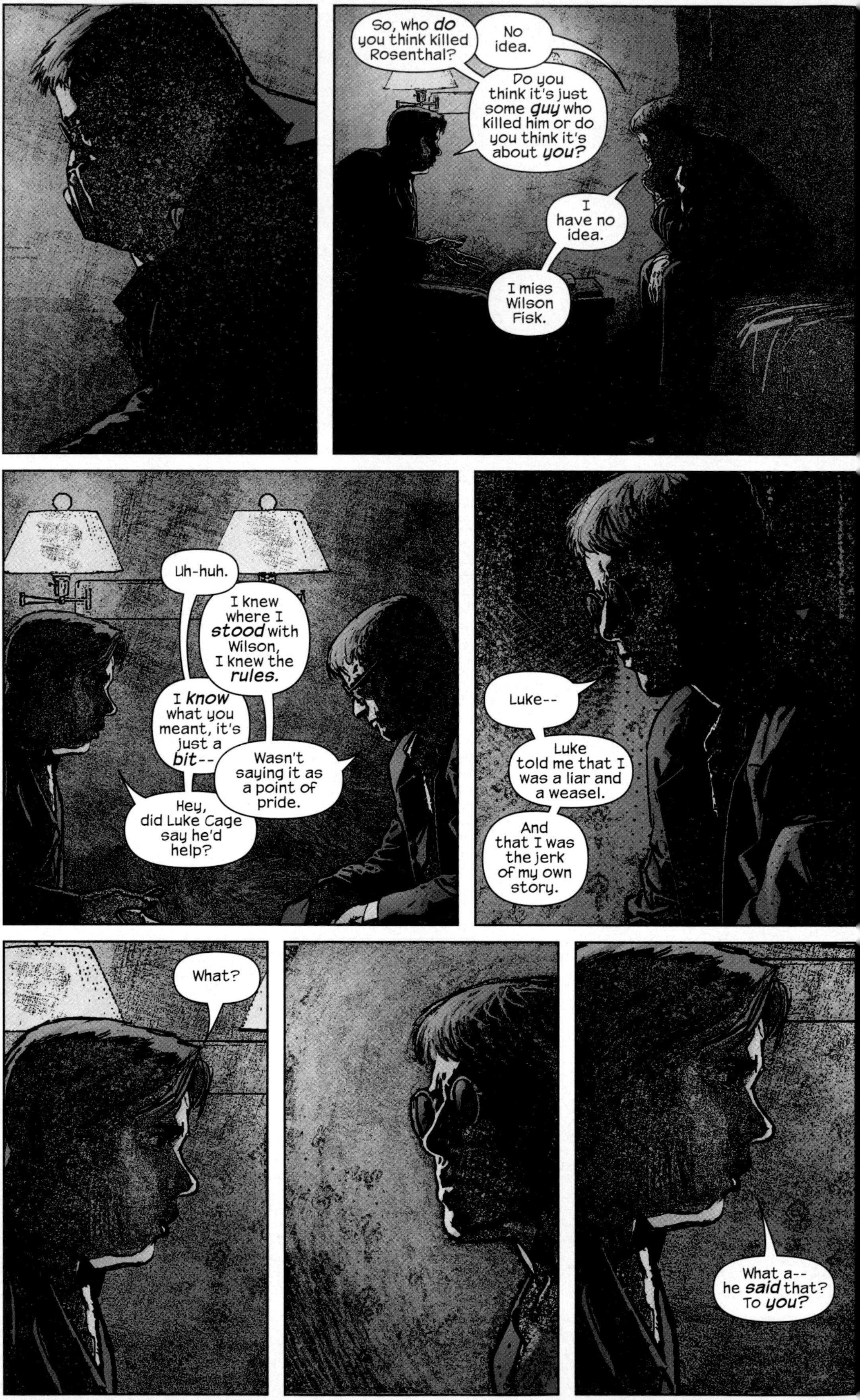
So, who do you think killed Rosenthal?
No idea.
Do you think it's just some guy who killed him or do you think it's about you?
I have no idea.
I miss Wilson Fisk.
Uh-huh.
I knew where I stood with Wilson, I knew the rules.
I know what you meant, it's just a bit--
Wasn't saying it as a point of pride.
Hey, did Luke Cage say he'd help?
Luke--
Luke told me that I was a liar and a weasel.
And that I was the jerk of my own story.
What?
What a-- he said that? To you?

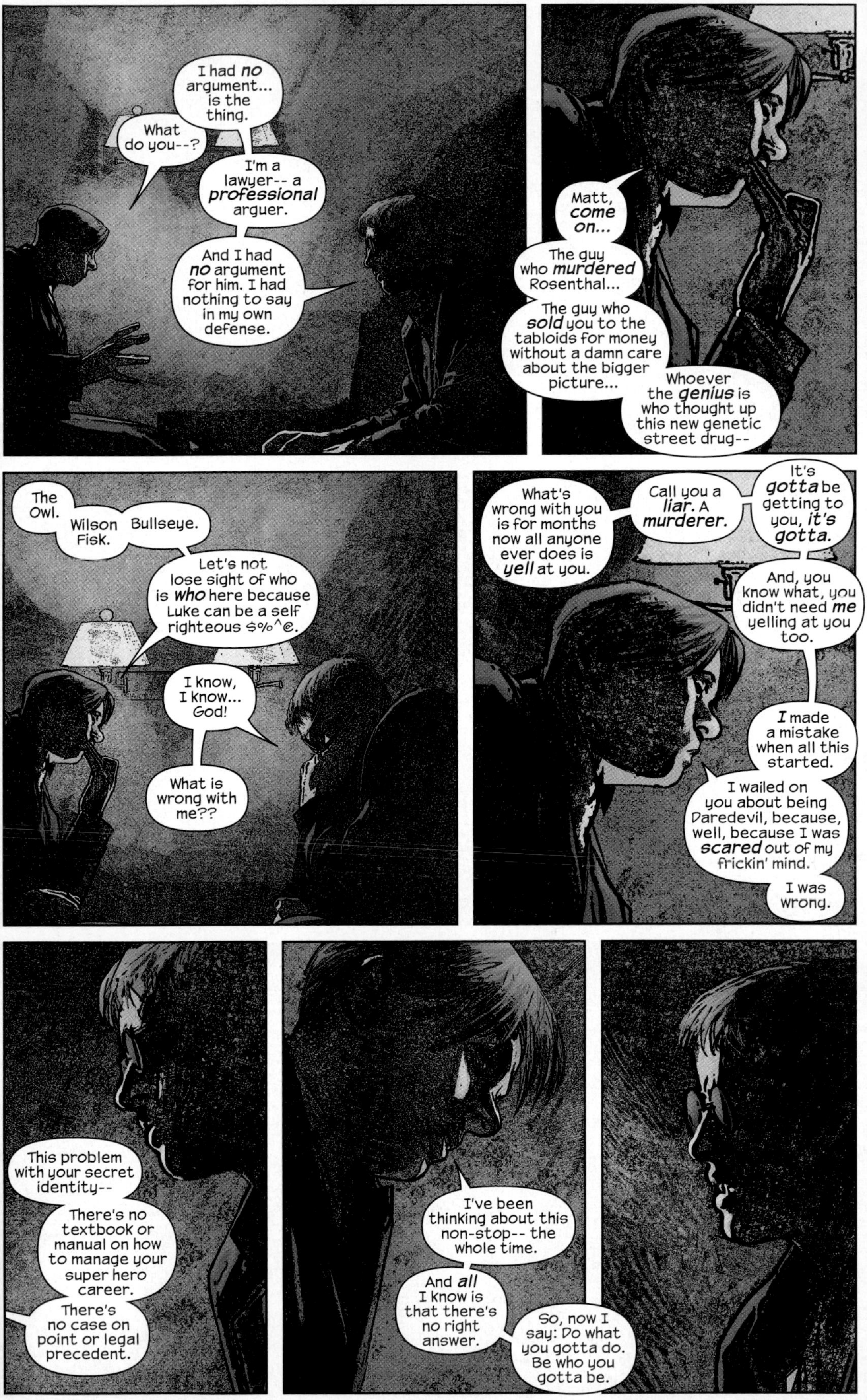
What do you--?
I had no argument... is the thing.
I'm a lawyer-- a professional arguer.
And I had no argument for him. I had nothing to say in my own defense.
Matt, come on...
The guy who murdered Rosenthal...
The guy who sold you to the tabloids for money without a damn care about the bigger picture...
Whoever the genius is who thought up this new genetic street drug--
The Owl.
Wilson Fisk.
Bullseye.
Let's not lose sight of who is who here because Luke can be a self righteous $%^@.
I know, I know... God!
What is wrong with me??
What's wrong with you is for months now all anyone ever does is yell at you.
Call you a liar. A murderer.
It's gotta be getting to you, it's gotta.
And, you know what, you didn't need me yelling at you too.
I made a mistake when all this started.
I wailed on you about being Daredevil, because, well, because I was scared out of my frickin' mind.
I was wrong.
This problem with your secret identity--
There's no textbook or manual on how to manage your super hero career.
There's no case on point or legal precedent.
I've been thinking about this non-stop-- the whole time.
And all I know is that there's no right answer.
So, now I say: Do what you gotta do. Be who you gotta be.

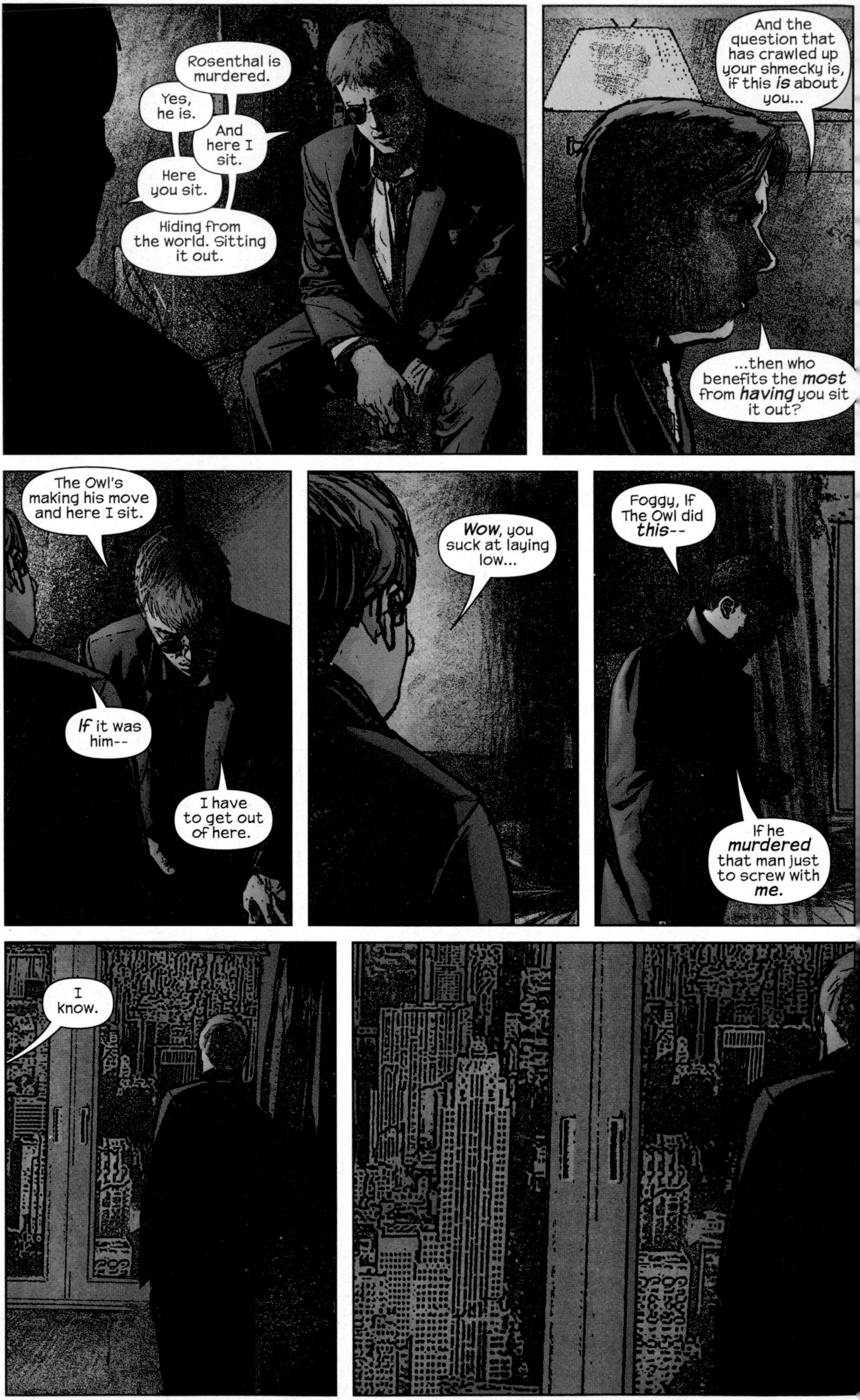
Rosenthal is murdered.
Yes, he is.
And here I sit.
Here you sit.
Hiding from the world. Sitting it out.
And the question that has crawled up your shmecky is, if this *is* about you...
...then who benefits the *most* from *having* you sit it out?
The Owl's making his move and here I sit.
If it was him--
I have to get out of here.
Wow, you suck at laying low...
Foggy, If The Owl did *this*--
If he *murdered* that man just to screw with *me.*
I know.

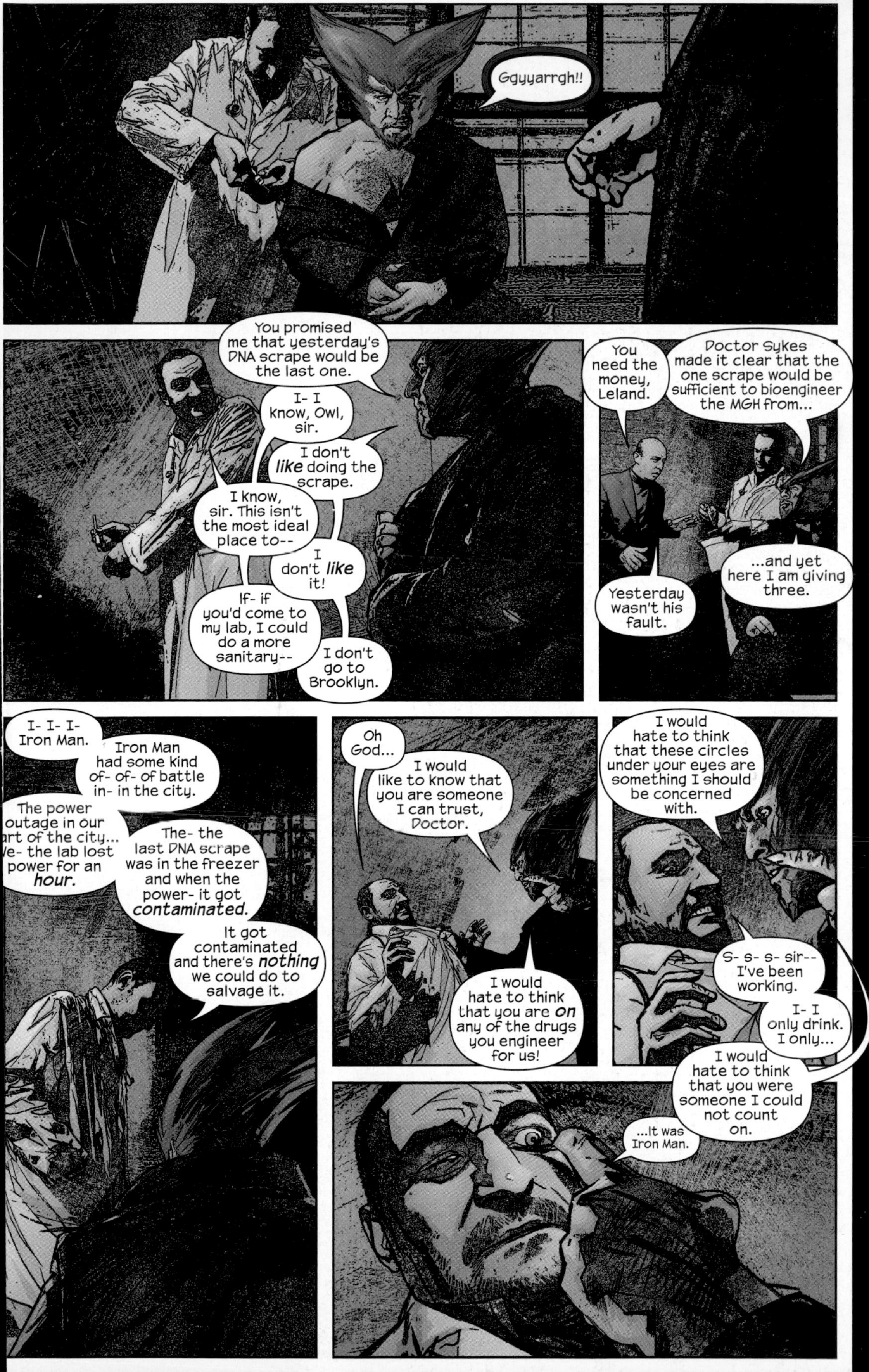
Ggyyarrgh!!
You promised me that yesterday's DNA scrape would be the last one.
I- I know, Owl, sir.
I don't *like* doing the scrape.
I know, sir. This isn't the most ideal place to--
I don't *like* it!
If- if you'd come to my lab, I could do a more sanitary--
I don't go to Brooklyn.
You need the money, Leland.
Doctor Sykes made it clear that the one scrape would be sufficient to bioengineer the MGH from...
Yesterday wasn't his fault.
...and yet here I am giving three.
I- I- I- Iron Man.
Iron Man had some kind of- of- of battle in- in the city.
The power outage in our art of the city... Ve- the lab lost power for an *hour.*
The- the last DNA scrape was in the freezer and when the power- it got *contaminated.*
It got contaminated and there's *nothing* we could do to salvage it.
Oh God...
I would like to know that you are someone I can trust, Doctor.
I would hate to think that you are *on* any of the drugs you engineer for us!
I would hate to think that these circles under your eyes are something I should be concerned with.
S- s- s- sir-- I've been working.
I- I only drink. I only...
I would hate to think that you were someone I could not count on.
...It was Iron Man.

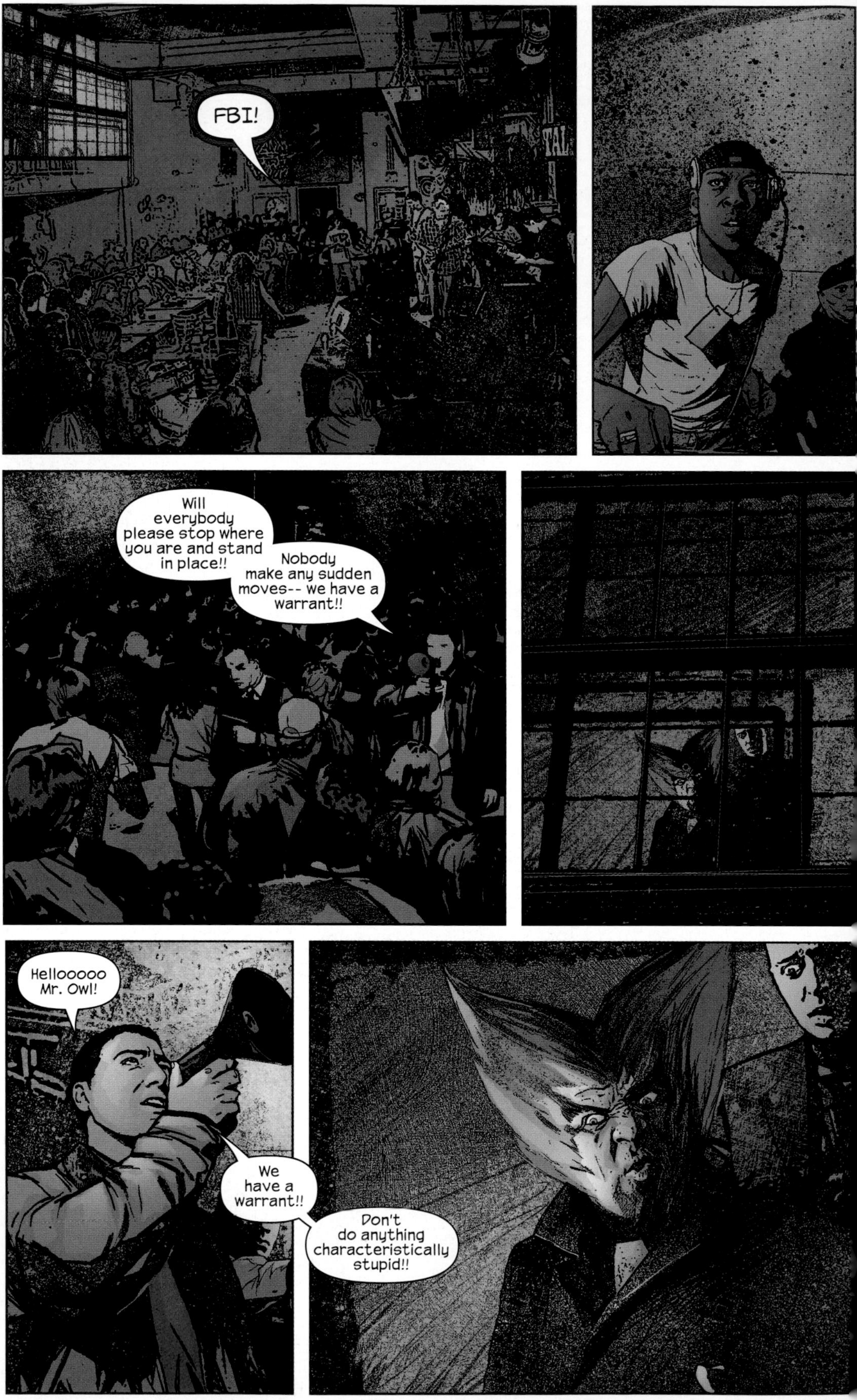
FBI!
Will everybody please stop where you are and stand in place!!
Nobody make any sudden moves-- we have a warrant!!
Hellooooo Mr. Owl!
We have a warrant!!
Don't do anything characteristically stupid!!

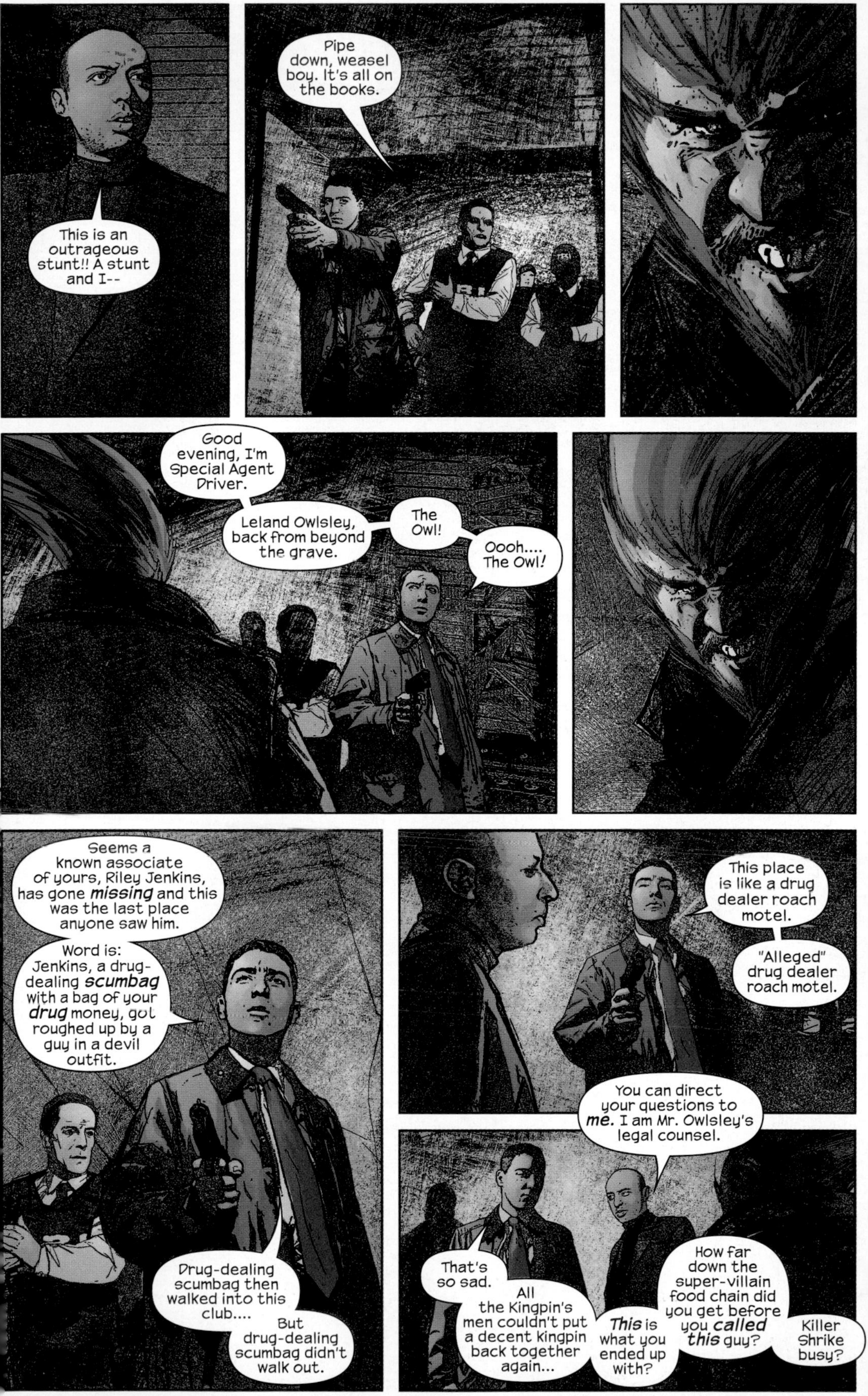
This is an outrageous stunt!! A stunt and I--
Pipe down, weasel boy. It's all on the books.
Good evening, I'm Special Agent Driver.
Leland Owlsley, back from beyond the grave.
The Owl!
Oooh.... The Owl!
Seems a known associate of yours, Riley Jenkins, has gone *missing* and this was the last place anyone saw him.
Word is: Jenkins, a drug-dealing *scumbag* with a bag of your *drug* money, got roughed up by a guy in a devil outfit.
Drug-dealing scumbag then walked into this club....
But drug-dealing scumbag didn't walk out.
This place is like a drug dealer roach motel.
"Alleged" drug dealer roach motel.
You can direct your questions to *me.* I am Mr. Owlsley's legal counsel.
That's so sad.
All the Kingpin's men couldn't put a decent kingpin back together again...
This is what you ended up with?
How far down the super-villain food chain did you get before you *called this* guy?
Killer Shrike busy?

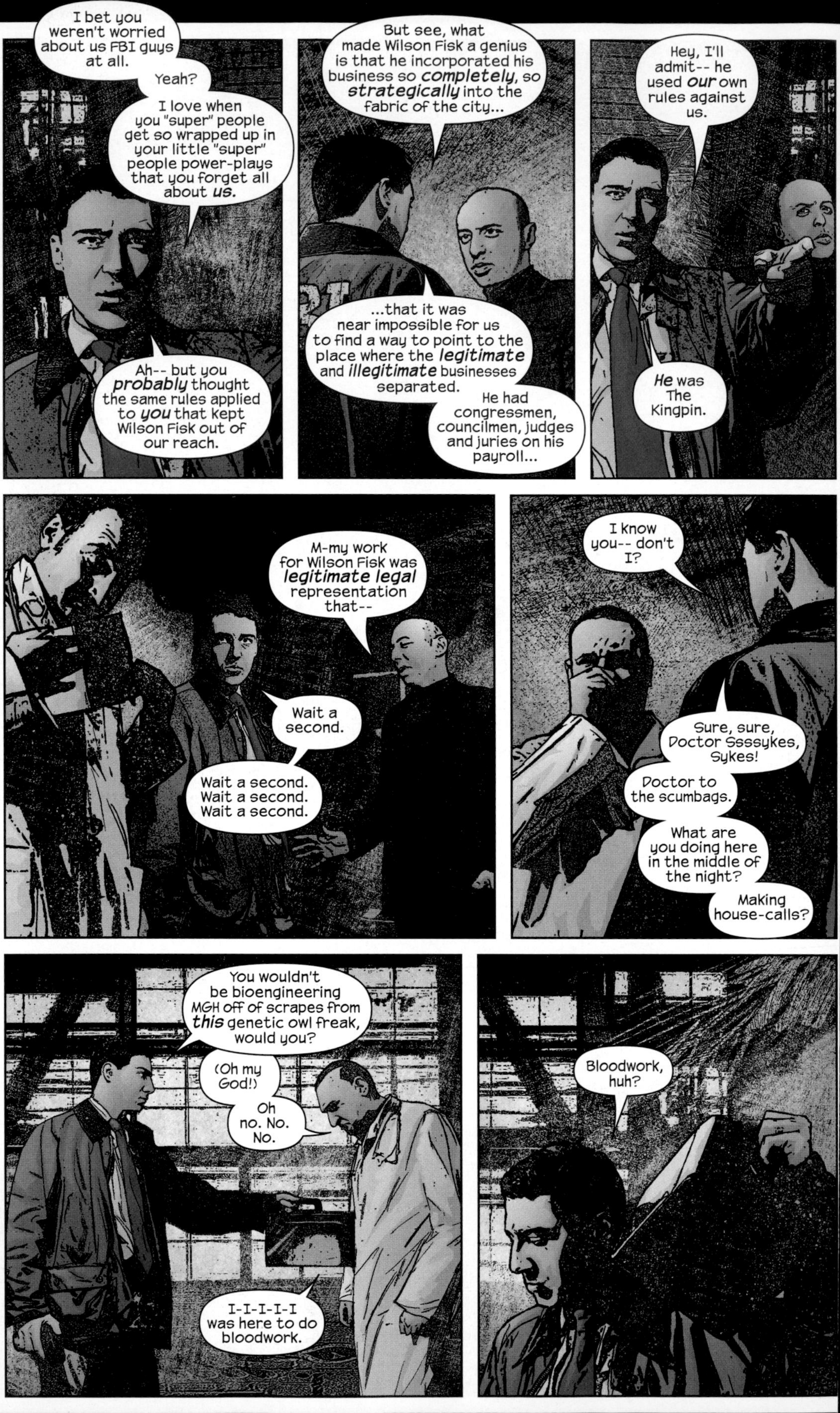
I bet you weren't worried about us FBI guys at all.
Yeah?
I love when you "super" people get so wrapped up in your little "super" people power-plays that you forget all about *us.*
Ah-- but you *probably* thought the same rules applied to *you* that kept Wilson Fisk out of our reach.
But see, what made Wilson Fisk a genius is that he incorporated his business so *completely,* so *strategically* into the fabric of the city...
...that it was near impossible for us to find a way to point to the place where the *legitimate* and *illegitimate* businesses separated.
He had congressmen, councilmen, judges and juries on his payroll...
Hey, I'll admit-- he used *our* own rules against us.
He was The Kingpin.
M-my work for Wilson Fisk was *legitimate legal* representation that--
Wait a second.
Wait a second. Wait a second. Wait a second.
I know you-- don't I?
Sure, sure, Doctor Sssykes, Sykes!
Doctor to the scumbags.
What are you doing here in the middle of the night?
Making house-calls?
You wouldn't be bioengineering MGH off of scrapes from *this* genetic owl freak, would you?
(Oh my God!)
Oh no. No. No.
I-I-I-I-I was here to do bloodwork.
Bloodwork, huh?

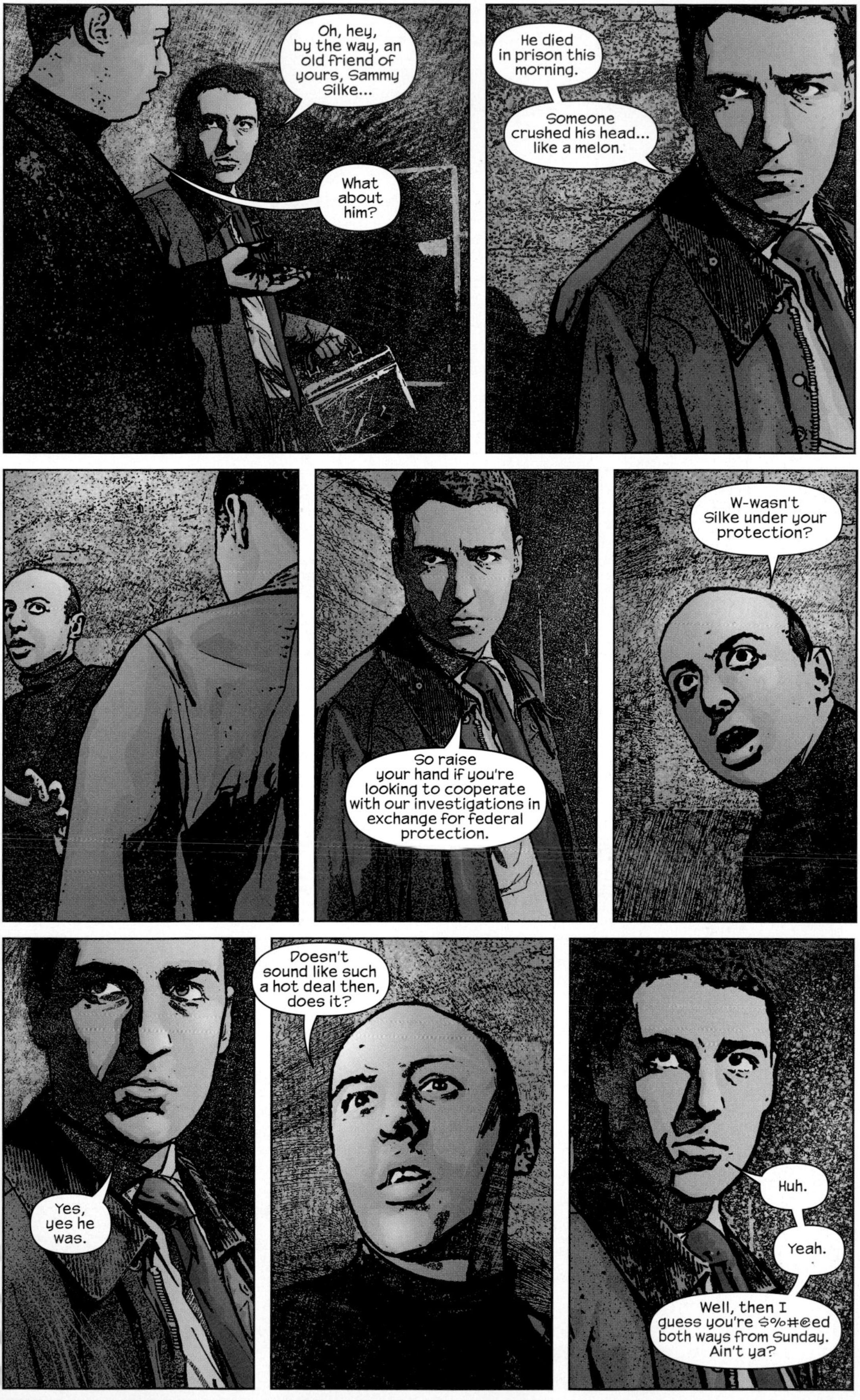

Oh, hey, by the way, an old friend of yours, Sammy Silke...
What about him?
He died in prison this morning.
Someone crushed his head... like a melon.
So raise your hand if you're looking to cooperate with our investigations in exchange for federal protection.
W-wasn't Silke under your protection?
Yes, yes he was.
Doesn't sound like such a hot deal then, does it?
Huh.
Yeah.
Well, then I guess you're $%#@ed both ways from Sunday. Ain't ya?

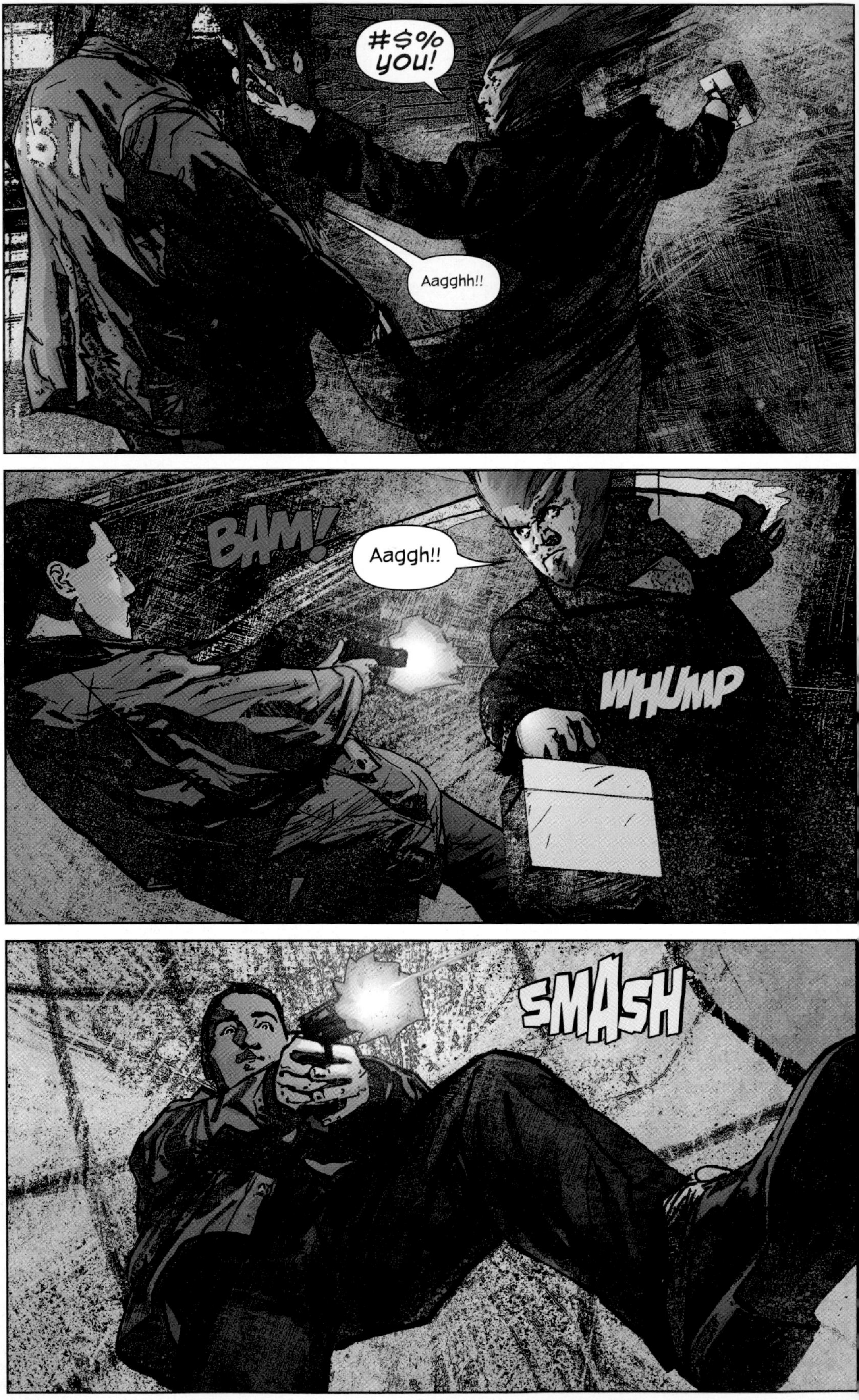
#$% you!
Aagghh!!
BAM!
Aaggh!!
WHUMP
SMASH

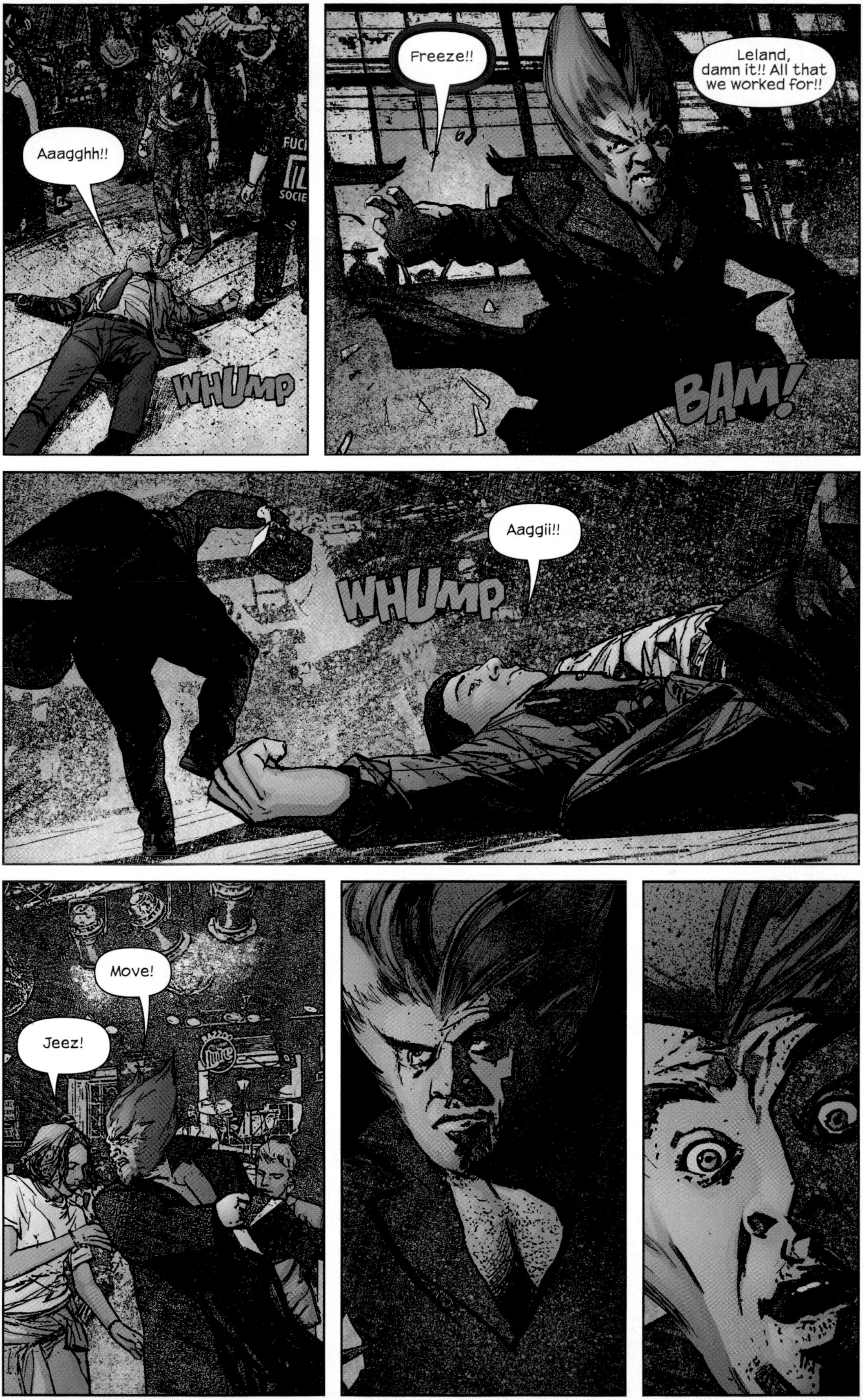
Aaagghh!!
WHUMP
Freeze!!
Leland, damn it!! All that we worked for!!
BAM!
Aaggii!!
WHUMP
Move!
Jeez!

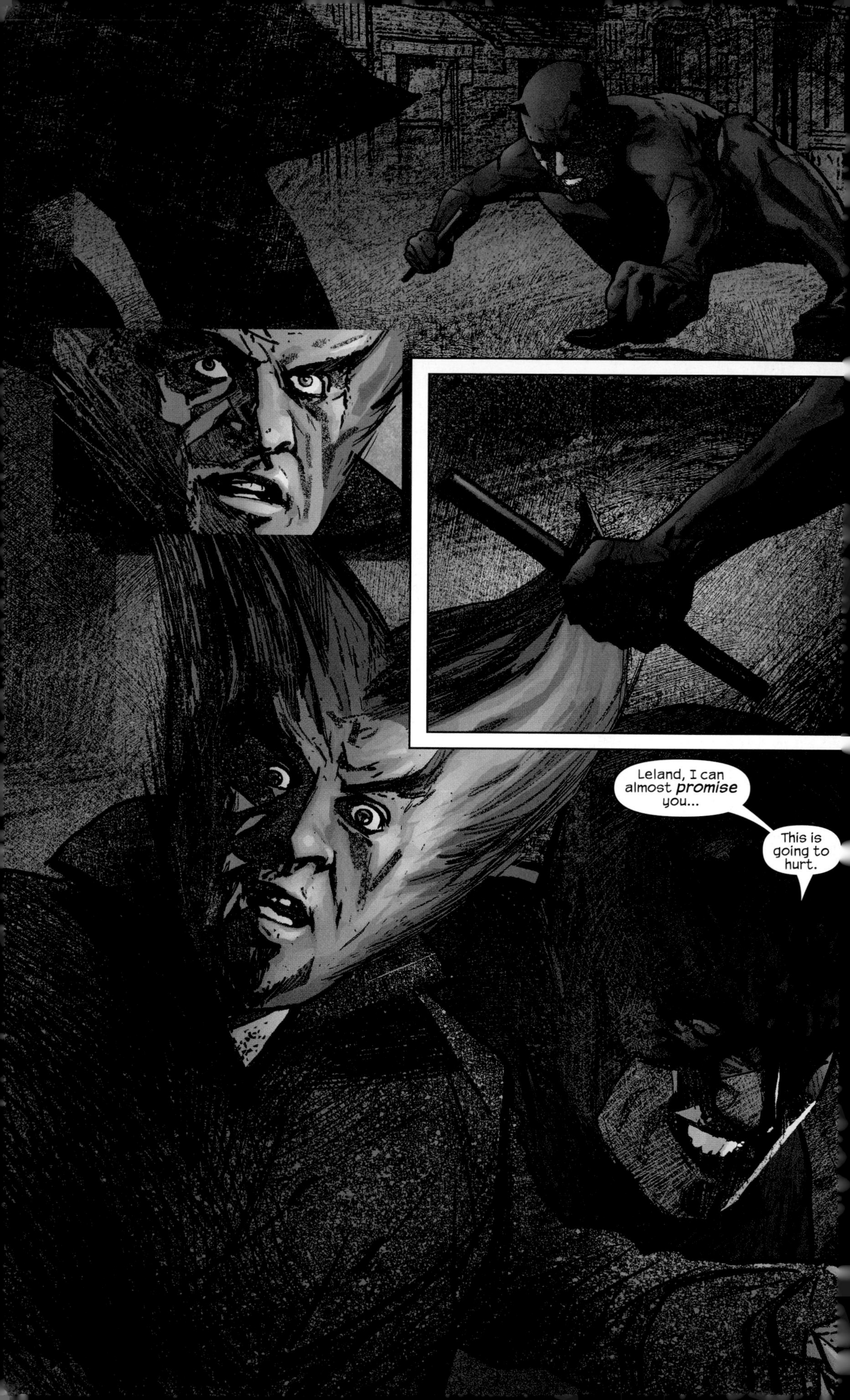
Leland, I can almost *promise* you...
This is going to hurt.

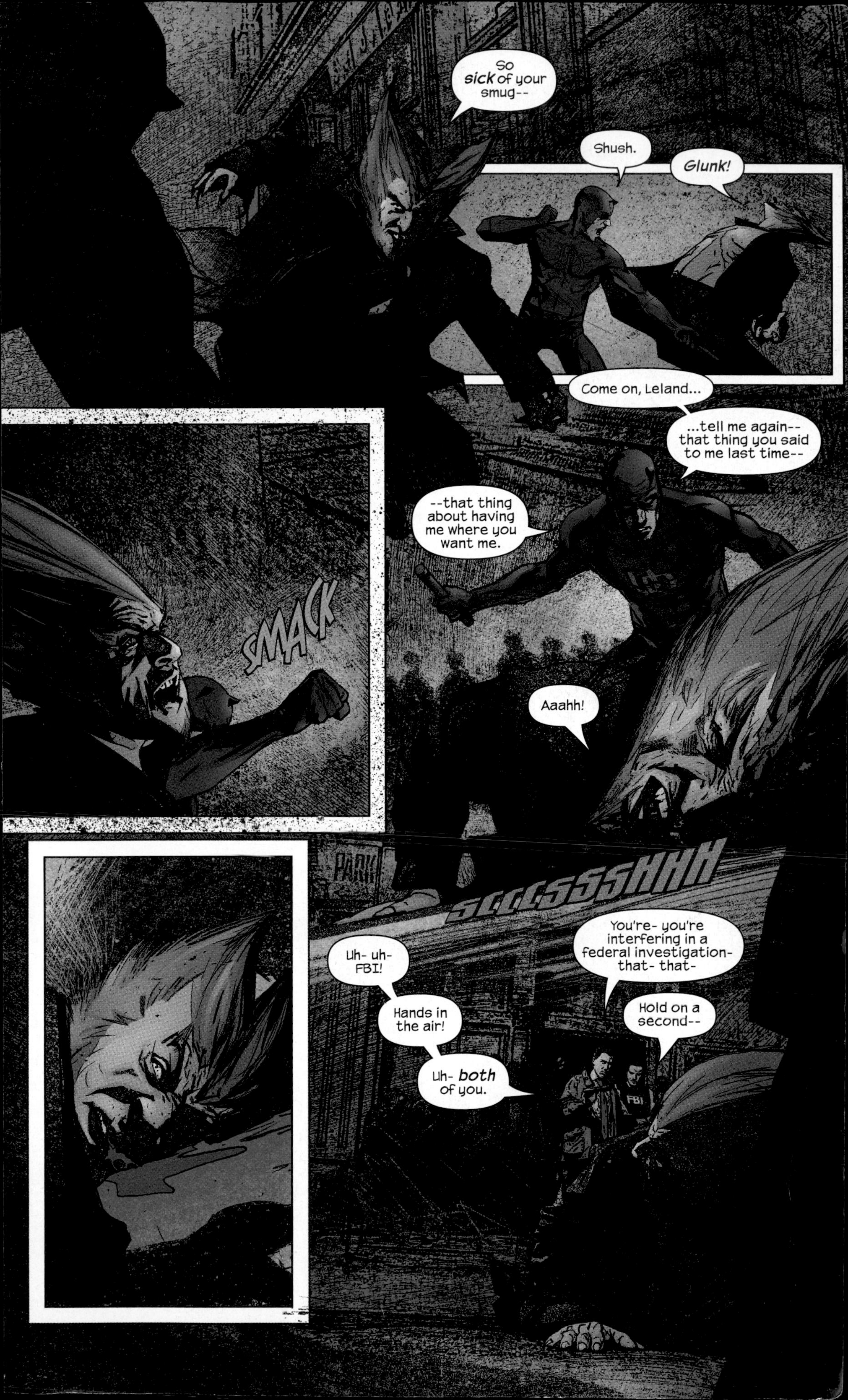
So sick of your smug--
Shush.
Glunk!
Come on, Leland...
...tell me again-- that thing you said to me last time--
--that thing about having me where you want me.
SMACK
Aaahh!
SCCCSSSSHHH
PARK
Uh- uh- FBI!
Hands in the air!
Uh- both of you.
You're- you're interfering in a federal investigation- that- that-
Hold on a second--
FBI

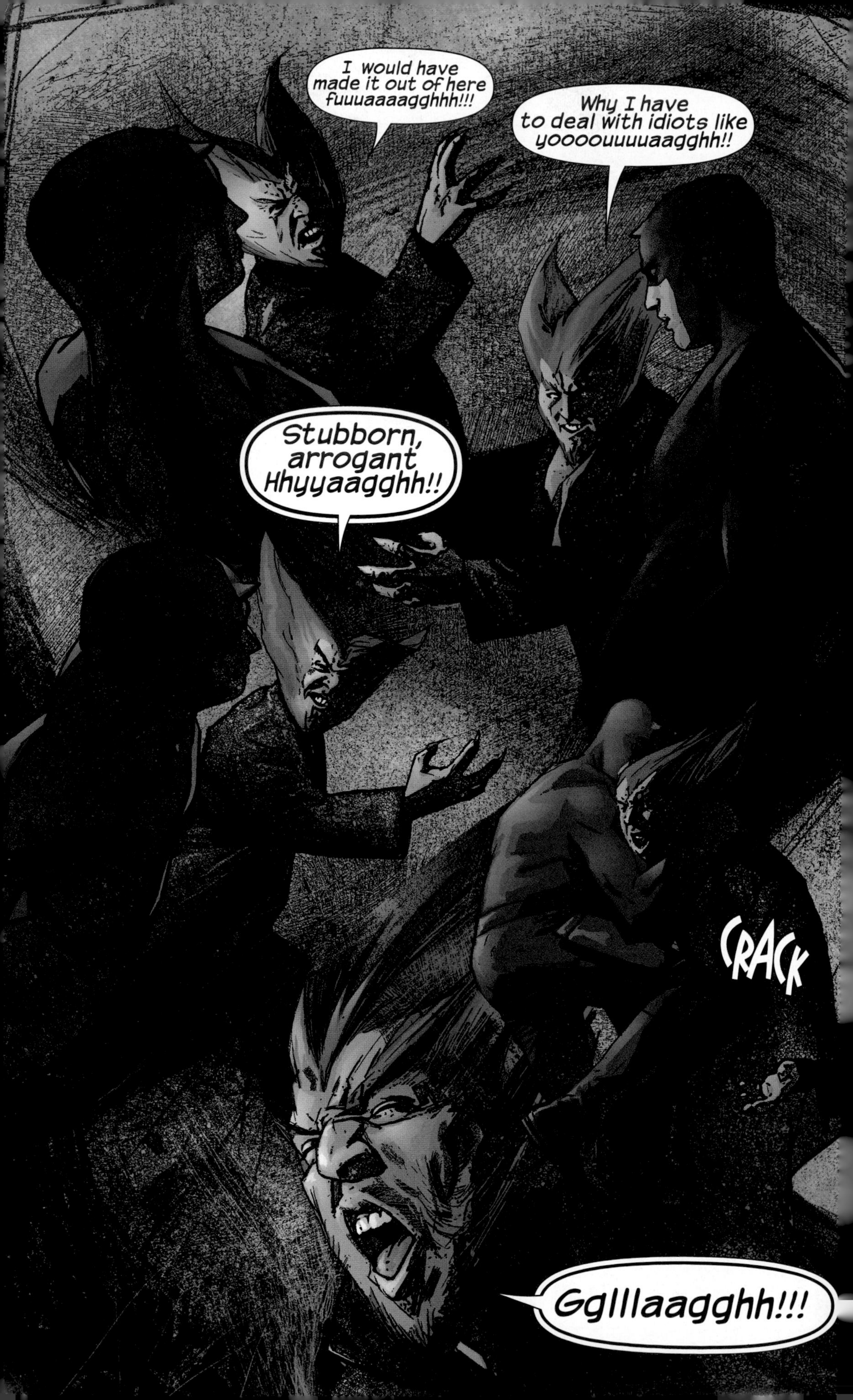
I would have made it out of here fuuuaaaagghhh!!!
Why I have to deal with idiots like yoooouuuuaagghh!!
Stubborn, arrogant Hhyyaagghh!!
CRACK
Gglllaagghh!!!

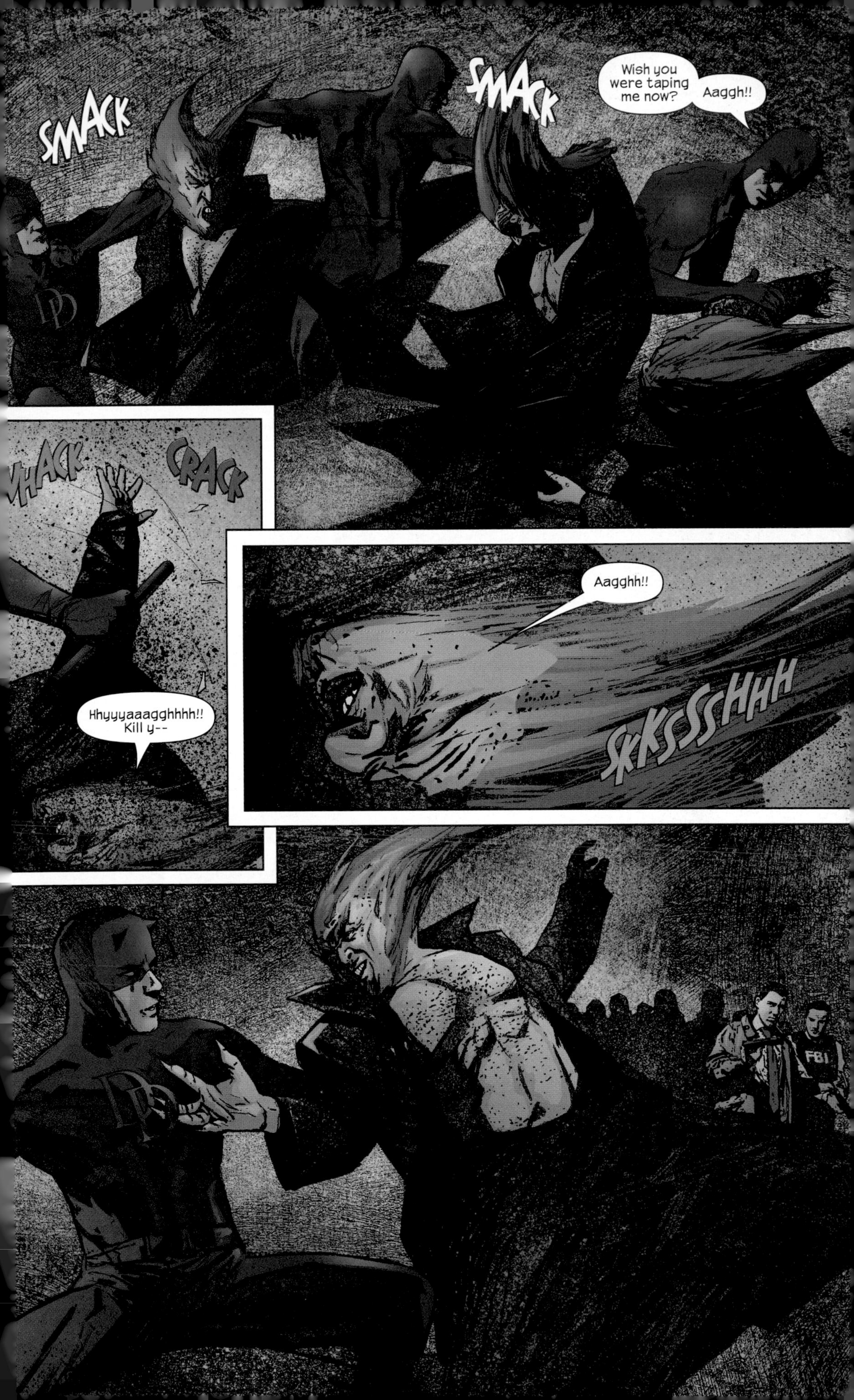
SMACK
SMACK
Wish you were taping me now?
Aaggh!!
CRACK
Hhyyyaaagghhhh!! Kill y--
Aagghh!!
SKKSSSHHH

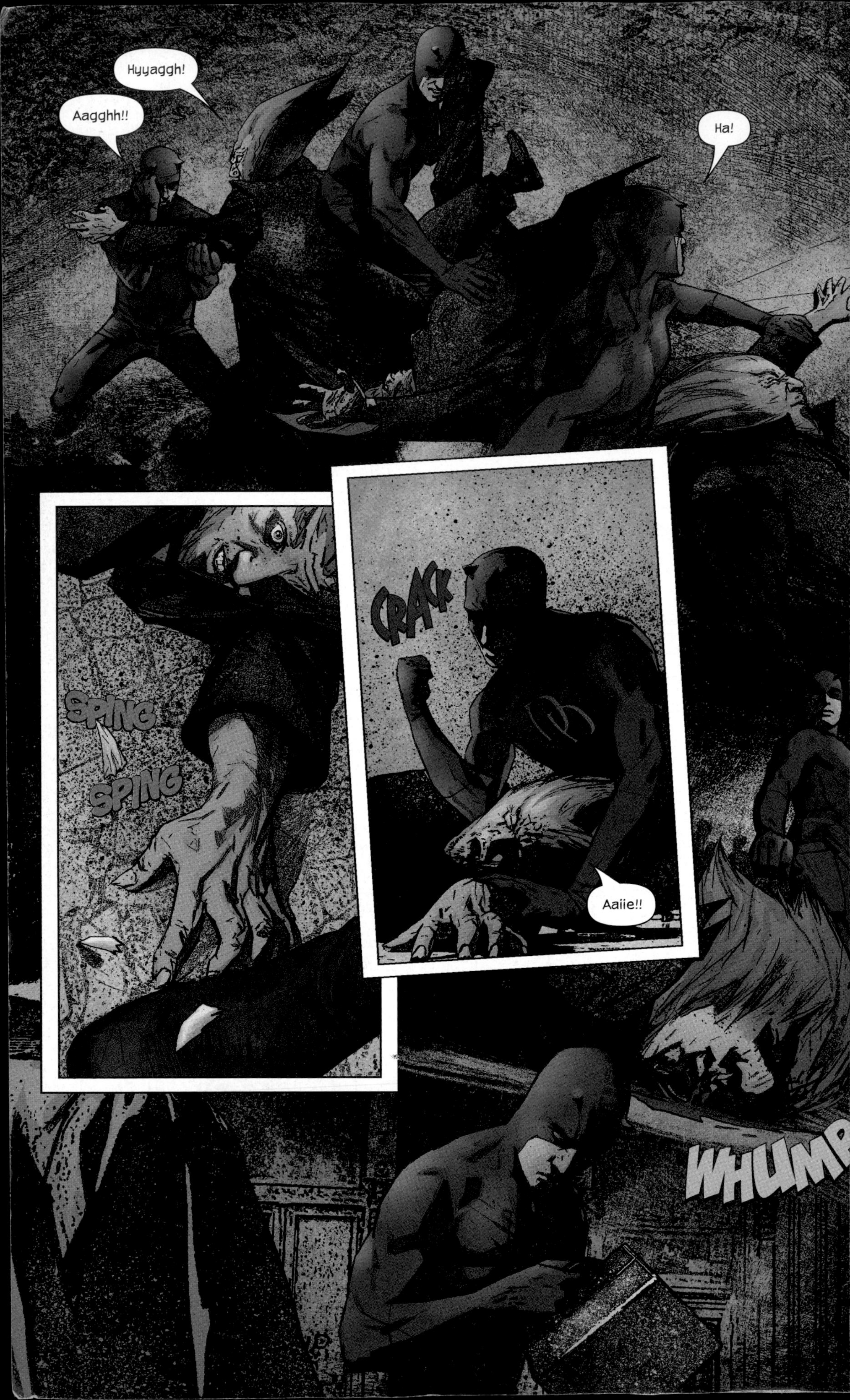
Hyyaggh!
Aagghh!!
Ha!
SPING
SPING
CRACK
Aaiie!!
WHUMP

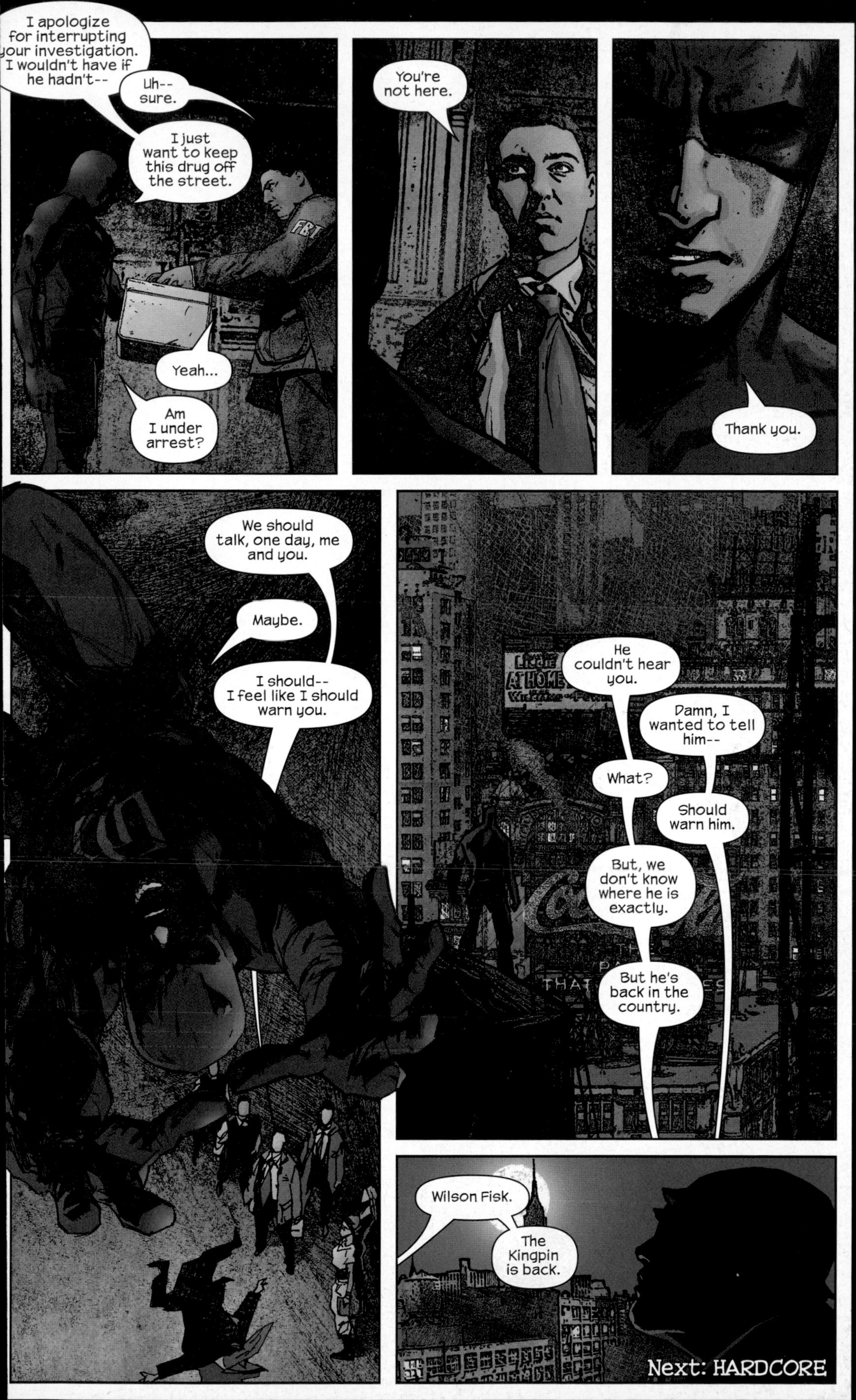
I apologize for interrupting your investigation. I wouldn't have if he hadn't--
Uh-- sure.
I just want to keep this drug off the street.
FBI
Yeah...
Am I under arrest?
You're not here.
Thank you.
We should talk, one day, me and you.
Maybe.
I should-- I feel like I should warn you.
He couldn't hear you.
Damn, I wanted to tell him--
What?
Should warn him.
But, we don't know where he is exactly.
But he's back in the country.
Wilson Fisk.
The Kingpin is back.
Next: HARDCORE

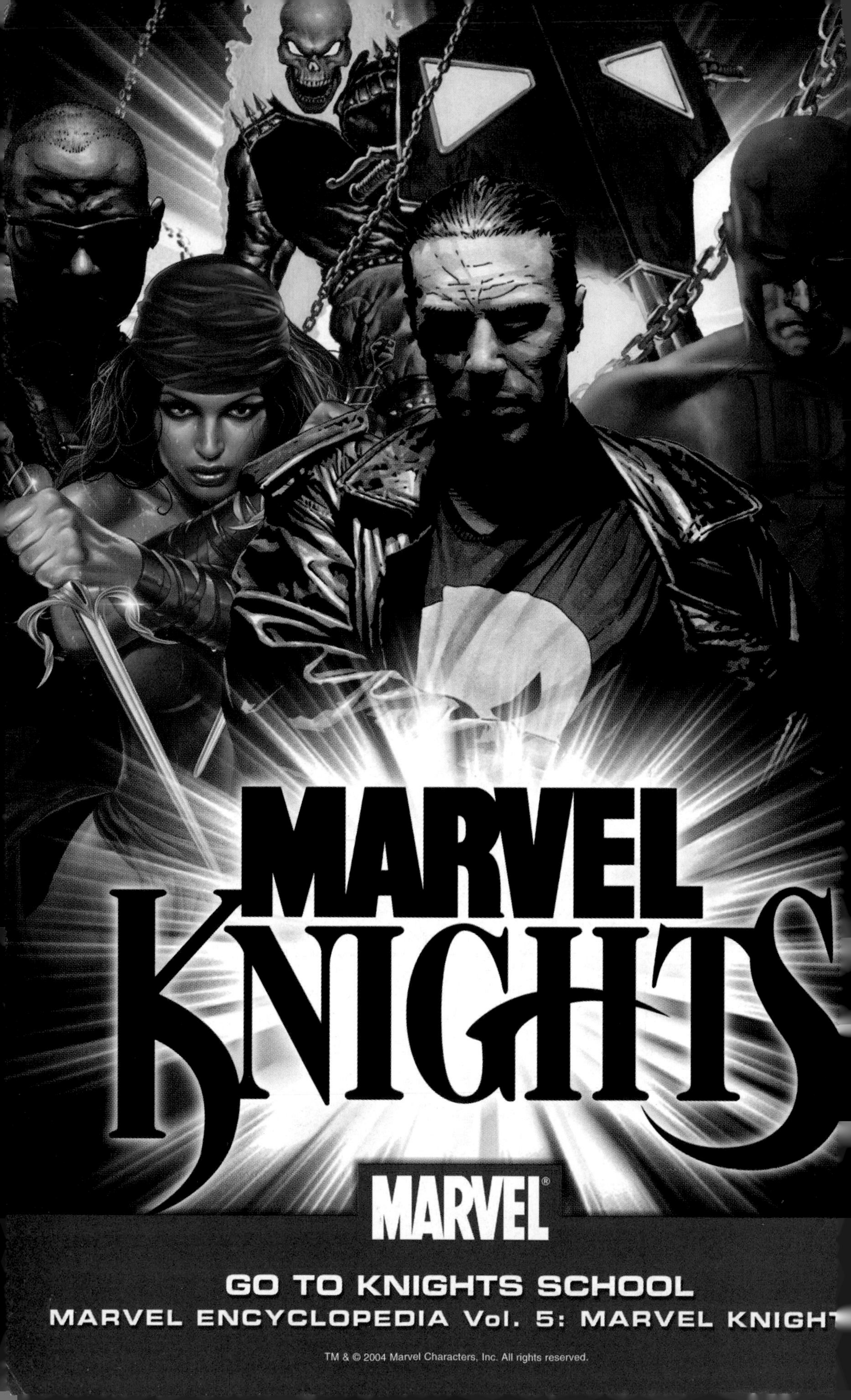
MARVEL
KNIGHTS
MARVEL®

MARVELS
10TH ANNIVERSARY EDITION

MARVEL®

CELEBRATE 10 YEARS OF MARVELS!
KURT BUSIEK • ALEX ROSS

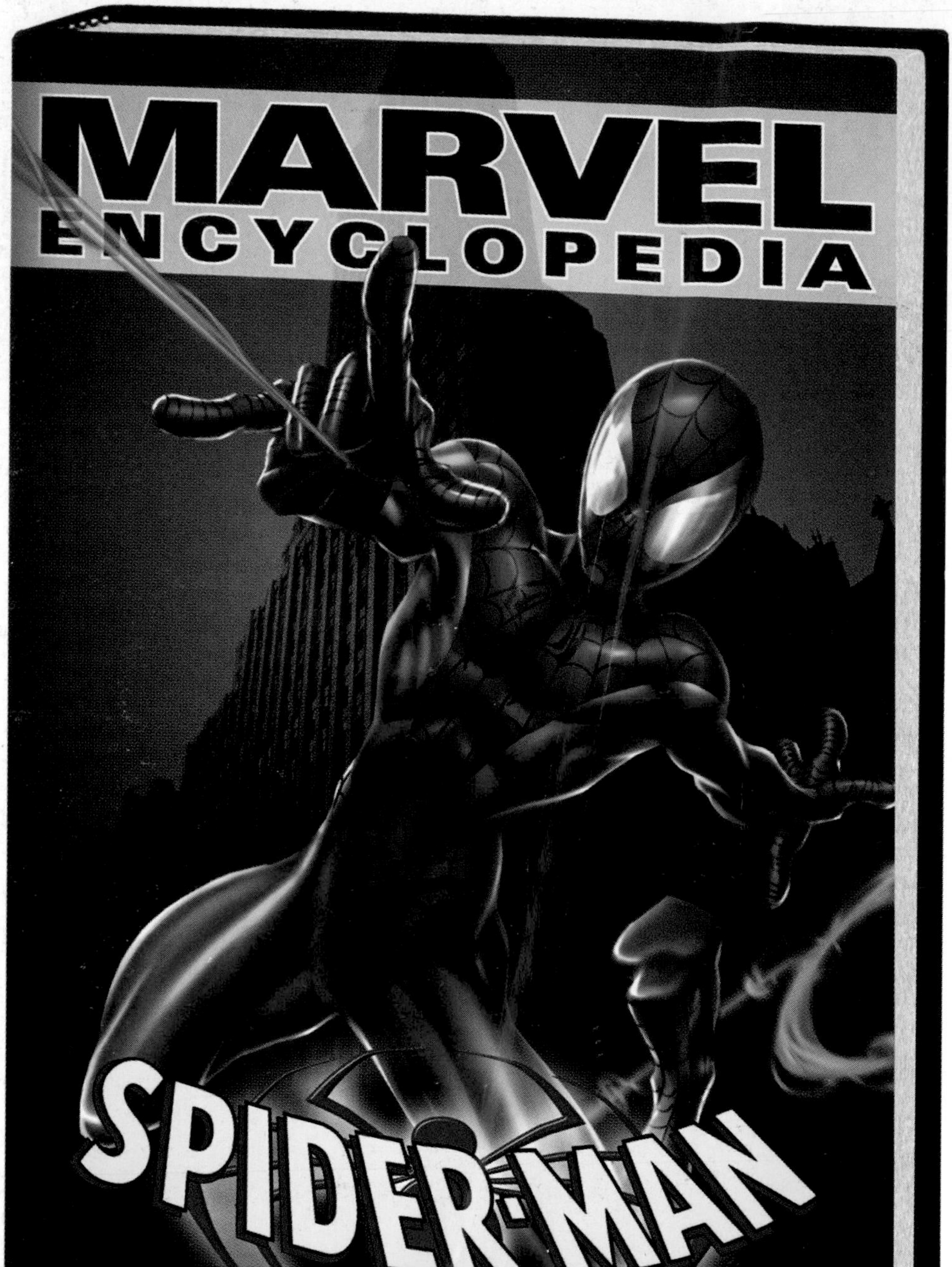
MARVEL ENCYCLOPEDIA
SPIDER-MAN